Guide to Lump Sum Investment

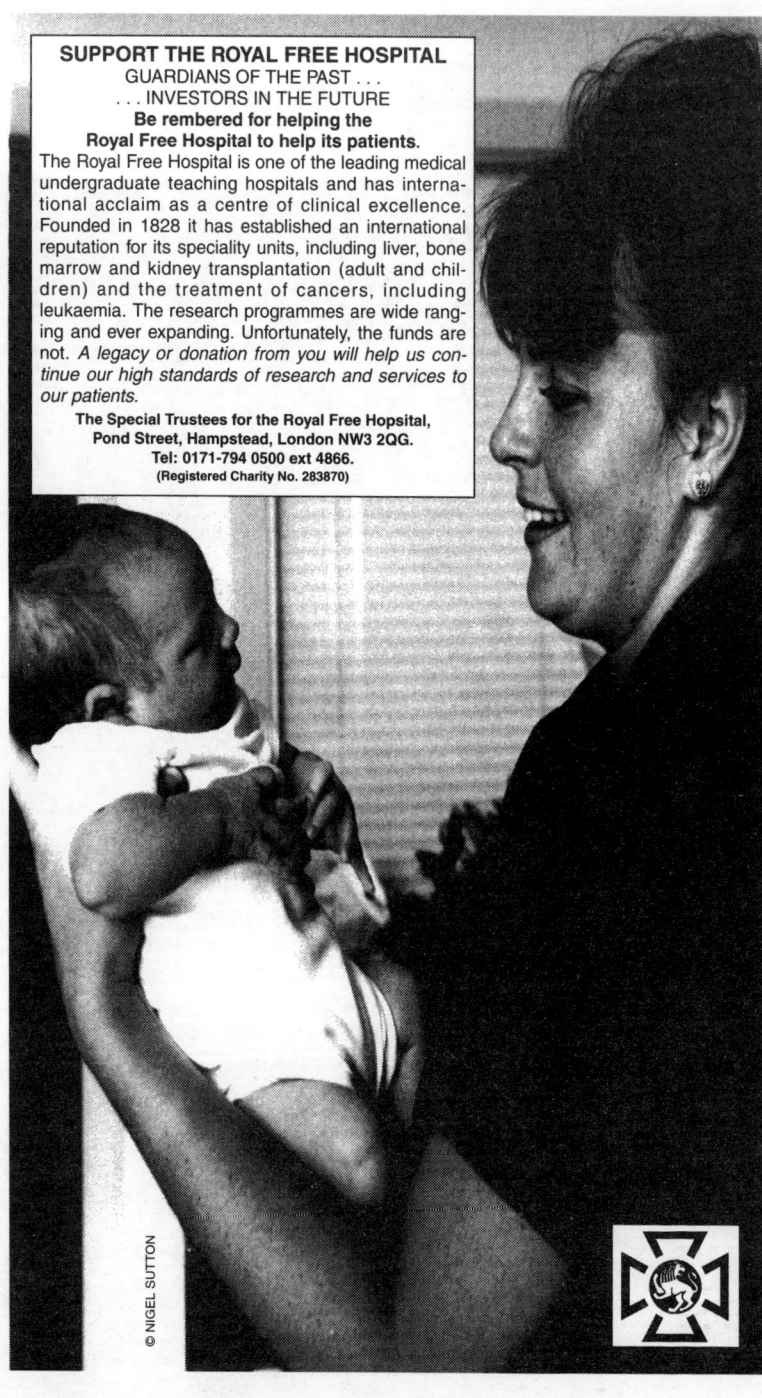

The Daily Telegraph
Guide to Lump Sum Investment

EIGHTH EDITION

Liz Walkington

First published in 1985
by Telegraph Publications
Author: Diana Wright

Eighth edition 1996
Author: Liz Walkington

Apart from any fair dealing for the purposes of research or private study, or criticism or review, as permitted under the Copyright, Designs and Patents Act, 1988, this publication may only be reproduced, stored or transmitted, in any form or by any means, with the prior permission in writing of the publishers, or in the case of reprographic reproduction in accordance with the terms of licences issued by the Copyright Licensing Agency. Enquiries concerning reproduction outside those terms should be sent to the publishers at the undermentioned address:

Kogan Page Limited
120 Pentonville Road
London N1 9JN

© The Telegraph plc 1996

British Library Cataloguing in Publication Data

A CIP record for this book is available from the British Library.

ISBN 0-7494-1968-7

Typeset by DP Photosetting, Aylesbury, Bucks
Printed and bound in Great Britain by Clays Ltd, St Ives plc

ONE OF THE BEST FINANCIAL ADVISERS IN THE COUNTRY AND THAT'S OFFICIAL

Following a national survey, Leathes Prior was selected as one of 19 independent Financial Advisers who provided outstanding quality, depth and breadth of financial advice.

FOR PROFESIONAL, INDEPENDENT ADVICE ON:–

Investments	Inheritance Tax and Estate Planning
Pensions	Tax Planning
Mortgages	Commercial Finance
Life Assurance	Business Planning
Income Protection	Accounts
Wills, Probate and Trusts	General Insurance

"Free initial consultation without commitment"

John Gaskell BA FIFP CFP
Certified Financial Planner
74 The Close
Norwich BR1 4FR

LEATHES PRIOR
Financial Planning
SOLICITORS & NOTARIES
Personal Financial Planning
(Written details on request)

Alan Winstanley MLIA (DIP)
Financial Planning Manager
Canada House
4 Grammar School Road
North Walsham
Norfolk NR28 9JJ

Tel: 01603 610911

Tel: 0692 404351

Leathes Prior is regulated by the Law Society in the conduct of investment business

---

Choosing a financial adviser:

Selecting a Financial Adviser should be likened to choosing a Doctor or Dentist: the value of personal financial advice is dependent upon establishing a trusting relationship between a competent adviser and his or her client. After your health and emotional well-being, finances probably present the most important set of decisions we are all faced with. Good advice is never free and rarely comes cheap. However, the following checklist of questions should help you avoid the charlatans and incompetents and steer you towards the Financial Planner who is right for you:–

1. Are you authorised to provide advice under the Financial Services Act and who is your regulatory body?

2. Are you an Independent Financial Adviser?

3. What range of services do you offer and do they include ongoing management and regular reviews of my personal circumstances?

4. What experience do you have of advising on investments and other related financial matters such as taxation?

5. Do you have professional qualifications and if so what are they?

6. How do you earn a living from the services you offer and are you happy to work on a fee rather than commission basis?

7. What level of Professional Indemnity Cover do you have and what procedures exist if I am unhappy with the service I have received?

8. Am I the sort of client you are looking for?

A full list of Certified Financial Planners can be obtained from:– The Institute of Financial Planning, Whitefriars Centre, Lewinsmead, Bristol BSl 2NT. Tel: 0117 930 4434 Fax: 0117 929 2214

UNITED TRUST BANK LIMITED
Founded in 1955

STERLING DEPOSITS
(Minimum Deposit – £5,000)

FIXED DEPOSIT ACCOUNTS

The choice of 1 Year, 6 Month or 3 Month periods

Excellent rates of return

NOTICE DEPOSIT ACCOUNTS

A choice of either 90 days or 180 days

Superior rates of return

Our sterling deposit facilities are designed to provide competitive rates of return with flexibility, whilst providing and maintaining the highest standard of customer care and service.

For further details please contact:
Sally Johnson – Manager, Sterling Deposits
United Trust Bank Limited
1 Great Cumberland Place
London W1H 7AL

Telephone: 0171 258 0094
Facsimile: 0171 262 4273

Authorised under the Banking Act 1987

Contents

1. **Introduction** 15
   Risk and protection *16*
   Tax *20*
   Layout of the book *29*

2. **Fixed Capital Investments (1)** 36
   Fixed versus variable interest *36*
   The tax position *38*
   Banks *39*
   Building societies *42*
   Tax exempt special savings accounts *45*
   National Savings *48*
   Where to find out more *64*

3. **Fixed Capital Investments (2)** 65
   Local authority bonds *65*
   Guaranteed income and growth bonds *66*
   Cash unit trusts *70*
   Offshore deposit accounts *70*
   Offshore money funds *74*
   Where to find out more *76*

4. **The Gilts Market** 78
   Terminology *78*
   Types of gilts *80*
   Gilt prices *81*
   The yield *83*

Gilts and tax *84*
Why buy gilts? *86*
Conventional versus index-linked *87*
Buying and selling *89*
Permanent interest bearing shares *90*
Where to find out more *92*

5. **Equities**   93
   The Stock Exchange *93*
   Rolling settlement *94*
   The Alternative Investment Market *96*
   Market indices *97*
   Private investors *100*
   Ordinary shares *101*
   Dividends *103*
   Price/Earnings ratio *104*
   How to buy and sell *105*
   Computer software for investment tracking *106* (by Andy Webb)
   Finding a broker *110*
   Costs *112*
   Shares in a portfolio *113*
   Other ways to play the market *115*
   Other types of share *118*
   Stock market terms *119*
   Where to find out more *119*

6. **Unit Trusts and Offshore Funds (1)**   123
   Unit trust regulations *126*
   Charges *128*
   Bid and offer *129*
   Different types of unit *132*
   Funds of funds *134*
   Cash trusts *134*
   Index trusts *136*
   Futures and options trusts *136*
   Warrant trusts *139*
   Unit trusts and tax *139*
   Special facilities for the investor *140*

Keeping track of your investment *142*
  Offshore funds *143*
  Umbrella funds *148*
  Open-ended investment companies *149*
  Where to find out more *150*

7. **Unit Trusts and Offshore Funds (2):**
   The Investment Choice   **152**
   Unit trust categories *153*
   Investment aims *158*
   Income trusts *158*
   Generalist trusts *164*
   Growth trusts *165*
   Management style *168*
   Are you an active investor? *170*
   Offshore funds *174*

8. **Investment Trusts**   **177**
   The share price and the discount *180*
   Investment characteristics *182*
   Investment range *184*
   How to invest *186*
   Keeping track of prices *187*
   Variations on a theme *187*
   Lloyd's trusts *191*
   Venture capital trusts *192*
   Housing investment trusts *193*
   Lifestyle products *194*
   Where to find out more *195*

9. **Personal Equity Plans**   **197**
   PEP rules *198*
   Types of plan *199*
   Choosing a PEP *210*
   PEP facilities *215*
   Keeping track of your investment *215*
   Where to find out more *216*

10. **Life Assurance and Friendly Society Investments**   **217**
    Single premium bonds *220*

Taxation *222*
　　　Bonds versus unit trusts *224*
　　　Variations on the bond theme *226*
　　　Broker bonds *234*
　　　Annuities *234*
　　　Variations of annuities *235*
　　　Hybrid plans *239*
　　　Second-hand endowments *240*
　　　Friendly societies *242*
　　　Private health care *242*
　　　(by Richard Willsher)

11. **Retirement Planning** — 256
　　　Personal pensions *257*
　　　Contracting out of SERPS *262*
　　　Additional contributions *266*
　　　How much to save *267*
　　　Where to find out more *268*

12. **Tangibles and Other Investments** — 270
　　　Tangibles *270*
　　　Precious metals *273*
　　　Diamonds *274*
　　　Wine *279*
　　　Forestry *280*
　　　Theatre productions *281*
　　　Enterprise Investment Scheme *282*
　　　Enterprise zone trusts *283*
　　　Lloyd's of London *284*
　　　Charitable giving *285*
　　　Ethical investment *286*
　　　(by Richard Willsher)
　　　Investing in property *295*
　　　(by Richard Willsher)

13. **Where to Go for Professional Advice** — 334
　　　The Financial Services Act *335*
　　　Polarisation *337*
　　　Merchant banks *340*

Chartered Accountants.

For People With More Sense Than Money.

If you want independent financial advice
talk to a Chartered Accountant.
For details of authorised firms in your area contact
The Institute of Chartered Accountants
in England and Wales on 0171 920 8711.

Only use a Chartered Accountant

Stockbrokers *341*
Accountants and solicitors *345*
Independent financial advisers *345*
Insurance brokers *352*
Choosing an adviser *354*
Types of service *354*
Commission versus fees *355*
Making complaints *361*
Useful contacts *362*

Further Reading from Kogan Page   **363**

Index   **364**

Index of Advertisers   **372**

For Award-winning Fund Management...

Micropal
1st Unit Trust Management Group (over one year) Category-Large Group

"The Sunday Telegraph"
2nd Top Unit Trust Group over One Year-Large Groups (Average % Sector Ranking)

"The Sunday Times"
2nd Top Unit Trust Managers (International)

Micropal
2nd Income Distribution Fund (over 10 years)

Micropal
1st Emerging Companies Fund (over one year) out of 238 funds in the Micropal Life Fund "UK Equity" sector.

"What Investment"
2nd Specialist Unit Trust Managers 1994

Micropal
2nd Individual Pension Fund Management Group (over one year)

...*ring* the Royal.

For more information about our award-winning funds
Call 01733 283688

Royal Insurance

Royal Life Insurance Limited is part of the Royal Insurance Life & Pensions Marketing Group.
Registered Office: New Hall Place, Old Hall Street, Liverpool L69 3HS. Telephone: 0151 239 3000
Registered in England No.1565099
Members of the Royal Insurance Life & Pensions Marketing Group
are regulated by the Personal Investment Authority and IMRO.

1

Introduction

Money makes the world go around, or so the song says, and it is a valid point of view. But from another angle, the world makes money go around, and many of us, in different ways, are playing catch-as-catch-can trying to get a share of it. This book is, in very broad terms, about making the most of that share.

Given the chance, most people like to save money, whether it is for a short-term purpose, such as a holiday, a long-term purpose, such as retirement, or simply for unspecified 'emergencies'. Saving is effectively deferred consumption: you save today to spend tomorrow. This is true even if your savings pass on to a future generation and 'tomorrow' is 50 years hence; sooner or later, the savings will be spent.

While savings could be simply money stuffed under the mattress, investment implies some added value – either actual or potential. Generally, this would take the form of a monetary reward; *Chambers English Dictionary*, for example, defines investment as 'the placing of money to secure income or profit'.

But for some people, the actual rewards may be secondary in importance to the pleasure of going after them. Just as there is enjoyment to be had from horse-racing, so there is in, say, playing the stock market, and there are similar opportunities to study 'form' and look for attractive odds. Of course, it is always good to win, but there can be pleasure in taking part even if some ventures fail.

So before you can decide how to invest, you need first to be clear why you want to. It may be to fulfil a particular need at a specific time, for example, to meet expected school fees; it may be

Lump-Sum Investment

a less definite saving for retirement or for the future in general; it may be that you have spare money you feel should be put to good use; or it may be simply for the fun of it.

Having settled the why, you should then have some idea of what you expect to achieve from the investment, which is a first step to deciding the how. Other factors to take into account are:

- the amount of money you have available;
- your attitude to risk;
- your tax position;
- the time you are prepared or able to devote to managing your investments.

As regards the size of investment, there are few limits in either direction. Much of the information in this book could be as well used by someone with just a few hundred pounds to invest as someone right at the other end of the scale, although the majority of readers will perhaps fall into the middle band, with somewhere between a few thousand and a six-figure sum.

Risk and protection

As to risk, again the book aims to cover a wide range. To start with, Chapters 2 and 3 look at various types of investment which provide capital security. Those who prefer rather more spice to life may want to skip these and move straight on to unit trusts or shares. Nevertheless, most people will find some use for this type of investment.

As well as short-term cash-flow management – putting aside money for bills and so on – vehicles such as bank and building society deposits can be useful over the longer term for 'emergency' cash. Most of us like to feel we have some money that is not only safe, but also readily accessible; fixed capital investments can provide this security while also offering some return.

Phone ShareLink for the best
0121 200

Introduction

The drawback is that security can become a habit. The amount of safe money that it is sensible to have will differ from person to person: single people with no dependants may need less than families, while those whose only recourse for loans is the bank manager may want to tuck aside rather more than those who have obliging relatives. Deciding when you have enough and can start to move up the risk scale can be like letting go of the side of the swimming pool.

The other important point to remember is that 'safe' investments that guarantee capital security are almost always open to a different kind of danger – inflation. An investment that is not growing in money terms will be shrinking in real terms, as measured by its purchasing power.

To get an idea by how much, you need only look at Table 1.1,

Table 1.1 *Inflation*

What £1000 would be worth in the future, in today's terms

Years ahead	Annual rate of inflation		
	3%	5%	8%
1	971	952	926
2	943	907	857
3	915	864	794
4	888	823	735
5	863	784	681
6	837	746	630
7	813	711	583
8	789	677	540
9	766	645	500
10	744	614	463
15	642	481	315
20	554	377	215
25	478	295	146

introduction to stocks and shares. 2242.

Lump-Sum Investment

which shows how much £1000 would come to be worth, valued in today's terms, given different rates of inflation. Even at the modest rate of 3 per cent, more than a quarter of the value would be eroded over 10 years. At 8 per cent, more than half would be lost.

So far, the 1990s have seen reduced inflation and it is tempting to think that it has been controlled, if not wholly overcome. But the long-term record, as shown in Table 1.2, should act as a warning. After the extreme levels seen in the 1970s and at the beginning of the 1980s, inflation reached a low point in 1986 that was similar to the current level. Yet four years later it had climbed back up to 9.5 per cent, and there is no guarantee the same thing could not happen again. As it is, the rate has crept steadily up from the low of 1993 and this could accelerate in the run-up to the next General Election, as government spending is likely to be increased.

It is possible to have an inflation-proofed investment, in the shape of index-linked National Savings Certificates (outlined in Chapter 2) or gilts (outlined in Chapter 4). These will guarantee

Table 1.2 *Average annual inflation rates*

Year	%
1980	15.1
1981	12.0
1982	5.4
1983	5.3
1984	4.6
1985	5.7
1986	3.6
1987	4.1
1988	4.9
1989	7.8
1990	9.5
1991	5.9
1992	3.7
1993	1.6
1994	2.5
1995	3.4

to give you back your capital uprated by inflation, so in real terms you get back what you started with.

The downside is that this security comes at a price. The current ninth issue of index-linked National Savings Certificates pays tax-free interest equivalent to 2.5 per cent a year compound, for five years, on top of the index-linking. This may currently look better than some building society accounts that lack the inflation proofing, but if inflation rises, so will interest rates, so in neutralising the inflation risk you are paying an opportunity cost.

Once you venture beyond the realms of fixed capital investments, you lay yourself open to investment risk. Broadly speaking, this operates on a tit for tat basis – the greater the potential for capital growth, the greater the potential for capital loss. In theory, the upside and downside should be roughly in balance, either in actual amount or when adjusted for likelihood. For example, if an investment is more likely to lose than gain, the possible gain needs to be larger than the possible loss to persuade people into it.

In practice, there are other factors to take into account, not least of which is the investment period. Take, for example, the UK stock market, as measured by the FTSE-Actuaries All-Share index. Over the long term, the trend is broadly upwards; the 1987 crash, for instance, appears on a long-term graph as only a temporary blip. But for an investor who put money into the market in, say, July 1987 and took it out again at the end of October that year, the loss would have been considerable.

The lesson from this is that the odds improve if you are prepared to commit your money for some time and to be patient. If the market turns down, you may be tempted to cut and run, but if you hold on, the loss is only on paper and may eventually turn round to profit. Conversely, if you have only a short time horizon, the risk becomes much greater and you may be better advised to stick to fixed capital investments. The stock market is not the best home for money that may be needed at short notice.

Another means of controlling risk is to spread your investments around. One of the drawbacks of privatisation issues is that many people who buy them own no other shares. So if the company does badly, they stand to lose a disproportionate amount. At the worst, if you put all your money into a single company that then goes bust, you will lose everything. If, on the other hand, you hold a collection of several different shares, a loss on any one will only be a small part of your investment and may be counteracted by gains elsewhere.

This is the principle behind collective or 'pooled' investments such as unit trusts and investment trusts. Small investors, who lack the resources to achieve a wide spread of direct shareholdings, can instead buy a stake in a large portfolio. A trust will usually have at least 40 different holdings, so the chances of them all failing together are pretty small.

Again, of course, there is a price for safety. If you hold ten shares and one doubles in value, you may wish you had backed it to the hilt and not bothered with the other nine. But if one out of the ten halves in value, you will be grateful for the insurance of the other holdings.

Even with banks and building societies, you should not take safety for granted, bearing in mind the collapse some years ago of the Savings and Investment Bank in the Isle of Man and the more recent crash of the merchant bank Barings. In the UK, and nowadays in several other locations, there is a deposit protection scheme, which guarantees you will get back some, if not all, of your money. But if you are putting money offshore, you should check whether such a scheme applies; if not, only put in as much as you would be prepared to lose, or steer clear altogether.

Tax

Tax is the next factor to consider. A few investments, such as National Savings Certificates and personal equity plans, are tax free; some are subject to income tax, while others are liable to capital gains tax. Depending on your particular tax circumstances, this can influence the net returns you will make and therefore your choice. The main tax rates and allowances are summarised in Table 1.3.

Interest payments and dividends from shares are treated as income and taxed at your highest rate. Interest from bank and building society accounts is normally paid net of basic rate tax, although you can register for gross payments if you are a non-taxpayer, while higher rate taxpayers will have to pay the

Introduction

SELF ASSESSMENT
Getting up to date

Would you like a tax system that is easier to follow?

The Inland Revenue is making the tax system clearer for everyone who has to complete a tax return through a new system called Self Assessment. This is a more straight forward and efficient way of calculating and paying tax for up to nine million people.

You get a tax return to fill in if you are self employed (that includes business partners), a director, or an employee or pensioner with more complex tax affairs. If you are a Self Assessment taxpayer, in April 1997 you will get a new-look tax return and a guide which will show you how to complete it.

You will also be able to work out your own tax bill. But you won't have to do this. If you want the Inland Revenue to calculate your tax as they do now, all you will have to do is fill in the tax form and send it back by 30 September 1997. This will give time to work out your bill and let you know how much to pay by 31 January 1998 when any tax is due. If you want to work out your own tax bill then you will need to send back your tax return by 31 January 1998 with your calculation and any payment due.

What do you need to do now to get ready for Self Assessment?

There are two important things that everyone must do now to get ready for Self Assessment. The first thing is that from April 1996 everyone should, by law, keep records so they can fill in a tax return if they get one. If you are an employee these records have to be kept for about two years after the end of the tax year to which they apply. Self employed people and business partners will have to retain their records for about six years.

Remember – new record keeping requirements start now.

If you don't already do this, you should
- **set up a** system for keeping your tax records

- **maintain** records throughout the year
- **retain** your records for as long as necessary

It's a good idea to keep everything together in a tax file or large envelope

You should keep records of
Everyone (including trustees)
- all sources of income
- payments for which you will claim tax relief, for example, payments to charities or private pensions
- bank and building society interest and dividend vouchers

If you are self employed
- business earnings and expenses plus sales invoices and receipts

If you are an employee
- income and benefits from your employer, for example, payslips and other documents, plus a note of tips and expenses

These records will help you complete your April 1997 tax return if you are a Self Assessment taxpayer.

The second thing is to make sure that your tax affairs are up to date.

Your tax affairs are <u>not</u> up to date if you've still got a tax return which you should have filled in and sent back, or if you haven't sent in your accounts and other outstanding information.

You are also behind with your tax affairs if you haven't paid the tax on an agreed assessment or replied to one of our letters or telephone calls.

What can you do if you are behind with your tax affairs?

You can get your tax affairs up to date by filling in any tax returns you have, sending in your accounts and paying any tax that you owe.

If you need help with any of this, then talk to your financial adviser if you have one or contact your Tax Office.

The staff at the Tax Office will be happy to work out a plan with you of what needs to be done and the best way of doing it.

And the offices have a full range of all our booklets on Self Assessment.

The address and telephone number of your nearest Tax Office or Tax Enquiry Centre are in your local phone book under Inland Revenue.

Introduction

From April you must get
into this routine

Jump to it, the first Self Assessment tax year has now started. If you usually receive a tax return form, you'll need to make a record of your income and expenses.

What records do you need to keep?

They include bank and building society statements, dividend vouchers, business earnings and receipts, payments to employees or sub-contractors, cashbooks and any other documents that could relate to your tax.

How to avoid penalties.

There will be a clear timetable setting out what you have to do by when. Keeping to the right dates for sending back your tax return and making payments will mean you avoid interest and penalties.

Read the leaflet in your latest tax return.

Find out more by reading the special leaflet included with your latest tax return.

Alternatively, for free information guides, just send us the coupon or telephone our special number anytime. (All calls are charged at the local rate.)

☎ **0345 16 15 14** ☎
http://www.open.gov.uk/inrev/irleaf.htm
......24hr......24hr......24hr......24hr......

Inland Revenue

Please send me more information about Self Assessment. Please tick a box if you are:
Self-employed ☐   Employed ☐   A Pensioner ☐   Seeking work ☐

Name (Mr/Mrs/Miss/Ms) _____
Address _____
                                    Postcode _____ SA/DTGLI/1/C/1
PLEASE RETURN COUPON TO: SELF ASSESSMENT PO BOX 555 BRISTOL BS99 5UJ

Self Assessment - a clearer tax system

Lump-Sum Investment

Table 1.3 *Income and capital gains tax*

Rates of income tax 1996/97

Taxable income £	Rate %	Cumulative on top of band £
0–3900	20	780
3901–25,500	24	5964
Over 25,500	40	—

Main tax allowances

Personal allowance	£3,765
Personal allowance (age 65–74)	£4,910
Personal allowance (age 75+)	£5,090
Married couple's allowance	£1,790*
Married couple's allowance (age 65–74)	£3,115*
Married couple's allowance (age 75+)	£3,155*
Single parent allowance	£1,790*
Widow's bereavement allowance	£1,790*
Blind person's allowance	£1,250
Age allowance income limit	£15,200

(Allowance is reduced by £1 for every £2 of additional income above the income limit.)

* Tax relief is restricted to 15 per cent

Capital gains tax

Annual allowance for individuals	£6,300
(Excess, after indexation allowance, is charged at the individual's highest rate of income tax.)	
Annual allowance for trusts	£3,150
Chattel exemption	£6,000
Retirement relief (age 55+)	£250,000 plus 50% of gains between £250,000 and £1,000,000

Major exemptions
- Principal private residence
- National Savings Certificates
- Assets gifted to charity
- Life assurance policies, for the original owner
- Betting winnings, including the pools and premium bonds

Introduction

difference. Share dividends are also paid net and accompanied by a tax credit, with which non-taxpayers can reclaim what has been paid.

In the 1993 Budget, the basic rate tax charged on dividends was reduced from 25 per cent to 20 per cent. For basic rate taxpayers, there is no material difference, since the value of the tax credit has also been reduced and therefore matches the liability just as it did before. Non-taxpayers, though, are only able to reclaim 20 per cent, while investors subject to higher rate tax now have to pay out an extra 20 per cent, to bring the total up to the 40 per cent rate, instead of the 15 per cent that applied before.

One consequence of this is that personal equity plans, on which all dividends are tax free, are now slightly less attractive than before to basic rate taxpayers, as the tax saving is only 20 per cent, which may be offset by the plan charges. Conversely, they are a little more attractive to higher rate taxpayers, because of the higher tax bill they face on shares not held through a plan.

Capital growth on investments is generally subject to capital gains tax at the time the profit is realised. This is charged at the same rate as income tax, but in practice it is paid by very few investors. This is because there are two types of allowance which, combined with a little management, can allow you to avoid a liability.

First, there is an indexation allowance, designed to avoid tax being charged on gains which are due only to inflation. The base date for the calculation is 31 March 1982; assets held since before then are assessed as if they had been bought at the market value on that date and gains made previously are no longer taxable.

For assets acquired after March 1982, the original purchase price is scaled up in line with the change in the Retail Price Index. Only gains made above that are liable to tax. If you make a loss on selling an asset, it can be used to offset any gains you have made elsewhere. But a provision in the 1993 Autumn Budget means that you can no longer use the indexation allowance to create or increase a loss to offset gains.

There is also an annual exemption allowance, currently £6300 a year, which applies to all individuals. Taking this together with the indexation allowance means you would have to make very profitable disposals in one year to become liable. If it does seem

Lump-Sum Investment

DEFENDING YOUR WEALTH – PRE-ELECTION PLANNING

Those involved in tax planning for wealthy individuals are likely to be very busy between now and next General Election. A few months ago most pundits were predicting that this Government would continue for the full five year term, ie. until April 1997 but this is now beginning to look less certain. What is looking more certain is that barring some extraordinary revival of the fortunes of John Major and his Government, Mr Blair will be the next Prime Minister.

Before the last election, Labour made the mistake of announcing that it would increase the top rate of income tax to 50% and introduce an investment income surcharge of 9%. It is quite possible that this tipped the balance and kept the Conservatives in power. It seems unlikely that this mistake will be repeated, indeed Mr Blair has been at pains to assure the electorate and the world at large that his "new Labour" would not impose high direct taxes.

Nevertheless, the top rate of income tax is low by the standard of most developed countries, and some modest increase is quite possible, even probable. In a paper entitled "Tackling Tax Abuses Tackling Unemployment" issued in November 1994, the Labour party pointed out that the top one percent of families earning more than £120,000 had benefited from substantial reductions in tax since 1979.

With employment income taxed on a receipts basis rather than an earnings basis, the payment of bonuses, or indeed salaries in advance could be considered, although this may not be practical for larger companies.

Inheritance tax planning
Although we have relatively little specific information as to Labour's intentions for income tax, there is much more guidance on its intentions for Inheritance Tax (IHT) and a clear difference in view between the two main parties. On the one hand John Major has declared his intention to scrap IHT and Capital Gains Tax (CGT) when circumstances allow – Labour on the other hand in the 1994 document made it clear that many of the apparent loopholes in the current legislation would be closed.

Lifetime gifts
One specific area to be targeted by a Labour Government is the use of Potentially Exempt Transfers (PETs). Under existing legislation it is possible for an individual to make gifts during lifetime of any amount, without liability to IHT arising on the gift. Most gifts – if not already covered by an annual exemption – are treated as PETs when made. They become wholly exempt provided that the transfer or is still alive seven years after the date of the gift. This rule was introduced in 1986. It is a far cry from the capital transfer tax introduced by the last Labour govern-ment when tax was charged on all lifetime gifts in excess of £15,000, with rates rising from 5% to 75%. Labour has said that it would be its intention to remove the ability to make PETs, and to reintroduce an automatic charge on lifetime gifts.

Business and agricultural property
Another area which may be susceptible to change is the transfer of business or agricultural property. Current reliefs are generous: for certain categories, relief is available at 100%, making such assets effectively exempt from IHT. The business property relief is available for transfers of unincorporated businesses, and shares in unquoted trading companies. (In the case of minority holdings below 25% the relief will be raised from 50% to 100% on 6 April which is remarkably generous.) Under the last Labour government the equivalent rate for these reliefs was 30%.

Rates of IHT
The indications are that rates of IHT would also increase. Under the present legislation individuals can give away up to £154,000 (£200,000 from 6 April) without liability. For amounts in excess of this there is a flat rate charge of 40% for transfers on death. This would be increased for "larger estates". No specific indication has been given yet of what constitutes a larger estate, and what the revised rates may be, but it is safe to assume that for estates over say £1m there would be a substantial increase..

Clearly anyone who has not yet taken estate planning steps should do so straight away. Not only may IHT become more stringent if there is a change of government but also capital gains tax reliefs such as retirement, hold over and reinvestment reliefs, may be withdrawn or modified. There really is no time like the present – a delay could be costly.

Estate planning using lifetime gifts needs to be undertaken carefully, to ensure that the rules for obtaining relief are obeyed, and professional advice should be sought. *Binder Hamlyn is a leading firm of chartered accountants with offices in London, Croydon, Newbury, St Albans, Manchester, Leeds and Newcastle and is part of Andersen worldwide.*

Advertisement feature

Introduction

Defend your wealth against political change

At Binder Hamlyn we understand that every client has individual financial needs.

We also understand that the prospect of a change of Government might require timely action for certain individuals.

If you are looking for a personal service and practical advice on any aspect of your financial situation, we can help.

We offer advice on:

- financial gifts
- estate planning and inheritance tax
- the transfer of business and agricultural property
- retirement and pension planning
- reinvestment matters
- school fee and trust arrangements
- lump-sum investments

Let us take the weight off your mind before an election decides matters for you.

If you think we can be of assistance, please contact Frank Akers-Douglas at the address below.

BINDER HAMLYN

20 Old Bailey, London EC4M 7BH
Telephone: 0171 489 6423

Binder Hamlyn is a leading firm of chartered accountants with offices in London, Croydon, St Albans, Newbury, Newcastle, Leeds and Manchester.

Andersen Worldwide

Authorised by the Institute of Chartered Accountants in England and Wales to carry on investment business likely to happen, one way round the tax is to sell assets up to the point where you fully use the exempt allowance and buy the same assets again the next day. Your overall portfolio is then the same as before, but you will have established a new purchase price for the assets you sold and bought, on which the indexation allowance will be based in future.

This technique, known as 'bed and breakfasting', enables you to neutralise up to £6300 of gains over and above inflation, for the price of the dealing costs – and, as special deals are widely offered towards the end of the tax year, these are very small compared to the potential tax liability.

Tax should not be the only criterion when choosing an investment, nor even necessarily the prime one. But as a broad rule, the higher rate taxpayer will do better from a growth investment, where he can use the capital gains exempt allowance, than from one that produces income on which he will immediately lose 40 per cent.

There are two other factors which may influence choice. First, since 1990, married couples have been taxed independently, whereas before that all investment income was imputed to the husband. They are still entitled to a married couple's allowance, but since the start of the 1995/96 tax year this has qualified for tax relief of only 15 per cent.

Meanwhile, each of the couple has his or her own personal allowance, capital gains tax exempt allowance and tax rate. As a result, there may be benefits in transferring investments between you and your spouse – particularly as such transfers are exempt from inheritance tax. For example, income-producing investments could be put in the name of whichever partner has the lower tax rate, while those producing capital growth can be split so as to make the most of the annual CGT allowance. Bear in mind, though, that if you give assets away to your partner, you are not entitled to ask for them back if the marriage breaks down.

The other issue is age allowance. Individuals are entitled to a higher personal tax allowance when they pass the age of 65, with another increase when they reach 75, while a higher married couple's allowance is given where either partner reaches 65 or 75 during the tax year. The trap is that there is an annual income limit (based on the husband's income for the married couple's

Introduction

allowance). If income goes above this level, the allowance is reduced by £1 for every £2 of excess income – a heavy penalty. Hence those who are at or near the limit may do better from growth-oriented investments which they can cash in if they need extra income.

Finally, there is inheritance tax. This does not affect an investor directly, since it only comes into play on death, and gifts between husband and wife are exempt. Nevertheless, with the increase in home ownership, many people may find their total assets go beyond the nil rate band, and it may be worth taking note of the exemptions, particularly if your investment plans extend to your heirs. Details are given in Table 1.4.

Layout of the book

Investments can be categorised in a number of different ways: by product type, by what they achieve in terms of income or growth,

Table 1.4 *Inheritance tax rates*

Amount of transfer	Tax rate
Up to £200,000	Nil
Over £200,000	40%

Relief on transfers made within 7 years of death

Years between gift and death	% of full tax charge
0–3	100
3–4	80
4–5	60
5–6	40
6–7	20

Main exemptions
Transfers between husband and wife
Transfers of up to £3000 a year
Gifts to anyone of up to £250 a year
Gifts out of income forming 'normal expenditure'
Gifts on marriage – up to £5000 for parents, £2500 for grandparents, £1000 for anyone else

Lump-Sum Investment

or by risk factors. For the most part, this book goes by product type, although Chapters 2 and 3, as mentioned above, lump together investments that offer capital security. Chapter 2 covers high street institutions, such as banks, building societies and National Savings products which are largely available through post offices; Chapter 3 goes further afield into local authority bonds, insurance company guaranteed bonds and offshore money funds.

Chapter 4 covers gilts, which come halfway between fixed capital and risk investments. If you hold on to a gilt to its maturity date, you will get a fixed return, but meanwhile gilts can be traded, for profit or loss.

Chapters 5 to 9 deal with equity-based investments: shares themselves, unit trusts, offshore funds, investment trusts and personal equity plans, which can be based on individual shares or trusts. While the chapter on equities is largely based on the UK market, a point to bear in mind is that the advantages of spreading your investments can apply equally well on a global scale as on a domestic one.

These days, the major world markets have a tendency to move roughly in line with each other, but there can still be short-term differences, as well as currency factors that will affect the returns. Smaller markets are a law unto themselves, usually displaying significant volatility.

'Smaller', however, is a relative term; the so-called emerging markets currently account for around 5 per cent of total world market capitalisation and the proportion is steadily increasing. While direct investment into these markets – and to some extent, any overseas markets – can be difficult, expensive and risky for the private investor, pooled funds such as unit and investment trusts offer a sensible and accessible route in. A glance at Table 1.5, which shows the capitalisation of the main markets, provides a clear picture of what you are ignoring if you focus on the UK alone.

Moving on, Chapters 10 and 11 cover investments with life assurance companies, which might more immediately be associated with regular savings. This is particularly true of pension plans, covered in Chapter 11; however, retirement planning can be so important, and so few people can expect the maximum

Introduction

This is Bill, taking good care of his tax affairs.

Bill has no worries about tax.

He knows that his Returns are up to date and that he hasn't paid a penny too much, there's no way he's adding to the hundreds of thousands of pounds worth of unclaimed refunds held by the Inland Revenue.

Even though, in trials of the new Self Assessment Tax Returns, 46% contained errors and 10% were completed so badly they were impossible to process, Bill knows his forms will be correct.

But, most importantly, he knows that by using a personal taxation service like Just Tax, his affairs couldn't be in better hands leaving him free to get on with far more enjoyable things!

For further details, please call
*Free*fone **0800 716 961**

Just Tax

 Just Tax is a division of Seymour Taylor Chartered Accountants. Registered to carry on audit work and authorised to carry on investment business by the Institute of Chartered Accountants in England and Wales.

Lump-Sum Investment

Table 1.5 *World stock markets*

Exchange	Capitalisation (US$bn)	% of World Index
Australia	178.8	1.46
Canada	180.8	1.48
France	403.0	3.29
Germany	428.0	3.50
Hong Kong	251.6	2.06
Italy	136.8	1.12
Japan	2842.2	23.23
Malaysia	132.9	1.09
Netherlands	243.2	1.99
South Africa	140.8	1.15
Sweden	140.2	1.15
Switzerland	346.9	2.84
UK	1086.5	8.88
USA	5185.0	42.38

Note: Figures are as at 29 March 1996.

Source: The Financial Times

benefits allowed, that topping-up provision should feature high on the list of priorities for investing windfall cash.

Chapter 12 rounds up so-called alternative investments, including tangibles such as precious metals and diamonds.

The final criterion for choosing investments that was mentioned at the outset of this chapter is the time you have to devote to your portfolio. While some investments take a while to come good, few selections will be right for all time, particularly as your own circumstances and needs will change over time. Constant chopping and changing will generally lose more in costs than it gains; nevertheless, reviews are an important part of the process.

It is not only your own circumstances that will change; the market is also in constant flux. In the past half-dozen years, there have been two major upheavals: Big Bang, which reorganised the operations of the Stock Exchange, and the Financial Services Act, which set up a new system of regulation for the industry.

Neither of these has proved conclusive, in that adjustments are still going on. In March 1993, the Stock Exchange abandoned

Introduction

INFORMATION ABOUT ST. MARY'S HOSPICE

- St. Mary's is a Registered Charity (No. 503456). It is Birmingham's only independent adult Hospice offering the very best package of palliative care available in the city to patients and support to their relatives and friends for as long as they need it. All services are free.

- Care is given by a highly competent and skilled team using the latest knowledge to ensure patient comfort so that they really live until the moment they die.

- As well as 25 in-patient beds and 20 day care places, St. Mary's has a team of 7 Home Care Nurses offering skilled support for around 250 people in their own homes. The team are on-call 24 hours a day, 7 days a week – thus help is just a 'phone call away.

- The Education Department offers courses in palliative care up to and including degree level for Doctors, Nurses, Social Workers etc.

- Please help us to continue our work which this year will cost £2.5 million. In addition to this a further £2.5 million is needed for major upgrading to enable us to continue to offer the sort of care we are famous for.

For further details please contact Barry Shuttleworth, Head of Funding Development.

St. Mary's Hospice, 176 Raddlebarn Road, Selly Park,
Birmingham B29 7DA.
Tel: 0121-472 1191. Fax: 0121-472 5075.
Patron: Her Grace, The Duchess of Norfolk

Reg. Charity No. 503456

PALLIATIVE CARE IN THE WEST MIDLANDS

The pioneering work of Dame Cecily Saunders and the 'Hospice Movement' started some 25 years ago. Form this was born the concept of "palliative care" which is rapidly developing and facing the challenges of patient and carer needs, advancing knowledge and changes in the health and social care systems.

Palliative care is the active, total care of patients with advanced, progressive illness which is not curable and for whom the focus of care is on quality of life for them and their carers. The components of such care involve:

    Management of pain and other physical symptoms.
    Integration of physical, psychological, social and spiritual care needs (holistic care).
    Individually planned, patient led care including meeting cultural and religious needs.
    Support to families and carers including day and inpatient respite care.
    Care of dying patients.
    Bereavement care.
    Liaison between and integration of primary healthcare teams, secondary services and specialist palliative care services.

The draft Calman Report on the commissioning of services for patients with cancer has included reference to palliative care needs. The essence of the report is to provide a smooth, expert equitable and seamless service for all patients. Access and appropriate current service provision for ethnic minorities particularly needs to be addressed. Cancer has traditonally been the largest part of the workload for many palliative care services but the needs of patients with non-malignant illnesses must be considered and provided for.

Research and education are corner stones of improvement and development and the University of Central England with help from Cancer Relief Macmillan Fund launched "The Centre for Palliative Care Educaton and Research" in 1994. The centre aims to foster and co-ordinate multidisciplinary education and research in the Region and has as its flagship a B.Sc. in palliative care nursing. This degree is a joint enterprise between the University, Saint Mary's Hospice, Birmingham and Saint Richards Hospice, Worcester.

The financing of palliative care services is complex and the future for this exciting! Most hospices are charitable organisations although some are solely NHS funded. The "Bottomley" monies and the subsequent ringfenced monies to health authorities allowed most hospices to receive health funding in the form of a grant. The government stated a philosophy of a move towards 50:50 funding in the future. The NHS reforms have allowed hospices to formalise contracts with NHS purchasers. In the 95/96 financial year the financial provision for purchase of palliative care services will no longer be ringfenced although the remit for purchasing services remains with the health authority. Whatever happens to funding from NHS sources hospices will undoudtedly remain dependent on the charitable donations.

the development of Taurus, a proposed electronic dealing system, and is now about to introduce a different and rather less ambitious system called Crest.

The Financial Services Act has undergone a series of alterations since it was introduced. The Act set up a system of self-regulation under the auspices of the Securities and Investments Board (SIB), which in turn delegates authority to self-regulatory organisations. Before 1994, there were four of these: the Financial Intermediaries, Managers and Brokers Regulatory Association (Fimbra), which looked after independent financial advisers; the Life Assurance and Unit Trust Regulatory Organisation (Lautro), which covered insurance companies and unit trust groups; the Investment Management Regulatory Organisation (Imro), which covered fund management groups (including some unit trust groups); and the Securities and Futures Association (SFA), which covered stockbrokers and the like. In addition, the SIB itself regulated a small number of companies.

In July 1994, a new body, the Personal Investment Authority (PIA), came into operation. This is responsible for all retail investment services, encompassing the operations of former Fimbra and Lautro members, plus Imro firms which primarily deal with private, rather than institutional, investors.

While all these initials may be bemusing, they are not without relevance to private investors in general, and the time factor in particular. The less time you are able to devote to looking after your investments, the more you may need to rely on the services of an adviser, and the Financial Services Act aims to ensure that the advice you will receive is honest and competent. It also provides for redress in the case of malpractice.

Details of how the Act and its various creations operate are given in Chapter 13. This also discusses the various types of advice available and how to choose between different services. For example, one of the main planks of the Act is that advisers are 'polarised' into two categories: completely independent, which means offering advice across the full range of the markets in which they operate, or tied to a single company and able to offer only the products it supplies.

At the outset, one of the cardinal rules for independents was that they should offer 'best advice' – the best possible product, in

Introduction

Table 1.6 *Past performance comparisons*

Value of £100 invested over periods to 29 February 1996

	3 years	5 years	10 years
Building society (90-day account)	114.2	133.2	211.1
Investment trust	152.2	211.8	369.3
Unit trust (offer to bid basis)	135.5	186.6	289.7
Retail Price Index (previous month)	108.9	115.4	156.1
FT-SE Actuaries All Share Index	144.5	188.5	338.0
MSCI World Index (£)	144.7	198.0	304.1

Source: Association of Investment Trust Companies

terms of type and supplier, to fit their customers' needs. This has now been adjusted to read 'good advice', in recognition of the fact that no one can be expected to pick in advance the product which will turn in the best performance in some years' time.

While you may be happy to trust your adviser's judgement, you are likely to get more out of the relationship if you understand the basics of the selection process. This book is designed to help in that, and at the end of each chapter there are suggested sources of further information.

One final word of warning. The book only deals with lump-sum investments, hence it does not cover regular savings by way of monthly or annual premiums on life assurance policies or pension plans, or outgoings such as a mortgage. In practice, these may all impinge on your overall financial picture and any part should not be viewed in isolation from the rest.

Having said that, lump-sum investments may arise out of windfall gains such as inheritance and therefore be additional to existing regular, and planned, savings. If you are happy that your basic needs are already catered for, you may be prepared to take a different tack with the lump sum, perhaps involving more risk.

Because the choices are so wide, it is impossible to categorise potential gains. But to whet your appetite, Table 1.6 gives a few key statistics. While there is no guarantee that taking risks will always provide rewards, it does suggest that, over the long term, a little care and imagination can prove fruitful.

2

Fixed Capital Investments (1)

As a starting-point, this chapter will look at the more familiar varieties of investment available through high street outlets. In particular, it will deal with fixed capital products: those which guarantee that the capital you get out will be the same as the capital you put in.

This can be reassuring, but the drawback is that old hidden enemy, inflation, which will progressively erode the value. The rate of inflation is one factor which influences the general level of interest rates; they are rarely substantially above inflation for very long, which means that the real rate of return on the investments discussed here is usually pretty small. Indeed, it can even be negative: in October 1990, for example, the gross return on an instant access deposit of £5000 hit a high of 14 per cent, but inflation was then running at 10.9 per cent – above the net return to a basic rate taxpayer. So these investments are suitable chiefly for short periods, 'emergency' money or the extremely cautious.

Fixed versus variable interest

Most of the investments covered in this chapter pay variable interest, which will move up and down in line with general market rates. But there are a few, including some National Savings products and fixed term deposits, which pay fixed interest over a predetermined period of time.

Fixed interest rates, like fixed mortgage rates, are something of a gamble: if general rates subsequently go up, you lose; if they go down, you win. As a gambler, you are probably betting on fairly

Fixed Capital Investments (1)

Since being established in 1976, Concern Universal, a Christian ecumenical organisation, has been saving lives and helping local communities build a better future. It exists to help the vulnerable, improve education and healthcare and provide basic amenities. In short Concern Universal responds to the needs of local communities.

The variety and scope of our work is ever broadening reflecting the priorities of the different communities in which we work. As a result we have programmes in twenty countries covering areas such as the rehabilitation of child soldiers; children affected by war; water; health; training; agriculture and small enterprise development.

Our work relies on voluntary donations. We use these to secure funds from the major European donors. Using this method we can double, treble even quadruple the value of your donation. Then we work wherever possible with the Church in the field. This makes your money work as hard as possible.

There are many ways to help us – some are as easy as signing a cheque – some are more difficult such as organising a fundraising event. Others are tax-efficient like Gift Aid, while a Covenant can help us plan for the future. *All are worthwhile.*

For a copy of our 1994/95 Annual Review or for more information on how we could help each other please write or phone –

Concern Universal, 14 Manor Road, Chatham, Kent ME4 6AN.
Phone 01634 813942. Fax 01634 813942   *Concern Universal is a registered charity No 272465*

ARE YOU CONCERNED . . .

One of the most disturbing aspects of civil war in developing countries is the use of children, girls as well as boys, some as young as seven, as frontline troops. The degree of trauma and brutality endured by these children is too horrific to describe.

. . . ENOUGH TO CARE

Do whatever you can, however small it seems. A kind word. A friendly gesture. A simple donation.

Please accept by donation of £ _____

Name _____

Address _____

_____ Postcode _____   kp/sp/96

Please charge my Visa/Access/Switch/Delta/Barclaycard No: *Delete as applicable*

_____

Expiry date _____ Signature _____

Please send your donation to: **Concern Universal, Freepost 115, Chatham, Kent ME4 6AN**
A company limited by guarantee registered in London No. 1278887. Registered charity No. 272465

long odds, since the rate offered will ultimately depend on the view of the money market, which has no crystal ball but is generally in a better position to make predictions than the average investor. On the whole, it is better to be guided by your needs and decide whether or not the certainty of a fixed income would outweigh any possible loss.

Variable rates tend to reflect the general economic environment, but different institutions react at varying speeds to underlying changes. It may seem that mortgage rates move up faster than down, while investment rates are sticky in the other direction; in practice the institutions are simply balancing their borrowing and lending against the demand and supply in the market. Broadly, when they are looking to attract investors they will be quicker to raise their interest rates; when they are seeking to increase their lending they will try to hold rates down.

Neither pattern is likely to be consistent for all time, so this should not be a prime factor in deciding where to invest. Of course, it is possible to gain by monitoring all the rates available and switching your investments around accordingly, but this is more valuable if you are locking into a fixed rate; with variable rates, the benefit is likely to be small and short-lived compared with the time and energy you would spend on the research.

The tax position

Until April 1991, bank and building society accounts paid interest net of composite rate tax. This was calculated by the Inland Revenue on the basis of the proportion of savers who were non-taxpayers and therefore worked out at slightly less than basic rate income tax, but the major drawback was that it could not be reclaimed by those not liable for tax.

Nowadays, non-taxpayers can register to have interest paid gross by completing the Inland Revenue Form R85, available at banks and building societies. Otherwise, interest will normally be paid net of basic rate tax, which can be reclaimed by those who are not liable to some or all of it. Basic rate taxpayers themselves will have no further liability, while higher rate taxpayers will have to pay the difference.

National Savings Certificates and tax exempt special savings

Fixed Capital Investments (1)

accounts (TESSAs) are free of both income and capital gains tax (CGT), while the return on gilts is liable only to income tax and will be paid gross if they are held through the National Savings Stock Register (see Chapter 4). A handful of other products pay interest gross, although it will still be liable for tax. These include National Savings accounts, offshore bank and building society accounts (see Chapter 3) and fixed-term bank and building society deposits amounting to £50,000 or more.

Accounts that pay gross have the advantage that you can enjoy the money for a while before the tax falls due, but there is also a potential drawback. In the first year, and the second if you so elect, the tax charged is based on the actual interest received, but thereafter it moves to a 'preceding year' basis. So, for example, in the tax year 1996/97 your tax charge for the account will be based on the interest you actually received in 1995/96. When interest rates are rising, this means you will effectively pay too little tax, but conversely when they are falling you will be overcharged. In this case there is no right of appeal, because the procedure counts as an actual tax charge, rather than a provisional assessment. The only way around it, if interest rates are dropping and you are therefore losing out, is to close the account, as the tax will be calculated on the interest actually paid in the final year. However, the Inland Revenue is then entitled to reassess the previous year's charge and adjust that to the true amount if it is in its own favour to do so (note that it will not offer a rebate if you paid too much!).

In the long run, the overpayments and underpayments should tend to even out. However, when you decide to close the account, you should try to do so in a year when rates have been falling so that any final swing will be in your favour. If you subsequently open another account, this will not affect the tax assessment of the first.

Banks

Current accounts

Time was when a current account was simply a convenient alternative to keeping your money under the mattress. You earned no interest on it, but neither did it cost you anything to

Lump-Sum Investment

run, as long as you kept the account in credit. The high street banks, at least, offered services that were more or less identical to each other, so most people picked the one that was nearest to their home or workplace, or possibly the one their parents used, and then stuck with it for life. This had the advantage, in theory at least, that if you established a track record with your bank you were likely to be looked on more favourably if you needed a loan.

Nowadays, competitive pressures have swept all that aside. There are a host of different accounts offering a variety of facilities and there is more point in shopping around to find one that suits your needs. For instance, there are some that offer, within limits, an interest-free overdraft, particularly on student accounts – students being potentially lucrative customers in the future. Others are linked to a savings account, with an automatic sweep between the two, or provide telephone banking through which you can juggle your money between accounts.

Also, since building societies began to provide cash card and cheque-book facilities, banks have introduced interest payments on current accounts. On the basic accounts, however, the rates are very low, so they should be considered as purely for cash flow purposes, not as investments.

Higher interest accounts

Just as current accounts have burgeoned, so have deposit-style accounts. These offer better rates of interest but do not normally provide cheque-book or money transmission facilities, though they may have a link to a current account and some offer a cash card.

For instant access accounts there is usually no minimum deposit. Notice accounts, where withdrawals require between one and three months' notice, may require a minimum of £1000 or £2500. Generally, these will allow immediate access with loss of interest equivalent to the notice period, but the penalty may be waived if there is a balance remaining in the account of £5000 or £10,000.

Interest rates rise with the amount deposited and the length of notice; examples of rates offered at the time of writing are shown in Table 2.1.

Fixed Capital Investments (1)

Table 2.1 *Bank account rates*

Amount deposited (£)	Instant access (%)	60 days' notice (%)	90 days' notice (%)
500–999	2.24	2.55	—
1000–2499	2.24	2.55	—
2500–4999	2.56	2.55	3.38
5000–9999	2.67	2.81	3.38
10,000–24,999	3.16	3.38	3.68
25,000–49,999	3.35	3.75	4.13
50,000+	3.46	3.94	4.13

Note: Rates net of basic rate tax, applicable as at March 1996. Bank base rate: 6%.

Source: Money Facts

Money market and high interest cheque accounts
These were once the preserve of merchant banks and licensed deposit-takers, and there are still some that are essentially deposit accounts for large sums of money, with no money transmission facilities. However, most of the major banks now offer some form of high interest cheque account. The services provided are usually more limited than the standard current account; there may be a minimum withdrawal or cheque amount of anything up to £250, or only a limited number of withdrawals free of charge, so for daily purposes you would probably need an ordinary account as well.

But, as in other spheres, competition is leading to improved options and there are a growing number of accounts which have no minimum withdrawal and offer a full range of facilities such as overdrafts, cash card, cheque card, standing orders and direct debits, with free banking as long as you remain in credit. On top of this, the interest rates can be substantially more than the token offerings on basic current accounts.

The one drawback is that they do require a relatively high initial deposit, generally of £1000. There are one or two which offer respectable rates of interest on sums from £1 upwards, but these do not provide the full range of services.

Lump-Sum Investment

Term deposits
Fixed-term deposits pay a fixed rate of interest for a specified period of time, which may be anything from one month to five years. Some of the smaller banks offer these for as little as £500 but the minimum is usually £2500 or £5000. As a rule, no withdrawals are allowed during the term and the interest rate is fixed at the outset, but rates can vary on a daily basis, so check before you invest.

Very large sums of money, upwards of £50,000, can be placed in money market time deposits through banks. While these may be for a period of some months, it is also possible to place money on overnight deposit with automatic renewal on a daily basis, so that you can leave the money for as long as you like while having instant access to it. Interest rates are set daily or sometimes more frequently and, provided the deposit is at least £50,000, interest can be paid gross.

Building societies

Like the banks, building societies have vastly expanded their range of products in recent years. In terms of the banks versus building societies 'savings war' the societies have largely been the aggressors, moving in on the banks' traditional territory of cheque accounts. They were also granted wider powers by the government, allowing them, for example, to own a domestic bank and to raise more money from wholesale markets. But at the same time, they have faced considerable competitive pressure from each other, with the result that there has been a number of mergers, not only among smaller societies but also between the large ones, a prime example being the recent Halifax–Leeds tie-up. One society, Abbey National, has changed its status to become a bank and three others, Halifax, Woolwich and Alliance & Leicester, intend to do so next year.

Banking accounts
Banking accounts come in two types: those which are more or less deposit-style accounts but provide cash card facilities; and those which offer a cheque-book and other banking facilities such as standing orders, direct debits and even overdrafts, though this

Fixed Capital Investments (1)

last is rather less common. The services are generally free as long as the account is in credit, but there may be a minimum opening balance – normally not more than £200.

Interest is paid on these accounts and, while it can be rather more generous than bank current accounts, the same caveat applies, that rates are too low for these accounts to be considered as investments proper. For larger deposits, however, the rates offered are comparable to banks' high interest cheque accounts, or similar facilities may be offered through a separate account. The minimum deposit in this case is generally upwards of £2500. Some societies offer postal accounts, which may still provide instant access but carry higher interest rates than the basic cheque account.

Instant access and notice accounts

Despite the vast array of different accounts that come under this heading, there are just three main points to consider in making a choice: the minimum investment, the period of notice required for withdrawals and the interest offered. Table 2.2 shows examples of the better offerings around at the time of writing. As can be seen, the general rule is that interest rates increase with the amount deposited and the length of notice period, though there

Table 2.2 *Building society variable interest account rates*

Amount deposited (£)	Instant access (%)	60 days' notice (%)	90 days' notice (%)
500–999	2.06	3.00	2.48
1000–2499	2.06	3.00	3.30
2500–4999	2.25	3.00	3.30
5000–9999	2.40	3.00	3.30
10,000–24,999	2.70	3.56	4.43
25,000–49,999	2.70	4.13	4.65
50,000+	3.00	4.28	4.80

Note: Rates net of basic rate tax, applicable as at February 1995.

Source: Money Facts

Lump-Sum Investment

can occasionally be anomalies where one society's instant access account offers more than another's notice account.

Notice accounts usually allow withdrawals within the notice period subject to an equivalent loss of interest, but the penalty may be waived if, say, £5000 or £10,000 remains in the account. There are also some which offer a bonus if no withdrawals are made during the year. This can be attractive if you do not expect to need access to your money but are not quite prepared to tie it up in a longer term bond.

Deposit accounts are not shown in the table as they are scarcely heard of these days. Although some instant access accounts require a minimum of £500, a number are available for smaller sums, right down to £1, so they have largely superseded the older deposit and paid-up share accounts.

When comparing interest rates you should always go by the Compound Annual Rate (CAR) figure. This takes into account how often interest is credited, whether monthly, half-yearly or annually. If interest is credited more than once a year, the interest paid will itself start to earn interest, so the total return over a year will be that little bit higher.

One other point to watch for is when an account is closed to new business in favour of a new version. Often the old account will carry a lower rate of interest than the new one, although the terms and conditions may be identical. Not all societies inform their investors in this case – the argument being that the postage would prove prohibitive – so you need to keep an eye on developments and be prepared to switch if necessary. Local society branches will have up-to-date information on closed and new accounts.

Fixed-term accounts
Fixed-term accounts fall into two types: those which offer a fixed rate of interest during the term and those on which the interest is variable but guaranteed to be a fixed percentage above the ordinary share account rate. The minimum investment is generally £1000 and terms may run from six months to five years. Withdrawals during the term may be disallowed altogether, or may be subject to a penalty (commonly of 90 days' interest). Examples of fixed rates are shown in Table 2.3.

Fixed Capital Investments (1)

Table 2.3 *Building society fixed-term account rates*

Term	Minimum investment (£)	Net rate (%)
6 months	2000	4.28
6 months	10,000	4.43
1 year	1000	4.58
2 years	1000	4.8
3 years	1000	5.06
5 years	10,000	5.18

Note: Rates net of basic rate tax, applicable as at February 1995.

Source: Money Facts

Like banks, the larger building societies offer money market time deposits for sums from £50,000 upwards. Rates change frequently but, once you invest, are fixed for the full term.

Tax exempt special savings accounts

Tax exempt special savings accounts (TESSAs) first appeared in January 1991, having been announced in the previous year's Budget. In a way, they are like a little sister to personal equity plans (PEPs, detailed in Chapter 9); PEPs offer tax-free returns from equity-linked investments, while TESSAs offer tax-free returns from bank and building society deposit accounts.

TESSAs are available to any UK resident over the age of 18 and run for a period of five years. The maximum investment that can be made is £3000 in the first year and up to £1800 in each subsequent year, subject to an overall maximum of £9000. You may have only one TESSA, which must be held individually (ie not in joint names), but if you become dissatisfied with your current provider, you may transfer the account to another, although not all institutions are prepared to accept transfers.

For more flexible tax free investment phone ShareLink PEPs on 0121 233 9955.

45

Provided the capital is left intact for the full five years, all the interest earned is tax free. You may make withdrawals equivalent to the interest earned net of basic rate tax, but any larger amount will invalidate the TESSA which will then revert to being an ordinary taxable deposit. However, if you die within the five years, the TESSA will be treated as maturing at that point. All interest earned to date will be free of tax, but from then on it will become taxable as usual.

The first TESSAs matured in January 1996 but the 1994 Budget introduced a follow-on opportunity. Once you have held a TESSA for five years you may use the capital, but not the accumulated interest, to open a 'TESSA 2'. So, if you invested the maximum in your first plan you can transfer the full £9000 into a new one on which all interest will again be tax free, provided that the capital is left untouched for five years.

You must open the new TESSA within six months of your old plan maturing, but you do not have to put the full £9000 in at once: you can add in the balance up to 12 months later. If you have less than £9000 from your first TESSA you may invest extra money in the second and subsequent years of the new plan, up to a maximum of £1800 a year and £9000 overall. Finally, you may choose a different bank or building society for your new TESSA, as long as you obtain a certificate from your current provider to show that you are entitled to open the Mark 2 version.

Whether or not it is worthwhile to have a TESSA depends very much on your personal circumstances. Some of the returns from the first TESSAs have been rather disappointing; accounts paying a variable rate have been hit by the plunge in interest rates over the past five years. Conversely, fixed-rate plans have turned out unexpectedly well. Over the next five years, however, the opposite could prove true, as interest rates may well rise from their current very low level.

If you are going to hold money in a deposit account anyway, you may as well hold it in a TESSA, particularly if you pay higher rate tax. Even if you suddenly need access to the money, and therefore lose the tax advantage, you will be no worse off than if you had put it in an ordinary account in the first place.

You may, however, find that the rate of interest does not turn out to be so good. This is because a number of TESSA providers

Fixed Capital Investments (1)

1st FOR ALL YOUR FINANCIAL NEEDS

Many happy returns

WE'RE WORKING HARD TO MAKE YOUR MONEY WORK HARDER

Leeds & Holbeck Building Society offer a comprehensive range of investment products. Whether you're looking for an account with instant access, a monthly income, or a home for your Tessa money - you'll find our rates highly competitive, ensuring you many happy returns.

LEEDS & HOLBECK BUILDING SOCIETY

Leeds & Holbeck Building Society, Holbeck House, 105 Albion Street, Leeds LS1 5AS.

IN PARTNERSHIP WITH LOCAL PEOPLE

TO FIND OUT MORE, CALL US NOW
0113 225 7777

Lump-Sum Investment

offer a special bonus at the end of the five-year term, at the expense of a lower rate meanwhile. Transferring the account to a new provider may also trigger a penalty, sometimes in addition to a stipulated period of notice, so to get the full benefit, as well as the tax exemption, you have to be prepared to stay the course.

Because of these bonuses, and the various terms attached, it is difficult to compare different TESSAs to determine the best buy. Also, where interest rates are variable, there is no guarantee that today's best offer will still be among the leaders in a year's time. Since you are effectively locked in once you start a plan, providers may be rather more interested in attracting new business than looking after their existing customers; it has been known, for example, for a provider to close an account to new business and then drop the rate paid on it, while offering a more attractive rate on a new product. Although you can transfer in that instance, the penalty charged may mean you lose out anyway.

The choice may be influenced by how much you want to invest. TESSAs may be opened with as little as £1 or £10 a month for those that offer a regular savings option. Some of the best rates, though, apply only if you make the maximum £9000 investment over the term and a number require you to set up a separate 'feeder' account which itself carries a minimum balance, and from which withdrawals are made to fund the TESSA.

You should also bear in mind that, if you are willing to tie your money up for five years, many advisers would consider the stock market was a more natural choice than a deposit account. A couple of TESSA providers have addressed this by creating plans that are linked to stock market performance. These offer a low guaranteed return, of 4 or 5 per cent a year, but with the possibility of a great deal more, depending on how the stock market moves.

The terms of these accounts will vary over time, so check carefully if you are planning to invest. They also carry stiff penalties for withdrawing your money early, so you must be prepared for a full five-year commitment.

National Savings

National Savings products can be divided into three categories:

Fixed Capital Investments (1)

Save money with Barclays Savings

If you are thinking of saving up for that exotic holiday, a new car or a kitchen and don't want to pay tax on your hard-earned money, then you should be considering opening a TESSA account. TESSAs are a simple and safe way to save money and, provided you keep your money in the account for five years, you won't pay a penny in tax on the interest you earn.

Barclays has a range of TESSAs, all offering competitive rates of interest. You can also choose whether to invest a lump sum, or simply put away as little as £25 each month. Jon Green, a personnel manager from London, was one of the thousands of people who invested in a Barclays TESSA when they were first introduced in 1991. Jon was immediately attracted to the idea of saving in a TESSA and was not disappointed with his tax-free earnings when his TESSA matured earlier this year.

"I originally invested in a Barclays TESSA because it was such a safe, easy way to save money – and it offered a good rate of interest" said Jon. "By investing a little each month, I really didn't miss the money.

"When TESSAs were launched, they seemed a little too good to be true. But, once I had sat down with a personal banker at my Barclays branch, who explained exactly how they work, I was very keen to open one. It was no real hardship keeping my savings tied up for five years – especially as I knew I wouldn't have to pay a penny in tax at the end of it. Investing in a TESSA meant my savings would go further".

"My TESSA matured in January, which was perfect timing for me. I had just moved house after getting married last year and we badly needed a holiday from the decorating. Thanks to my TESSA, we will be sunning ourselves in Cuba this year and still have money left over. I've decided to reinvest that money in a new TESSA, so who knows where we'll be off to in five years time."

TESSAs have proved such a popular way of saving money that two thirds of Barclays customers who took out a TESSA when they were launched in 1991 are deciding to reinvest their capital in a new Barclays TESSA. Barclays has a range of competitively priced fixed and variable rate TESSAs. Overall, TESSAs have proved to be a real winner with consumers.

Currently, more than two and half million people have a savings account with Barclays. They chose Barclays because it offered:

• *Competitive rates* – many of Barclays savings products, especially TESSAs and Savings Bonds, are regularly featured in "Best Buy" tables in the national press

• *Convenience* – as a Barclays saver, you can deposit money in any of Barclays 2,000 strong branch network

• *Choice* – Barclays has a large range of savings products to suit every need

If you would like to know more about Barclays range of TESSAs or other savings accounts, call the Barclays Information Line on 0800 400 100.

Lump-Sum Investment

those that pay a return completely free of tax, those that are taxable but pay interest gross, and a couple of one-offs, the First Option Bond and Premium Bonds, which do neither of these things.

Tax-free investments

National Savings Certificates

National Savings Certificates can currently be bought for a minimum of £100, with units of £25 thereafter. Recent issues have followed the same pattern: they run for five years with a fixed rate of return in each year. The return increases over the five years, so although you can cash units in at any time, you lose out by doing so. Table 2.4 shows the interest build-up on the current 43rd issue.

As Table 2.5 shows, issues are available for varying lengths of time and give different rates of return, depending on the market rates at the time and how anxious the government is to get a slice of the savings market. In 1993, it took a more aggressive stance by doubling the maximum holding in current issue certificates to £10,000 and also doubling the reinvestment limit to £20,000.

Reinvestment is an option at the end of the fixed period, when certificates mature. Instead of taking out your money, you can either continue to hold the certificates or reinvest in the latest issue, for which there is a £20,000 maximum holding on top of the £10,000 for new investment.

Once an issue has reached the end of its fixed period, the interest rate moves to the general extension rate, which is variable

Table 2.4 *National Savings Certificates 43rd issue*

Years after purchase	Value at end of year (£)	% yield for year	Compound yield % pa
1	103.75	3.75	3.75
2	108.06	4.15	3.95
3	113.46	5.0	4.30
4	120.44	6.15	4.76
5	129.77	7.75	5.35

Note: Value for a £100 certificate; tax-free return.

Fixed Capital Investments (1)

Table 2.5 *National Savings Certificates, past issues*

Issue number	Dates of issue	Value of £100 certificate after 5 years (£)	Compound annual return over 5 years (%)
33rd	1.5.87–21.7.88	140.26	7.0
34th	22.7.88–16.6.90	143.56	7.5
35th	18.6.90–14.3.91	157.42	9.5
36th	2.4.91–2.5.92	150.37	8.5
37th	13.5.92–5.8.92	146.94	8.0
38th	6.8.92–4.10.92	143.57	7.5
39th	5.10.92–12.11.92	138.63	6.75
40th	13.11.92–16.12.93	132.25	5.75
41st	17.12.93–19.9.94	130.08	5.4
42nd	20.9.94–25.1.96	132.88	5.85

and currently 3.51 per cent for the 7th to 35th issues. The 1st to 6th issues come under different rules and are subject to a lower rate of interest. So you will do better to cash in any of these and reinvest in the current issue, rather than retaining them. More recent issues that are still within their fixed period are worth holding on to up to maturity, because the guaranteed return is higher than anything you could currently get from a comparable investment.

Index-linked certificates
Like the ordinary savings certificates, the current 9th issue of index-linked certificates has a minimum investment of £100 and a maximum of £10,000, with a further £20,000 allowed for reinvestment from mature certificates. The difference is that here the return is linked to movements in the Retail Price Index over the five-year period. In addition, extra interest is added at a guaranteed rate, which increases for each of the five years. Currently the compound return above inflation is equal to 2.5 per cent a year and is free of tax. All the interest earned is added to the capital value – so that after year 1 you are earning interest on the interest – and repaid in total when you cash in.

Lump-Sum Investment

"Why TESSA?"

The acronym TESSA stands for "Tax Exempt Special Savings Account" and the key aspect is contained in the first two words – Tax Exempt. Introduced by the Government to promote good savings habits, the product allows the interest earned on the account to be paid entirely free of income tax, provided the conditions of the account are met.

The account, aimed at 18-year olds and over and first launched in 1991, is designed to run for a five year period, with a maximum amount which can be saved over this time of £9,000; this is composed of various amounts which can be saved in each of the five years. Currently, amounts from £10 per month to a lump sum of £3,000 in Year 1, of £1,800 in each of years 2, 3 and 4 and of £600 in Year 5 may be saved; while the lesser sums are very welcome, higher rates are on offer to those who can invest more. The choice will depend very much on whether you have capital to invest at the outset or whether you intend to build up your savings over the five year period. An individual may only hold one TESSA and therefore only benefit from one tax incentive at any one time.

The maturity of the original first generation TESSAs in January 1996 will demonstrate how well such an investment can perform and the same format has been continued for a further five year period. Investors can 'roll-over' all of their existing capital sum (up to the maximum £9,000) into TESSA 2 which will then continue to qualify for the tax-free incentive. Only the capital sum can be carried forward and in order for it to escape the income tax net, interest from the old TESSA must be moved before the new account is opened. Savers then have six months from the original TESSA maturity date to open a new account, during which time, earned interest is subject to tax. The importance of timing here is crucial, for in order to qualify for 'wall to wall' tax free savings, a follow-up account must be opened on the day your existing TESSA matures.

Most institutions offering TESSAs accept deposits into the account in a number of ways: either a lump sum deposit at the commencement of each year, irregular deposits made throughout the year or regular weekly/monthly/quarterly sums perhaps saved from salary payments. In some cases, bonus payments are on offer when certain minimum deposit levels are achieved during a period.

The basic TESSA is available from most, if not all, financial institutions; why then should an investor opt to hold a TESSA with any one society or bank? The answer in most cases is the rate of return offered by the institution, although there may be some conditions, for example in the event of accounts being moved from one institution to another.

Although TESSAs are mobile accounts, in that the savings built up may be moved from one organisation to another to achieve the benefit of improved interest rates, beware; certain institutions will not accept transferred TESSAs partway through their five-year term while others charge a transfer fee – £25 is not an uncommon amount for a variable rate TESSA being moved. Fixed rate accounts are more expensive to transfer, in that, because the society or bank has budgetted for having your funds over the five year period, early closures will attract penalty charges.

Rates quoted for TESSAs may be either fixed, variable or escalating. They can be fixed for the five-year life, despite and regardless of any fluctuations in money market rates or actions taken by other institutions. This is an option chosen by a small number of institutions who have taken a long term view as to what will happen to rates over the next five years and offers a guaranteed return, albeit at what might appear to be, a not very attractive rate. You have to decide when opening your TESSA, whether you agree with this view or not.

More common is the variable rate TESSA, where rates will alter periodically, to reflect what is happening to interest rates in general or market changes such as special offers by other institutions. This is the option offered by the majority and because of this, a walk down the High Street or a quick look at the financial press will show what rate each is offering *at this point in time*.

In order to maximise the return on your investment, it is important to choose an organisation which has consistently paid above-average rates and with the second generation of TESSA becoming available this year, few organisations can demonstrate a better track record than the Dunfermline. The Dunfermline TESSA has consistently led in terms of paying higher rates during the past five years and has been identified as an outstanding performer by independent financial analysts.

Existing investors are also free to switch their savings at this point, without penalty, to anyone offering better rates of interest and there are many offers of both fixed and variable rates. Organisations will also offer a variety of inducements, aimed at attracting investors currently with other institutions as well as retaining their own investors.

The Dunfermline will continue to offer attractive rates of interest for the new-style TESSA in 1996, with the aim of ensuring that our members achieve maximum returns – tax free whenever possible!

Advertisement feature

52

Fixed Capital Investments (1)

Our new high interest, savings account.

For anyone with a letterbox.

The Dunfermline Direct High Interest Postal Savings Account Rates.		
Over £100,000	£50,000 - £99,999	£25,000 -£49,999
6·60% gross*	**6·45%** gross*	**6·25%** gross*
£10,000 -£24,999	£5,000 -£9,999	£2,000-£4,999
6·05% gross*	**5·85%** gross*	**5·20%** gross*

Dunfermline Direct is a new postal savings account which offers high rates of interest from Scotland's leading Building Society.

We provide all that you'll need, even pre-paid envelopes. So there's no more trekking to your building society or bank, the nearest postbox will do. Which means it's convenient and very easy to use.

If you've got between £2,000 and £250,000 to invest it's the perfect savings account.

Withdrawals require 28 days notice. Immediate withdrawals forfeit 28 days interest. Interest is paid to you on 30th June each year, with a monthly interest option available.+

Of course, for the very best demonstration of how easy it all is, simply write to us at Dunfermline Building Society, FREEPOST DF2, Dunfermline KY11 5BR. Or phone 0345 336688 (LOCAL RATE 24 hrs). It won't be long before the details pop through your letterbox.

DUNFERMLINE
SCOTLAND'S BUILDING SOCIETY

Dunfermline Building Society Caledonia House Carnegie Avenue Dunfermline
Fife KY11 5PJ Phone 01383 627727

* Gross - The rate of interest paid without the deduction of basic rate tax to eligible non-tax payers. Interest rates correct at time of going to press. +All gross rates are reduced by 0.5% with the monthly income option.

Lump-Sum Investment

As mentioned at the start of this chapter, inflation can be a serious threat to fixed capital investments and the real returns above inflation offered by interest rates can be very small. So in principle, index-linking should be very attractive. In practice, though, it is like any fixed rate: in return for protection against doing worse, you give up the chance to do better. For example, if inflation remains at the current rate of around 2.9 per cent, the total return on index-linked certificates, including the extra interest, would be 5.4 per cent, just slightly above that offered on savings certificates. If inflation leaps up again, the in-built protection will be extremely worth while.

Taxable investments

Income bonds

Income bonds are available from a minimum of £2000 up to a maximum of £250,000 and offer a monthly income, paid on the 5th of each month. The interest rate is variable, but six weeks' notice is given of any change, which will be advertised in newspapers. The current rates are 6.25 per cent gross for sums up to £25,000 and 6.5 per cent gross for larger amounts, which compares reasonably well with banks and building societies. Income is paid (gross, but liable to tax) direct to a bank, building society or National Savings investment account.

Capital bonds

Capital bonds run for five years and offer a guaranteed rate of return if they are held for the full term. For the current Series J bonds this is 6.65 per cent gross. You can cash in a bond early, but this would mean you lose out, as the interest rate increases each year, and the amount you get on cashing in is the value at the last anniversary plus a special interest rate since then. No interest is paid on bonds encashed before the first anniversary.

The minimum holding is £100, with a maximum of £250,000. This maximum applies to total holdings of all capital bonds, with the exception of Series A. At the end of the five years bonds are repaid in full, together with all the interest accumulated; no further interest is earned after the fifth anniversary.

Fixed Capital Investments (1)

GARY HAS A LEARNING DISABILITY

HE LIVES IN A HOUSE IN SHEFFIELD WHICH HE SHARES WITH THREE OTHER PEOPLE. HIS AMBITION IS TO TAKE AN ENGINE FIREMAN'S COURSE, SO HE CAN SPEND HIS HOLIDAYS WORKING ON STEAM TRAINS AT PRESERVED RAILWAYS.

Gary has been with The Home Farm Trust for seven years and now enjoys a varied and independent life thanks to professional care and development.

Every year, thousands of people are born with a learning disability, and we aim to provide services to meet their needs as and when they grow up. HFT has homes and day services around the country, and also supports people with learning disabilities and their carers in a variety of other ways.

PATRON
HRH THE PRINCESS ROYAL

"For nearly 35 years, The Home Farm Trust (HFT) has provided care, homes and quality of life for people with learning disabilities (formerly known as mental handicap) in towns and villages throughout the country.

The HFT approach to care is centred on the needs and wishes of the people we are here to help. We give people a say in the kind of home they want, the activities, training and work they pursue and help them maximise their potential and achieve greater levels of independence, whatever their ability.

HFT's care takes many forms. Gillian spent a traumatic childhood in various forms of care, but has blossomed during her years with HFT and now lives in a flat in the community with her husband Paul and daughter Ruth. Gillian continues to receive help from HFT in a supported environment.

Others are less able. Ben cannot speak. After many years of frustration, he can now ask simple questions and express himself through a voice activated machine with touch pads.

Mary has a learning disability and is also physically disabled. Despite the many challenges she faces, she has integrated well with her local community and is a valued member of the indoor bowls league.

Work experience is beneficial to many and placements include work at bakeries, shops, playschools, builders, parks and many other venues. Families also play a very valuable role within HFT's philosophy, supporting the work of HFT through vital fundraising".

Please give us your support. Your donation will help us continue to provide a quality service to those men and women cared for by the Trust.

You can help us achieve our aims, by remembering us in your will or by sending a covenanted donation.

Please help us safeguard the future of more people with learning disabilities.

THE HOME FARM TRUST,
MERCHANTS HOUSE, WAPPING ROAD,
BRISTOL BS1 4RW.

TEL: 0117 927 37 46

REG. CHARITY NO: 313069.

Lump-Sum Investment

Index-linked certificates

Like the ordinary savings certificates, the current 9th issue of index-linked certificates has a minimum investment of £100 and a maximum of £10,000, with a further £20,000 allowed for reinvestment from mature certificates. The difference is that here the return is linked to movements in the Retail Price Index over the five-year period. In addition, extra interest is added at a guaranteed rate, which increases for each of the five years. Currently the compound return above inflation is equal to 2.5 per cent a year and is free of tax. All the interest earned is added to the capital value – so that after year 1 you are earning interest on the interest – and repaid in total when you cash in.

As mentioned at the start of this chapter, inflation can be a serious threat to fixed capital investments and the real returns above inflation offered by interest rates can be very small. So in principle, index-linking should be very attractive. In practice, though, it is like any fixed rate: in return for protection against doing worse, you give up the chance to do better. For example, if inflation remains at the current rate of around 2.9 per cent, the total return on index-linked certificates, including the extra interest, would be 5.4 per cent, just slightly above that offered on savings certificates. If inflation leaps up again, the in-built protection will be extremely worth while.

Taxable investments

Income bonds

Income bonds are available from a minimum of £2000 up to a maximum of £250,000 and offer a monthly income, paid on the 5th of each month. The interest rate is variable, but six weeks' notice is given of any change, which will be advertised in newspapers. The current rates are 6.25 per cent gross for sums up to £25,000 and 6.5 per cent gross for larger amounts, which compares reasonably well with banks and building societies. Income is paid (gross, but liable to tax) direct to a bank, building society or National Savings investment account.

Capital bonds

Capital bonds run for five years and offer a guaranteed rate of

Fixed Capital Investments (1)

Devon Air Ambulance

- Is a charity-funded helicopter ambulance used by West Country Ambulance Service for responding to '999' emegency calls.
- All helicopter costs have to be met by charitable contributions. No government, NHS, Local Authority or National Lottery funding is available to us.
- On average the helicopter is deployed three times a day throughout the year.
- The cost of the Ambulance service in Devon is £750,000 per annum.

Contact **Devon Air Ambulance Trust,**
Broadclyst, Exeter EX5 3LZ or Telephone 01392 46 66 66
to make a contribution or for further information

National Savings Bank ordinary account
With a basic interest rate of 1.75 per cent gross, the ordinary account is slightly more lucrative than a bank current account, although the facilities are more limited. Withdrawals are generally restricted to £100 on demand, with written notice required for larger sums, although if you have used the account for at least six months at one particular post office you can apply for a regular customer account, which entitles you to take out up to £250 on demand.

If you keep an account open for a full calendar year, you are then eligible for a higher interest rate for each month that the balance is £500 or more. Even so, this higher rate is only 2.75 per cent gross. The one feature that does add some attraction for higher rate taxpayers is that the first £70 of interest, or £140 for a joint holding, is free of tax. Otherwise, this is more a home for ready cash than an investment.

Lump-Sum Investment

National Savings Bank investment account
For smaller sums in particular, this can be an attractive alternative to bank and building society deposits, as the minimum is just £20. There are three tiers of interest rates which are currently 5 per cent for sums under £500, 5.5 per cent from £500 to £25,000 and 5.75 per cent for sums over £25,000. These are the gross rates; interest is credited gross, so you can enjoy the money for a short while before settling the tax bill. Withdrawals are at one month's notice and from May 1993 the maximum holding was increased to £100,000.

Pensioners Bond
The Pensioners Bond was announced in the 1993 Autumn Budget and introduced in January 1994. It is available only for people aged 60 or over, although it can be bought by trustees, as long as the beneficiary is over 60. The minimum investment is £500 and the maximum is £50,000 per series, or £100,000 for a joint holding, for which both savers must meet the age requirement.

The interest rate is fixed for the first five years that you hold a bond and for the current 3rd series is 7 per cent gross. The interest is taxable but paid gross and will be credited on the 19th of each month direct to a bank or building society account or a National Savings investment account.

At the end of five years, National Savings will write to tell you the guaranteed interest rate for the next five years. The money can then be reinvested or withdrawn without penalty. If you want to cash in at any other time, you must give 60 days' notice and no interest will be paid during those 60 days. Partial withdrawals can be made from a minimum of £500 as long as at least £500 remains in your holding.

At the time of writing, the Pensioners Bond has proved popular and the return is attractive compared with building society accounts. The drawback is that interest rates are currently exceptionally low and the trend could reverse over the next five years, leaving the bond looking uncompetitive. Although you can cash in early, the penalty is quite severe – the loss of interest would amount to about £115 on a £10,000 holding. For some people, the benefits of having a regular fixed income will

Fixed Capital Investments (1)

Save money with Barclays Savings

If you are thinking of saving up for that exotic holiday, a new car or a kitchen and don't want to pay tax on your hard-earned money, then you should be considering opening a TESSA account. TESSAs are a simple and safe way to save money and, provided you keep your money in the account for five years, you won't pay a penny in tax on the interest you earn.

Barclays has a range of TESSAs, all offering competitive rates of interest. You can also choose whether to invest a lump sum, or simply put away as little as £25 each month. Jon Green, a personnel manager from London, was one of the thousands of people who invested in a Barclays TESSA when they were first introduced in 1991. Jon was immediately attracted to the idea of saving in a TESSA and was not disappointed with his tax-free earnings when his TESSA matured earlier this year.

"I originally invested in a Barclays TESSA because it was such a safe, easy way to save money – and it offered a good rate of interest" said Jon. "By investing a little each month, I really didn't miss the money.

"When TESSAs were launched, they seemed a little too good to be true. But, once I had sat down with a personal banker at my Barclays branch, who explained exactly how they work, I was very keen to open one. It was no real hardship keeping my savings tied up for five years – especially as I knew I wouldn't have to pay a penny in tax at the end of it. Investing in a TESSA meant my savings would go further".

"My TESSA matured in January, which was perfect timing for me. I had just moved house after getting married last year and we badly needed a holiday from the decorating. Thanks to my TESSA, we will be sunning ourselves in Cuba this year and still have money left over. I've decided to reinvest that money in a new TESSA, so who knows where we'll be off to in five years time."

TESSAs have proved such a popular way of saving money that two thirds of Barclays customers who took out a TESSA when they were launched in 1991 are deciding to reinvest their capital in a new Barclays TESSA. Barclays has a range of competitively priced fixed and variable rate TESSAs. Overall, TESSAs have proved to be a real winner with consumers.

Currently, more than two and half million people have a savings account with Barclays. They chose Barclays because it offered:

• *Competitive rates* – many of Barclays savings products, especially TESSAs and Savings Bonds, are regularly featured in "Best Buy" tables in the national press

• *Convenience* – as a Barclays saver, you can deposit money in any of Barclays 2,000 strong branch network

• *Choice* – Barclays has a large range of savings products to suit every need

If you would like to know more about Barclays range of TESSAs or other savings accounts, call the Barclays Information Line on 0800 400 100.

Lump-Sum Investment

outweigh the possible loss if interest rates rise. Otherwise, you might do better with the Income Bond, which is currently paying slightly lower interest, but could pay more if rates rise and can be cashed in at three months' notice without any interest penalty.

First Option Bond

The First Option Bond was initially launched in July 1992 and caused something of a furore. The building societies saw it as a serious threat to their own ability to attract savings and Cheltenham & Gloucester took the bold step of raising its mortgage rate – on the grounds that it would have to raise its savings rate to compete with the bond and needed to maintain its margins. The last thing the government wanted, at a time when it was trying to bring down inflation, was to see mortgage costs rise, so it backed off and reduced the interest on the bond.

But governments do not remain intimidated for long and the bond was relaunched in the 1993 Budget. The minimum investment is £1000 and interest is fixed for 12 months at a time. At each anniversary, investors are notified of the new rate for the next year and have the option of continuing the bond or cashing it in. Between anniversaries, the return will be the full value at the last anniversary plus interest at half the fixed rate for the period since then, except that no interest is paid for encashments during the first year. Bonds can also be partially cashed in as long as the value remains above £1000.

Unusually for a National Savings product, interest is credited net of basic rate tax. Higher rate taxpayers will be liable for the difference, while non-taxpayers can apply for a refund. Interest is not paid out automatically, but you can apply for a part repayment equivalent to the amount earned. This should be timed for the anniversary date if possible.

At the time of writing the interest rate is 5 per cent net of basic rate tax, which compares well with building society accounts. There is also a bonus of 0.2 per cent where the value remains at least £20,000 during the year.

Premium Bonds

Premium Bonds are not exactly an investment, as there is no promise of a return – but then again, that could be said to apply

Fixed Capital Investments (1)

KENT AIR AMBULANCE TRUST
Registered Charity Number 1021367

KENT AIR AMBULANCE TRUST

Every second counts in the race to bring "immediate care" to the critically ill or seriously injured. Kent Air Ambulance responds swiftly to 999 calls delivering a parademic crew to incidents and transporting patients to hospital in a fraction of the time taken by a land ambulance.

But to maintain this life-saving service Kent Air Ambulance Trust has to raise up to £60,000 a month and relies on support from people who live, work, visit or travel in Kent.

YOU COULD HELP by making an individual gift – for example through Gift Aid or by leaving a legacy to pay for new equipment when needed or towards extending the helicopter's Operating hours.

YOU COULD HELP by pledging a regular contribution, via a Deed of Covenant or Payroll Giving.

For further information on how you can make a difference to a child hurt in a road accident, a man suffering from a heart attack, a woman unconscious after a fall:–

Please contact: **Kate Chivers,** Chief Executive, Kent Air Ambulance Trust, The Village Centre, High Street, Staplehurst, Kent, TN12 0BJ. Phone: 01580 893555.

Don't forget the life you save could be yours or a loved one's.

---

to equities and at least with Premium Bonds your capital is always safe. The odds on winning a prize also improve with the size of your holding: at the maximum of £20,000, you should on average win 14 prizes a year, while to win once a year on average you need to hold £1450-worth. Of course, averages do not always work out; although ERNIE is quite impartial, some people seem to be luckier than others.

The minimum investment is £100, with multiples of £10 thereafter. From 1 May 1996 the monthly prize fund will be calculated as equivalent to one month's interest on each eligible bond at an interest rate of 4.75 per cent. Bonds have to be held for one complete calendar month before they are entered for the draw. There are 350,000 prizes awarded each month, with 10 per cent of the fund allocated to prizes between £5000 and the £1 million jackpot, 15 per cent to prizes of £500 and £1000 and the remaining 75 per cent providing prizes of £50 and £100. All prizes are free of tax.

Lump-Sum Investment

Table 2.6 *National Savings guide*

Product	Minimum and maximum holdings	Who may buy or invest	Income fixed or variable
National Savings Certificates 43rd issue	Minimum £100, maximum £10,000 in addition to previous issues; may reinvest a further £20,000 from mature Savings Certificates	Individuals (also jointly), trustees	Increasing at fixed rate for initial term; variable extension rate thereafter
National Savings Certificates 9th index-linked issue	Minimum £100, maximum £10,000 in addition to previous issues; may reinvest a further £20,000 from mature Savings Certificates	Individuals (also jointly), trustees	Repayment value linked to changes in the RPI plus fixed annual supplement; variable after five years
National Savings income bond	Minimum £2000, maximum £250,000	Individuals (also jointly), trustees	Variable; paid monthly
National Savings capital bond Series J	Minimum £100, maximum £250,000 for holdings in all series, excluding Series A	Individuals (also jointly), trustees	Fixed if held for full five years; no interest paid after five years
Pensioners Bond 3rd Series	Minimum £500, maximum £50,000 in addition to Series 1 and 2	Individuals over 60 (also jointly), trustees	Fixed for five years at a time; paid monthly
National Savings First Option Bond	Minimum £1000, maximum £250,000	Individuals (also jointly), trustees	Fixed for 12 months at a time
National Savings Bank ordinary account	Minimum £10, maximum £10,000	Individuals (also jointly), children, trustees	Variable; credited annually
National Savings Bank investment account	Minimum £20, maximum £100,000	Individuals (also jointly), children, trustees	Variable; credited annually
Premium Bonds	Minimum £100, maximum £20,000	Individuals over 16; bonds can be bought for children by parents, guardians or (great) grandparents	No interest

Tax position	Notice of withdrawal	How to buy/sell
Free of income tax and CGT	At least eight working days	Buy: through post offices Sell: repayment form from post offices
Free of income tax and CGT	At least eight working days	Buy: through post offices Sell: repayment form from post offices
Interest is taxable, but paid gross	Three months; in the first year, interest paid at half rate from date of purchase to date of repayment	Buy: application form at post offices, send with cheque to Blackpool Sell: repayment form from post offices
Interest is taxable, but paid gross	At least two weeks; no interest paid if cashed in in first year	Buy: through post offices Sell: repayment form from post offices
Interest is taxable, but paid gross	60 days; no interest paid during notice period	Buy: application form at post offices, send with cheque to Blackpool Sell: repayment form on bond
Interest is taxable; paid net of basic rate tax which non-taxpayers can reclaim	No notice; no penalty if repaid on anniversary date, otherwise interest paid at half the fixed rate since the last anniversary; no interest if cashed in in first year	Buy: application form from post offices to be sent with cheque to National Savings, Glasgow Sell: repayment form on investment certificate
First £70 (£140 joint) of annual interest is free of income tax	Up to £100 on demand; larger amounts require a few days' written notice	Opening and withdrawals at post offices
Interest is taxable, but paid gross	One month	Opening: through post offices Withdrawals: form from post offices to be sent to Glasgow
Prizes free of income tax and CGT	At least eight working days	Buy: through post offices Sell: repayment form from post offices

Lump-Sum Investment

For a complete guide to all the National Savings products mentioned, see Table 2.6.

Where to find out more

Banks and building societies

Information on the types of account offered and current interest rates can be found in local branches. The Building Societies Association (0171 437 0655) can also answer general questions, but will not advise on current rates offered by individual societies. *Money Facts*, a monthly subscription magazine aimed chiefly at professional advisers, gives comprehensive listings of bank and building society accounts, TESSAs, offshore accounts and National Savings products. It is available from Moneyfacts Publications, Laundry Loke, North Walsham, Norfolk NR28 0BD, telephone 01692 500765.

Money market accounts

Information can be found in newspapers.

National Savings

Booklets on the various products are available at post offices. General information can be obtained by phoning the Sales Information Unit on 0500 500000 during normal office hours.

The latest interest rates are also quoted by recorded message on the following numbers:

London: 0171 605 9483/9484
Blackpool: 01253 723714
Glasgow: 0141 632 2766.

3

Fixed Capital Investments (2)

The last chapter covered the major institutions that offer fixed capital investments, most of which can be bought through high street outlets. Going a little further afield, there are a number of other products which also offer capital security, but may offer a more attractive rate of income than the standard bank and building society accounts, particularly for smaller investments.

Local authority bonds

Local authority bonds are issued for a fixed term of between one and ten years, over which the capital value remains constant. The minimum investment starts at £500 and the interest rate is fixed throughout the term. The bonds used to be a popular way for local authorities to raise funds, but in the 1980s the administration involved and the availability of cheaper loans from other sources led to a decline in the number of issues. However, there has recently been something of a revival and the bonds that are available are open to any investor – it need not be your own local authority that you buy from.

One drawback is that there is no facility to make withdrawals during the term of the bond, so your money is effectively locked in until the maturity date, although it may be possible to transfer it to a third party on written request. When the fixed term expires, there may be an opportunity to continue the investment for a further period at whatever the going rate of interest is at that time, otherwise you can simply have your original capital returned.

Lump-Sum Investment

As for the safety aspect, the bonds are backed by the local authority itself, not by central government. Hence they are marginally more risky than a government-issued security such as a gilt and usually offer slightly higher rates of return to reflect this. However, while there is no obligation for the government to help out or provide any compensation in the event of a default, there is a certain presumption that it would act if there was a danger of widespread losses, if only for the sake of political expediency.

Interest is paid out twice a year and will normally be paid net of basic rate tax. If you are a non-taxpayer, you can register to receive interest payments gross by completing Inland Revenue Form R85, in the same way as for bank and building society deposits. Once the bond has been issued, the interest rate will remain fixed for the full term. Hence the longer term bonds are most suitable for investors for whom security of income is a priority – others may find they lose out if interest rates rise in the future. The rates will vary between different authorities and across the different lifespans, and are reset on a regular basis – sometimes daily – so you should check the up-to-date position before investing. Examples of current rates at the time of writing are shown in Table 3.1.

Table 3.1 *Local authority bonds*

Years	1	2	3	4/5	6–8
Typical gross rates (%)	5.5	6.5	6.75	7.0	7.0

Source: Money Facts, March 1996

Guaranteed income and growth bonds

Guaranteed income bonds are issued by life assurance companies and are available for terms of between one and ten years, although the widest choice is for periods of four or five years. The minimum investment is generally around £5000 and the interest rate is fixed for the whole term, so these bonds are attractive to investors seeking a regular income, perhaps in retirement, to supplement a pension.

Not all life offices operate in this market and some that do issue

Fixed Capital Investments (2)

bonds only occasionally. In any case, specific offers will only be available for a limited period, as interest rates will be reviewed at regular intervals. The rates are generally based on the return available on gilts and should give a better deal than a building society deposit, but then again, you may be committing your capital for a longer period.

Interest payments are usually made once a year, though some bonds pay out half-yearly and there may also be a monthly income option on larger investments. Some examples of the rates available at the time of going to press are shown in Table 3.2. These are net rates and apply for an investment of £5000; in some cases higher rates may be available for larger sums.

You might expect that the longer you are prepared to tie up your capital, the higher the return should be, but, as the table shows, this is not always so. The companies have to match the rates that they offer to those they can obtain on their investments, so it depends on the pattern of market interest rates. Remember, too, that the rate is guaranteed throughout the term, so at the longer end you may be sacrificing a small measure of return in exchange for the security of a fixed income.

Once you buy a bond, you are effectively locked into it for the full term. Companies vary in their willingness to provide a surrender value on early encashment, but generally any amount offered will be small. Should the bond holder die, the original capital will be returned, but again, companies have different policies on whether they will add in any income accrued since the last payment. Where payments are annual, this could be a significant amount if the bond holder dies just before a payment is due. For married couples, one way around this problem is to take out a bond on a 'joint life, second death' basis, which means payments would continue to be paid to the surviving spouse for the rest of the term. Should both partners die, the capital sum

Phone ShareLink for a PEP talk on 0121 233 9955.

Lump-Sum Investment

Table 3.2 *Examples of guaranteed income bond rates*

Term	Income net of basic rate tax (%)
1 year	4.7
2 years	5.25
3 years	5.5
4 years	5.75
5 years	6.2

For comparison, these bonds were available when sample interest rates on competing products were as follows:

Product	Term or notice required	Rate net of basic rate tax (%)	Fixed/variable interest
NS Certificates 43rd issue	5 years	5.35[a]	Fixed
NS First Option Bond (£1-20,000)	1 year	5.0	Fixed
Building society instant access (min £5000)	None	2.4	Variable
Building society 90-day account (min £10,000)	90 days	4.43	Variable
TESSA (First issue)	5 years	7.25[a]	Variable

[a] Tax-free to all investors

would be repaid to the estate on the second death. As with annuities, however, this kind of 'extra' may mean the income level is slightly lower.

Another version is the guaranteed growth bond. This operates on a similar principle to the income bond, but the interest earned is accumulated within the bond rather than paid out, so at the end of the term you receive back your capital plus a guaranteed profit.

Tax treatment of guaranteed bonds

The tax position of guaranteed bonds can be complex, partly

> **ASSOCIATION FOR INTERNATIONAL CANCER RESEARCH**
>
> Cancer recognises no borders
> We fund vital basic research - worldwide
> Eminent scientists depend on us
>
> Help them conquer cancer with
> donations, covenants or bequests
>
> Charity No. SC022918
> Madras House, St Andrews, Fife KY16 9EH Tel: 01334-477910

because they are not all of the same structure. Longer term bonds are sometimes based on a combination of annuities: a temporary annuity, which provides the income payments, and a deferred annuity, which provides the return of capital at maturity. However, a change in the tax treatment of annuities at the beginning of 1992 made this route less attractive and the majority of bonds now issued are based on a single premium endowment policy with guaranteed bonuses.

For a basic rate taxpayer, the composition of the bond is of no concern. Income is paid net of basic rate tax, so you have no further liability. Non-taxpayers, however, cannot reclaim the tax paid from an endowment, so as a rule these bonds are not suitable to those investors.

Higher rate taxpayers are in a different position again. With an endowment, up to 5 per cent of the original sum invested may be withdrawn each year free of tax – it is counted as a return of capital – and any unused part of this allowance can be carried forward to subsequent years. Where a bond pays income annually, the mechanics are such that you will usually be 'in credit' with this allowance for most or all of the term. At maturity, however, tax may be charged on the 'profit', taking into account the money paid out and the amount originally invested. Further

Lump-Sum Investment

details of the taxation of single premium policies are given in Chapter 10.

Older investors who qualify for age allowance may also be affected by the tax rules. For these and higher rate taxpayers, an insurance broker or other professional adviser should be able to offer guidance on the best buy.

Cash unit trusts

Unit trusts are usually associated with equity investments, which are far from capital secure, but cash trusts are a fairly new breed. They invest chiefly in money market instruments and, by virtue of the size of the fund, they can secure top rates of interest. The minimum investment varies between £250 and £5000.

Cash trusts offer complete capital security and in most cases there is no initial charge. There is an annual management charge, which has to be met from the income the trust generates, but it is generally no more than 0.5 per cent. The return varies according to the interest rates available in the market; at the time of writing, gross yields go up to 6.15 per cent.

Income can be paid out or reinvested in the fund. Interest is credited net of basic rate tax, which can be reclaimed by non-taxpayers, while higher rate taxpayers will be liable for the extra amount due. A few trusts provide a cheque-book facility; otherwise, if you want to get your money out, the manager is obliged to issue a cheque within 24 hours of receiving the redemption form.

Further information on cash unit trusts can be found in Chapters 6 and 7.

Offshore deposit accounts

All the major banks and building societies now have offshore branches or subsidiary companies, situated in either the Isle of Man or the Channel Islands. Like their onshore parents, they offer a variety of accounts, depending on how much you want to invest and how quickly you want to be able to access your money. The choices include instant access, 90-day notice accounts, fixed interest term deposits with periods from a number of months to a number of years, money market accounts and high interest cheque accounts. All of these operate in very much the same way as their onshore equivalents.

As a rule, interest rates are tiered with the size of the deposit and the notice period (see Table 3.3 below). At the bottom end of the scale, minimum deposits start around £1000, while money market accounts start at around £2500 and can go up to more than £100,000.

Offshore deposit accounts enjoyed particular popularity when onshore accounts were subject to composite rate tax, which was deducted at source and could not be reclaimed by a non-taxpayer. Nowadays that advantage no longer exists and for UK residents the tax liability will be the same either way. However, offshore accounts do have the slight advantage that interest is paid gross, so the tax bill is deferred for a while.

The other important consideration is how safe your investment is. 'Offshore' used to be synonymous with shady, or at least dubious, dealing, but the image has been considerably cleaned up in recent years. The Isle of Man, which had a salutary experience with the collapse of the Savings and Investment Bank in 1982, now has a compensation scheme for bank and building society deposits. In addition, building society subsidiaries are covered by their parents for the full amount of their liabilities. The Channel Islands keep a tight rein on financial businesses by having a strict vetting procedure for any institutions applying to set up in the islands.

Table 3.3 *Examples of offshore deposit rates*

Type of account	Gross annual interest rate (%)
Instant access, min £1000	4.9
Instant access, min £5000	5.4
Instant access, min £50,000	6.6
60-day notice, min £10,000	5.65
90-day notice, min £10,000	6.4
Money market account, min £5000	4.25

Source: Money Facts, March 1996

Lump-Sum Investment

OFFSHORE PRIVATE BANKING INTERNATIONAL

As a private individual and international investor resident outside Denmark, you are in a special position to earn high returns on your funds by investing with JYSKE BANK.

All investors have different needs, here we offer a wide range of savings and investment schemes. 30 years ago, JYSKE BANK began to specialise in private deposits from abroad that yield high returns in Denmark. The long-standing commitment to offshore/international private banking has made us the leading Danish bank in this field.

We attach great importance to providing our customers with optimum benefits. Being far away does not prevent us from offering a personal and professional service.

JYSKE BANK is a well established Danish bank with a history spanning more than 100 years. The name originates from a merger of four Jutland based banks in 1967, which lead to the formation of JYSKE BANK, Bank of Jutland; making it the fourth largest Danish bank today.

Our head office is located in Silkeborg in Jutland, an area of outstanding natural beauty. From here, all central planning and liquidity functions are managed. In addition to our 133 branches in Denmark, JYSKE BANK has a branch in London, subsidiaries in Gibraltar, Zurich, Hamburg and representations in Spain and Portugal.

More than 35,000 international customers from 150 countries hold their savings and investments with JYSKE BANK, and every day new customers join us. The reason for this international success is simple. All our customers receive a personal service, and a choice from a range of different savings and investment schemes adapted to suit their financial requirements.

Many of our international customers have chosen JYSKE BANK on the recommendation of others. We see this as an expression of customer satisfaction with the high level of service and the products which we offer.

Denmark is a sensible choice when it comes to placing your money. Its strict banking laws and the Danish Financial Supervisory Authority provide substantial security. In addition, Denmark is an economically and politically stable country. Stability is provided through Danish membership of the Economic Community, NATO, OECD and the EMS which sets limits for exchange rate movements between the currencies of member countries.

The Danish economic policy to keep inflation low is a major factor behind the confidence we enjoy amoung our many overseas customers. By persuing this policy, Denmark has consistently obtained one of the lowest inflation rates of the world.

JYSKE BANK's Private Banking (International) Department is located in the centre of Copenhagen. All the staff have special training in banking and foreign languages. Many have English and German as their mother tongue. This means our customers can rely on professional advice in these languages. If you happen to be in the Danish capital, do please call in. You will find us at Vesterbrogade 9, a few minutes walk from the main central railway station and the famous Tivoli Gardens.

In addition to the personal contact with staff in Copenhagen, JYSKE BANK offers consultations outside Denmark, with our advisers regularly visiting the areas where most of our overseas customers and potential customers live.

Please contact us to receive information and how to become a customer with us, we would like to welcome you to high class private banking in JYSKE BANK.

Fixed Capital Investments (2)

PRIVATE BANKING (INTERNATIONAL)

Invest your funds with a Danish bank

- Low costs
- No account fees
- No Danish taxes
- Personal Account Manager
- 30 years experience with foreign clients
- 150,000 shareholders
- Customers in more than 150 countries
- 133 Danish branches

Please choose two of the investment opportunities listed below, and we will forward you the relevant information:

❏ **No 1 Account/Fixed Term Deposits**
High interest currency deposit accounts. 19 different currencies. Interest rates up to 8.00%/9.375% p.a.

❏ **Securities**
Trade, safe-keeping and portfolio management of international securities

❏ **Bond Funds**
6 bond funds in different currencies and with different compositions

❏ **Equity Funds**
2 equity funds: International Equity Fund and Emerging Markets Equity Fund

❏ **Geared Bond Funds**
2 geared bond funds: High-risk Investments in European currencies or in USD and USD - related currencies

The value of fund investments can go down as well as up and an investor may not get back the original amount invested. Depending on the investor's currency of reference, currency fluctuations may adversely affect the value of investments.

*Further information can also be obtained at Jyske Bank (London), FREEPOST LON5323, London, WC2A 1BR, England.
Tel.: 0171 831 2778
(FREEPHONE: UK ONLY 0800 378415).
Fax: 0171 405 2257. Member of S.F.A.*

Please send in the advert

Name _____
Address _____
Postal Code _____ City _____
Country _____
Tel. _____ Fax _____

Jyske Bank
Private Banking
(International)
Vesterbrogade 9
DK-1780 Copenhagen
Denmark
Tel. 0045 3378 7801
Fax 0045 3378 7811

207-498

COPENHAGEN · LONDON
ZURICH · GIBRALTAR · HAMBURG
FUENGIROLA · LISBON

Lump-Sum Investment

Offshore money funds

Sterling offshore money funds are similar to the money market funds mentioned in the last chapter, investing in much the same kind of holdings, such as bank deposits and certificates of deposit. In addition, however, there are offshore money funds denominated in a variety of different currencies. These range from major currencies, such as the US dollar, the German D-Mark, the Swiss franc and the Japanese yen, to the less obvious, such as the Belgian franc, the Danish krone and the Swedish krona.

After the UK left the Exchange Rate Mechanism in September 1992, there was increased interest in foreign currency funds, which may offer higher rates of interest than their sterling counterparts. However, there is a greater risk involved because of currency fluctuations. This may be reduced if you invest in a managed currency fund, where the manager will switch between various currencies according to their perceived prospects. Even so, while there is the opportunity for gain on the exchange rates, there is equally the chance of capital loss.

Some money funds have no set minimum investment, while others may require £1000 upwards. One point to watch for is that these funds carry an annual management fee. The usual figure is around 1 per cent and anything higher than this should be treated with caution, as it will cut into the returns available.

Taxation of offshore funds

The tax position of offshore funds is a little complex, as they are classified into two types: those with 'accumulator' status, also known as 'roll-up' funds, and those with 'distributor' status.

Prior to 1984, all funds were of the roll-up type, which meant that all interest earned was accumulated within the fund and added to the capital value. As a result, when investors came to sell, they were liable only to capital gains tax on the profits. Since there was the annual exemption allowance to make use of, and the top rate of capital gains tax at that time was only 30 per cent, this provided excellent tax efficiency, for higher rate taxpayers in particular.

Since 1984, however, the Inland Revenue has introduced new

Fixed Capital Investments (2)

tax rules based on the dual classification. Roll-up funds still accumulate all the interest in the old way, but when you come to sell your holding, all the profits – whether they arise from capital gains or interest – are taxed as income.

For investors who are not in need of a regular income, there are still some advantages in roll-up funds, because the tax liability is deferred until you cash in your investment. This means that, meanwhile, you continue to earn interest on the full amount. Also, you will benefit if you wait to sell until your tax rate is lower than it is now, perhaps after retirement. Better still, if you retire or move abroad and cease to be a UK resident, you can escape UK tax altogether by cashing in the holding after you have left the country.

Distributor status was introduced as a special concession. To qualify, funds must distribute at least 85 per cent of their income and this will be taxed in the hands of the investor at normal income tax rates. They must also not engage in 'trading' – primarily, procedures designed to convert income into capital gains and thereby reduce the tax liability. Distributor status is only granted in retrospect, so funds that could be borderline tend to opt for accumulator status rather than risk their investors being faced with an unexpected tax position.

Distributor funds can be useful for non-taxpayers. Even for those who do pay tax, there is a small benefit compared with onshore funds as interest is paid gross, so there will be a short period of grace before you have to give the taxman what is due.

Where to find out more

Information on all the products mentioned in this chapter, with details of current offers and interest rates, can be found in the financial pages of newspapers (advertising and editorial) and in specialist magazines. *Money Facts*, a monthly publication, gives a guide to investment rates, including local authority bonds and offshore deposit accounts. It can be contacted on 01692 500765. Alternatively, you should consult an insurance broker or other professional adviser.

Fixed Capital Investments (2)

AIB Grofund Currency Funds Limited

BEING ALLIED IRISH HAS ITS OWN REWARDS
(Twelve to be precise)

There are many advantages to being Irish and luck is sometimes considered to be one of them.

Looking back over the past five years, it would appear that the Irish luck has certainly blessed AIB's Managed Currency Funds.

Let us assure you – luck has nothing to do with it. Through the skill, determination, and expertise of our Fund Managers, we have consistently featured in the top three Managed Currency Funds and have scooped *Twelve* major awards.

Don't trust to luck, choose the fund manager with a proven track record and consistent high performance. Fill in the coupon below or call Ronan Walsh and he'll be glad to outline the advantages of being Allied Irish.

AIB's AWARD WINNING PERFORMANCE

CHARTERHOUSE COMMUNICATION
OFFSHORE MANAGED CURRENCY
FUND GROUP OF THE YEAR
1990 - 1st 1991 - 2nd 1992 - 3rd
1993 - 1st 1994 - 2nd 1995 - 1st

MICROPAL OFFSHORE FUND
MANAGED GROUP OF THE YEAR
1990 - 1st

MICROPAL FIVE YEAR
OFFSHORE SURVEY
Managed Currency Sector 1990 - 1st

MICROPAL FIVE YEAR
OFFSHORE SURVEY
Smaller Group Category 1990 - 1st

MICROPAL ONE YEAR
OFFSHORE SURVEY
Larger Group Category 1990 - 1st

MICROPAL ONE YEAR OFFSHORE
Managed Currency Fund Sector
1992 - 3rd

MICROPAL FIVE YEARS
OFFSHORE TERRITORIES
Managed Currency MM Sector
1995 - 3rd

AIB FUND MANAGERS (CI) LIMITED

AIB House, PO Box 468, Grenville Street, St. Helier, Jersey JE4 8WT, Channel Islands
Telephone: 0044 1534 883102 Facsimile: 0044 1534 874542 E Mail: aibjsy@itl.net

---

DT/6/96

Yes, I am interested in sharing in the success of AIB Fund Managers. Please send me more information on your award winning suite of Currency Funds as soon as possible.

Name: ....

Address: ....
....
.... Postcode: ....
Telephone: .... Fax: ....

AIB Grofund Currency Funds Limited is both a Recognised Fund under the Collective Investment Funds (Jersey) Law 1988 and a UK Recognised Collective Investment Scheme under Section 87 of the U.K. Financial Services Act 1986. Past performance of our funds is no indication of their future performance. The Value of this investment and the income arising from it may fall as well as rise and is not guaranteed. AIB Fund Managers (CI) Limited is a wholly owned subsidiary of AIB Bank (CI) Limited, a member of the AIB Group. A copy of the most recent audited accounts of AIB Bank (CI) Limited is available upon request. Issued by AIB Fund Managers (CI) Limited and approved for publication by AIB Investment Managers (UK) Limited. Regulated by IMRO

4

The Gilts Market

In recent years, the government has done a fair amount to encourage saving – with the introduction of personal equity plans and tax exempt special savings accounts. Yet the government itself frequently lives beyond its means by spending more than its revenues, hence the National Debt, which grows rather more often than it is reduced.

National Savings products, outlined in Chapter 2, are one form of borrowing by the government, but by far the biggest chunk is through gilt-edged securities, or gilts for short. These are issued regularly and come in a variety of types. Most have a lifespan of up to 20 years, though some last indefinitely, but although they cannot be cashed in before their maturity date, they can meanwhile be traded on the Stock Exchange.

Gilts are regarded as being one of the safest of all investments. This is not to say that you cannot make a loss on them – the prices fluctuate, so your capital is not guaranteed. But the promises made by the gilt itself – the interest payments and the redemption value – are as secure as you can get; the government has never yet been known to default.

Terminology

One of the off-putting things about gilts is the jargon. If you go along to a building society, the accounts may have fancy names, but the descriptions of 'instant access' or '90 days' notice' are usually pretty clear. In fact, the title of a gilt is descriptive of what it offers, but you need to be able to decipher the code. As an

The Gilts Market

The "NOT FORGOTTEN" Association helps Ex-Service Disabled from all the Wars

There are almost 300,000 disabled ex-service men and women in this country. They have been injured in conflicts from 1914 to the present day.

Many of them earned decorations. Most had terrible experiences which they will never be able to forget. They all went to war knowing the risks, yet they accepted these courageously so that the rest of us could enjoy peace and freedom. Surely we owe them a debt of honour for the sacrifices they made.

Now most of them are elderly and often frail. Their esential needs may be provided for, but what we at the "Not Forgotten" Association do is to give them some of the "extras" which most of us take for granted – like television, holidays, outings, entertainments.

In short, something to look forward to – something to make life worth living.

Please help us to make them feel that they matter – that they are "Not Forgotten". Call us on (0171) 730 2400 or write to:

The "Not Forgotten" Association,
158 Buckingham Palace Road,
London SW1W 9TR.

Patron HRH the Duchess of Kent GCVO.
Founded 1920.
Registered Charity No. 229666

---

example, let us suppose you are offered £100 nominal of Treasury $9\frac{1}{2}$ per cent 1999.

To start with, 'nominal' refers to the face value of the gilt, which is the amount the government will repay at the date of redemption. This is also called the 'par value'. But between now and the redemption date, the price of the gilt will vary and may be above or below par. So your £100 nominal may cost you more or less than £100, but if you hold it for the rest of its lifespan, that is what you will get back. It follows that, at the time you buy, there is an in-built capital gain or loss if the gilt is held to redemption.

The name 'Treasury' can effectively be ignored. Some gilts, like 'War Loan', have names which reflect the original purpose of the borrowing, while most that are around today are called Treasury or Exchequer. Either way, the name has no relevance to the investment characteristics.

The percentage, $9\frac{1}{2}$ per cent in this case, refers to the 'coupon', or the interest rate that will be paid on the gilt. The rate applies to the nominal value of the gilt, so £100 nominal at $9\frac{1}{2}\%$ will earn £9.50 interest a year. In practice, the true rate of return on your money will depend on the price you pay for the gilt. If you buy below the par value, you will be getting a higher rate than the one quoted. For example, if your £100 nominal costs you £98, the £9.50 interest works out at just under 9.7 per cent. This is known as the 'flat' or 'running' yield of the stock.

Finally, 1999 is the redemption date, when the nominal value will be repaid to whoever holds the gilt at that time. Some stocks are 'double-dated': they carry two redemption dates, for example, 2001–2004. This means that the government can choose to redeem the stock at any time between those dates, but no later than the second one. As a rule, if a stock is standing above its par value as redemption approaches, the earlier date is more likely; if it is below par, the later date.

Types of gilts

Conventional gilts are classified into four types, which are generally shown separately in newspaper price listings. Those with up to five years left to run before redemption are called 'short-dated' or 'shorts'; those with remaining lives of 5 to 15 years are called 'mediums'; 'longs' are those with more than 15 years to run; and half a dozen or so stocks are undated, which means there is no fixed redemption date.

The nearer a gilt is to its redemption date, the closer its price will get to the nominal value, in anticipation of the repayment due. So short-dated stocks should have the least volatile prices. Mediums and longs, on the other hand, may fluctuate substantially in either direction. Because of the difference in coupon, two stocks with the same nominal value and the same redemption date may have quite different prices on the market.

Undated stocks could in theory be redeemed at some point, but it seems very unlikely. The coupons are low, between 2.5 and 4 per cent, so there is no incentive for the government to redeem them, only to have to borrow new money at higher cost.

In addition to these various conventional gilts there is another category, index-linked stocks. With these, both the interest and the capital repayment value are adjusted in line with the Retail Price Index (RPI). In practice, the figure used is the level of the index eight months before payment is due, to ensure that the

The Gilts Market

Your voice for freedom of choice in medicine

You are concerned about health – your own, that of your family's and the people around you. You may have used alternative remedies, either on a casual basis or as a committed patient. But in all probability, you have never thought that supporting alternative medicine was a priority. The brutal fact is that, with your support, non-conventional therapies could be severely restricted or disappear.

People turn to alternative medicine for all sorts of reasons, mainly because orthodox treatment has failed to answer their problems. Most employ natural remedies alongside conventional methods, others use them exclusively, and growing numbers see them as their first choice, with orthodox medicine providing cover in emergencies or where surgery is indicated.

The NMS was set up in 1985 in response to consumer fears that natural remedies were about to be legislated out of existence. Without protest, this would almost certainly have meant the disappearance of most of these remedies. But we are far from home and dry. Scare stories about the dangers of natural medicines appear with alarming frequency in the Press, few of them with any foundation.

The Natural Medicines Society exists to protect the individual's right to have access to high quality alternative medical treatment and to extend the range of what is available within our healthcare system. We want a genuine choice of well-established high quality medicines and therapies administered by properly qualified practitioners, available to everyone.

The cause of natural medicines is not overtly emotional and yet, beneath the surface, our work is as vital to the health of the population as that of any other medical charity. Alternative medicine has answers that have eluded orthodoxy and the intelligent use of its techniques and remedies could contribute to the improvement of health and the saving of lives. The adoption of a genuinely holistic philosopy of health care and the integration of natural therapies into our healthcare system would bring incalculable benefits to everyone.

If, like us, you believe that is possible, please give your support and help us to lay a firm basis for future advances. The Natural Medicines Society represents the consumer voice for freedom of Choice in medicine. You have a voice – make it heard by supporting the NMS!

The Natural Medicines Society, (Registered Charity No 327468), Market Chambers, 13a Market Place, Heanor, Derbyshire DE75 7AA.

Advertisement feature

---

amount of payment is always known in advance. This is compared with the base index for the stock, which is the level of the RPI eight months before the stock was issued; the base index for each stock is shown in newspaper price listings.

The coupons on these stocks look lower than those for conventional gilts because the figure quoted is the unindexed amount, which is then multiplied up by the inflation factor. Like conventional stock, prices will vary and as the redemption date approaches will move towards the repayment value, but this will be the indexed value, not the £100 nominal.

Gilt prices

The prices of gilt stocks are listed in newspapers alongside other share prices, generally under the heading of 'British Funds'. Prices are quoted in pounds and fractions, which can look a bit bewildering; for example, a figure of 119 $3/_{32}$ signals a price of £119.09. As a rule of thumb, $1/_{32}$ of a pound is roughly 3p.

The prices listed are normally the mid-market prices that

applied at the close of trading on the previous day. This will give a reasonable guide, but prices are changing all the time; for an up-to-date figure you would need to consult a broker. You also need to remember that the actual buying and selling prices involve a spread – the buying price will be slightly above the mid-market figure quoted and the selling price slightly below it.

One other factor affecting the quoted price is the accumulated interest. Inevitably there is a time-lag involved in preparing and sending out interest payments and meanwhile stocks could change hands, so the rule is that payments are made to whoever was the registered holder 37 days before the interest payment falls due. At this point the stock becomes 'ex dividend', indicated in price quotations by the letters 'xd'. If you sell a stock that is ex dividend you will still receive the interest payment, but the part of it that relates to the period after you sold will be subtracted from the sale proceeds. Similarly, if you buy a stock ex dividend, this portion of interest will be deducted from the cost, to compensate for you not actually receiving it.

If you buy at other times, you will have to pay for the interest that has accumulated since the last payment date. For example, if you buy two months after the previous payment, your purchase includes two months' worth of interest and the value of this will be added to the price.

Aside from these factors, there are a number of influences on the general level of gilt prices, chief of which is interest rates. In simple terms, if bank interest rates are at 12 per cent, then a gilt with a coupon of 12 per cent should trade around its par value. If bank rates fall to 8 per cent, the gilt looks more attractive and this will drive the price up until the effective yield, based on the purchase price, comes into line with bank rates.

In practice, though, prices will reflect not only current interest rates but the market's expectations of future rates. Once you have bought a gilt, you have locked into a particular rate of return, so if general interest rates fall, you will be doing well. On top of this, a fall in interest rates will tend to mean a rise in gilt prices, so there will be a capital gain if you sell. Conversely, if interest rates are forecast to rise, the prospects are less attractive. Inflation will also affect the true value of both future income and capital value, so, again, prices will be influenced by the market's expectations.

The Gilts Market

The yield

As mentioned above, the flat yield on a gilt depends on the purchase price as well as the quoted coupon. It can be calculated by dividing the coupon by the price and multiplying by 100. This then represents the interest rate you will get on your investment. But the flat yield is not the whole story. The total return to be made from a gilt also depends on the change in the capital value between when you buy and when you sell or when the stock is redeemed.

If you hold the stock to redemption, you will make a known capital gain or loss depending on the price at which you bought it. Even if you stand to make a loss, this need not mean that stock is not worth buying. For one thing, if the maturity date is still some way off, the price may rise before then, allowing you to sell at a profit. Alternatively, if you hold on to the stock, the interest payments may be enough to outweigh the capital loss and still represent an attractive return.

This return can be judged from the redemption yield, which takes into account the capital gain or loss as well as the flat yield. The calculation is complicated, but figures are included in newspaper listings and can also be obtained from stockbrokers, who have computer programs designed for the purpose. The figures assume that all interest payments are reinvested in the same stock at the same redemption yield.

A comparison between flat yields and redemption yields is shown in Table 4.1. Here, the high coupon short-dated stocks are standing above their par value and the redemption yield is

Table 4.1 *Gross flat and redemption yields on gilts*

Stock	Price (£)	Flat yield (%)	Redemption yield (%)
Treasury 13.25% 1997	106.19	12.478	6.063
Exchequer 12% 1998	112.56	10.661	6.863
Treasury 8% 2000	102.98	7.769	7.246
Funding 3½% 2004	80.50	4.348	6.564
Treasury 9% 2012	107.10	8.404	8.207

Source: Money Facts, March 1996

Lump-Sum Investment

therefore a lot lower than the flat yield, though still competitive with, say, bank and building society accounts. The low-coupon Funding $3\frac{1}{2}$ per cent stock, on the other hand, offers only a modest running income but a much higher redemption yield, as there is a sizeable capital gain to be made.

These figures are for gross yields. When tax is taken into account, the picture can change again, as the next section will explain.

Gilts and tax

Interest payments on gilts are made twice a year. If the stock is held on the Bank of England register, interest is paid net of basic rate tax, with the exception of $3\frac{1}{2}$ per cent War Loan which is paid gross. Stocks held on the National Savings Stock Register, accessible through post offices (see 'Buying and selling' below), also have interest paid gross. In either case, taxpayers will be liable for any unpaid amount. Non-taxpayers can reclaim any tax already deducted, but may find the National Savings route more convenient.

Special rules apply to interest that has accrued shortly before you buy or sell. Where accrued interest has been allowed for in the purchase price, that part of the subsequent interest payment will not normally be liable for tax. Conversely, when you sell, you will be charged tax on the amount of interest earned before the sale, calculated on a daily basis. However, these rules do not apply when your holdings of gilts have not recently been worth more than £5000. In this case, tax applies only to interest that has actually been paid; so if the sale price includes an allowance for, say, three months' accrued interest, the profit is treated as a capital gain.

This is an advantage, as all capital gains made on gilts are tax free for private investors. The government caused a scare in 1995 by announcing that in future all gains would be subject to income tax, but eventually decided to exclude private investors from the ruling, although it does apply to companies.

As a result, higher rate taxpayers can continue to use gilts in a tax-planning strategy. By opting for a low-coupon stock and

The Gilts Market

"It simply isn't cricket not to make a Will!"

Receive a lapel badge when you send for this free booklet.

Far too few of us make Wills. In fact, only about one in three has made a record of their wishes. The trouble is that the two who don't may seriously increase the distress of those near and dear to them by adding insecurity to sorrow at the time of their death.

That's why The Royal London Society for the Blind has produced this useful booklet, full of sensible advice about making a Will. It is designed to be easy to read and is available free, by writing to the address below.

If you consider adding a Charity to your Will, I do hope you can support The Royal London Society for the Blind.

KP

Please help blind people. Return this coupon to:
David Gower, c/o Royal London Society for the Blind,
105 Salusbury Road, London NW6 6RH

Please send me___ copies of the booklet *A Simple Guide to Making a Will.*

Name _____

Address _____

_____

Post Code _____

Tel: _____

ROYAL LONDON SOCIETY FOR THE BLIND
Registered Charity No: 307892

holding it to maturity, they can ensure that most of the return will come in the form of a tax-free capital gain.

The tax change was intended as a prelude to the introduction of a gilts 'strip' market, now planned for early 1997. This allows the interest element to be stripped out from the capital repayment portion, with each part traded separately. It is likely to appeal primarily to institutions, but could also be useful for investors who have a set liability to meet in the future, such as school fees.

Why buy gilts?

The majority of gilt dealing is done by institutions such as pension funds and insurance companies, but individual investors can also take part. In fact, the Bank of England has made particular overtures to the private investor: it published a free booklet to explain how gilts work; the investment limit for buying gilts through the National Savings Stock Register was raised from £10,000 to £25,000 and the register was expanded to include all existing stocks; the Bank then introduced a simplified application form, published in newspapers, for a new stock issue.

But should you be tempted? When interest rates are low, high-coupon gilts compare very favourably to bank and building society accounts as regards the running yield they offer. If income is your priority, gilts certainly have an appeal, but remember that if high-coupon stocks are at a premium - the price is above the par value - and you hold the stocks to redemption, the high income will be achieved at the expense of a guaranteed capital loss.

This should be viewed in the context of future prospects from alternative investments. Any investment has an opportunity cost - by choosing one, you are giving up the chance of another. Of course, you can never be certain of getting the best, but you can consider probabilities. The lower the rates of interest and inflation, the more likely it is that they will rise in future. This will work against gilts in that the yield will become relatively less attractive, prices will fall, and the ultimate redemption value will be worth less in real terms.

Timing makes all the difference to a gilt investment. Ideally, they should be bought just as interest rates start to fall and sold

The Gilts Market

IT'S MIGHTIER THAN THE SWORD.

A signature on a will. It can go a long way to provide for the ex-servicemen and women of Erskine Hospital.
So next time one of your clients asks for advice on legacies, please remember our cause.
We need to raise more than £1 million worth of public donations every year.
We need to maintain expert medical care.
We need to provide the special facilities that our many disabled residents require.
That's why it's so important that people remember us when they make a will.
Please help us by jogging a few memories.
Legacies or bequests should be made payable to the Princess Louise Scottish Hospital (Erskine Hospital), Bishopton, Renfrewshire PA7 5PU. (Correspondence to the Treasurer, I. W. Grimmond, B. Acc, C.A., at the hospital. Tel: 0141-812 1100.)

Scottish Charity No. (SC 006609)

---

just as they are about to rise – even though they may appear most attractive when interest rates are at their lowest. But much depends on your investment criteria. On a long-term comparison, gilts have consistently performed less well than equities, but for some investors the fixed income and capital return may carry more weight.

Conventional versus index-linked

If inflation is the enemy of investors, index-linking should be the saviour. The return offered is guaranteed to stay in line with inflation, while the capital value at maturity is also protected from erosion. The redemption value of a conventional gilt, on the other hand, may be worth a lot less by the time it matures.

While current interest rates are influenced by current inflation, index-linked gilts look to the future in that prices will be influenced by expectations about the trend of inflation. Lately, index-linked stocks have tended to outperform conventional

Lump-Sum Investment

gilts; with the economy moving out of recession, and in the run-up to the next general election, inflation could start to pick up again. In this scenario, index-linked gilts look more attractive, as the inflation protection will prove rewarding, while if interest rates rise alongside inflation, the prices of conventional gilts are likely to fall, so they have less appeal.

One method used by stockbrokers to judge the relative merits of index-linked and conventional gilts is to calculate the 'break-even inflation rate'. This involves matching the index-linked stock with a conventional issue with the same or similar maturity date. Using a computer, they then work out what rate of inflation between now and redemption would make the (monetary) returns from the two stocks equal. If inflation runs above the break-even rate, the index-linked stock will give a better return.

Of course, it is still a matter of judgement whether inflation is likely to be above or below the break-even rate during the period in question. The further away the redemption date, the harder this is to judge, as inflation is likely to go both up and down more than once meanwhile. But you can at least assess the chances in the light of past experience.

Table 4.2 shows some examples of break-even rates for a basic rate taxpayer. To put these in context, the inflation rate at the time of writing is around 2.9 per cent; the January 1993 figure of 1.7 per cent was the lowest for many years, while in the worst days of 1980, the rate reached 21.9 per cent.

Table 4.2 *Break-even inflation rates.*

Stock	Price (£)	Comparison stock	Break-even inflation rate (%)
4.518% 1998	111.95	Treasury 7¼% 1998	2.71
2½% 2003	172.81	Treasury 8% 2003	2.83
2% 2006	181.00	Treasury 7¾% 2006	3.15
2½% 2013	138.19	Treasury 8% 2013	3.33
2½% 2016	147.19	Treasury 8¾% 2017	3.30

Note: Break-even rate applies at 20 per cent tax rate on interest.

Source: Money Facts, March 1996

Buying and selling

There are three ways of buying gilts: direct from the Bank of England when there is a new issue; through a stockbroker; or through the National Savings Stock Register.

When a new stock is issued, prospectuses are published in newspapers and are also available from the Bank of England. Stocks are auctioned, which means institutions register the price they are prepared to bid and only the highest bidders will receive stock if the issue is over-subscribed. Private investors, however, can register a non-competitive bid and they will then receive stock at the average of the successful bid prices. Usually they are asked to pay the nominal value up-front and the Bank then makes a refund or asks for more money, depending on the average price set.

For recent issues, the Bank has provided shorter application forms as a way of encouraging private investors. The advantage of buying new stock in this way is that there is no commission on the purchase.

For existing stocks, the National Savings Stock Register still offers the cheapest method of buying and selling for small sums although costs were recently increased. The costs are shown in Table 4.3. Aside from costs, there is the advantage that interest is

Table 4.3 *The cost of dealing in gilts through the Post Office*

Up to £5000	0.7% subject to a minimum of £12.50 for purchases (no minimum for sales)
Over £5000	£35 plus 0.375% of the amount in excess of £5000

Examples

Purchases		Sales	
Cost of transaction	*Commission*	*Proceeds of sale*	*Commission*
£250	£12.50	£250	£1.75
£1000	£12.50	£1500	£10.50
£5000	£35.00	£2500	£17.50
£10,000	£53.75	£7500	£44.38

Lump-Sum Investment

paid gross, which means non-taxpayers avoid the effort of reclaiming tax paid; taxpayers will still have to pay what is due, but benefit from a grace period.

There is a maximum that you can invest in any one stock through the register of £25,000 a day, but there is no limit to the total amount you can hold on the register. New stocks bought through a prospectus can normally be registered with National Savings rather than the Bank of England by ticking a box on the application form, subject to a limit of £25,000 in nominal value. Stocks held on the National Savings register can only be sold through it, while stocks held on the Bank of England register cannot be sold this way.

The drawback to buying and selling through National Savings is that it has to be done by post. While dealing will normally be carried out on the day instructions are received, you will not know until after the event what price applied.

The alternative is to deal through a stockbroker, which can be done by telephone at a known price. Commissions on gilt dealing are usually lower than for equities, but will still be subject to the broker's minimum, which can be £25 or more in London. Hence this is likely to prove an expensive route for small investments, especially as further commission will be payable when you come to sell.

One other route into the gilt market is through a collective investment such as an insurance company product or a unit trust. This gives you a stake in a portfolio of gilts for a much smaller outlay than buying your own collection, and with professional management as well, but, of course, there is none of the certainty you can get by buying stocks to hold to redemption.

Permanent interest bearing shares

Permanent interest bearing shares (PIBS) are issued by building societies as a means of raising permanent share capital. They are similar to gilts, in that they pay a fixed income, but the majority are irredeemable unless the issuing society is wound up. They can, however, be sold to a third party and are traded on the Stock Exchange.

Interest is paid twice a year and is paid net of basic rate tax, although non-taxpayers can reclaim it. Higher rate taxpayers will be liable for the extra amount. Hitherto, any profits made on the sale of shares have not been liable for tax, but this is set to change. Under the same proposals as for gilts, described on page 84, gains would become liable to income tax at the investor's highest rate.

The interest rates are more attractive than those offered on the standard range of building society accounts, but there is, of course, a capital risk. Share prices move inversely to interest rates and are particularly sensitive to long-term rates. So, for example, if market rates move downwards, prices will rise, which reduces the effective yield as a percentage of the purchase price. This is illustrated in Table 4.4, which shows the prices at the time of writing on a selection of shares and the corresponding yields. All the shares were issued at an original price of 100p, but falling market interest rates since issue have generally driven up the price. Equally, if rates rise again in future, the share prices will fall, so, unlike building society accounts, these are investments you should review regularly.

Currently, there are some 17 PIBS available. As the table shows, the yields vary, reflecting the market's view of the issuing society. Shares can be bought and sold through stockbrokers, who may advise on which appears most attractive. The minimum investment is generally £1000, but most stockbrokers have a minimum commission, which can be around £25, making

Table 4.4 *Examples of PIBS prices, coupons and yields*

Current price (pence)	Fixed coupon (gross)	Gross yield (%)
96.88	9.375	9.68
136.88	13.375	9.77
123.13	11.75	9.54
92.13	8.75	9.49
114.13	10.75	9.42
135.13	12.625	9.34

Source: *Money Facts*, March 1996

dealing expensive for small sums. PIBS are not normally liable to stamp duty.

Aside from the capital risk, there are other safety aspects. Interest payments are not guaranteed to be made if the board of the society decides payment would damage business interests or if interest has not been paid on shares and deposits. Also, PIBS are not covered by the building societies' investor compensation scheme, and if the issuing society were to go into liquidation, holders would be last in line for repayment, behind all depositors and ordinary shareholders. On the other hand, if the society is taken over by another, the PIBS will continue as the liability of the society making the take-over.

Recently an investment trust was launched that will invest in PIBS in the hope of benefiting from the spate of mergers in the building society world. At current prices at the time of writing, the trust should pay dividends of about 7 per cent a year, with the prospect of additional cash or shares from bonuses payable if any of the societies whose shares are held undergo a merger or conversion.

Where to find out more

Newspapers such as *The Daily Telegraph* and *The Financial Times* publish the prices of gilts on a daily basis, along with gross interest and redemption yields. Net redemption yields, break-even inflation figures and general advice on buying and selling can be obtained from a stockbroker. Stockbrokers can also provide information and advice on permanent interest bearing shares.

5

Equities

Equities could be said to come somewhere near the top of the investment tree. This is not because they necessarily demand a lot of money – privatisation issues have allowed people to own shares for a down-payment of just £100. But if you had only £100 to invest, the stock market would not normally be considered the ideal place to put it. Most investors come into equities only after they have built up more cautious funds elsewhere.

This chapter focuses mainly on the UK Stock Exchange. In fact, many of the points would apply in a similar way to overseas markets but, despite sophisticated communications technology, dealing in foreign shares tends to be both more expensive and more difficult. Unless you have a very large portfolio, it is more practical to invest abroad through pooled funds such as unit and investment trusts.

The Stock Exchange

The London Stock Exchange has its origins back in the eighteenth century, when people used to meet in coffee houses to exchange shares and arrange deals. It was formally constituted in 1802, in purpose-built premises on the same site as the current building, which was opened in 1973.

The exchange has two purposes: to act as a market for people wanting to buy and sell existing shares, and to raise money for companies by issuing new share capital. There are also two separate operations involved, jobbing and broking, corresponding to wholesale and retail functions. Jobbers are now known by the more descriptive name of market-makers; they make a market in shares by acting as primary buyers and sellers and holding stocks on their books. Brokers act as intermediaries between the market-makers and the end-clients, investors; they take orders from their clients and look for the best prices among the market-makers.

Trading used to take place physically on the Stock Exchange floor, but that came to an end with Big Bang, which reorganised the workings of the Exchange. Broking and jobbing firms were allowed to be taken over by companies, where previously they were partnerships, and both functions may now be carried out within a single company. They must, however, be kept separate, by means of a 'Chinese Wall'; this is to guard against any unscrupulous manoeuvring between them at the expense of the investor. If, for example, the broker knew that the market-maker wanted to get rid of some undesirable shares, he could connive at it by advising his clients to buy them.

Another effect of Big Bang was to remove the standard commission levels for buying and selling shares which were previously set by the Stock Exchange. Although some firms still roughly follow the old scales, there can now be wide differences. Much of the competition, though, is at the upper end and, for smaller investors, the general effect has been to increase costs. This is chiefly because brokers set a minimum commission, which can be as high as £40 for a London firm, making small transactions disproportionately expensive. Provincial brokers are generally cheaper, as they have lower overheads, and commission levels also vary according to the type of service provided.

Rolling settlement

The volume of shares traded has increased enormously since Big Bang. While prices are now posted on screens, dealing still involves a mass of paperwork and administrative logjams have not been uncommon, delaying the issue of certificates for shares bought and settlement for shares sold. The Stock Exchange planned to deal with this problem with the introduction of Taurus, a paperless dealing system which would have replaced certificates with electronic accounts, but after years of problems and delays it finally collapsed in March 1993.

Instead, it is set to introduce a system called Crest in July 1996. The first step towards this was taken in July 1994 with the introduction of a ten-day 'rolling settlement' period.

Previously, the settlement system was based on two- to three-week periods known as 'accounts'. Settlement of transactions undertaken during any one account would normally take place on a fixed account day, some ten days after the end of the period. Meanwhile, investors could enjoy credit for shares bought, but would be waiting for the proceeds of sales.

Under the new system, settlement for both sales and purchases has to take place within a set period from the transaction date – initially ten working days, reduced to five from June 1995 and due to shrink eventually to just three days.

Crest will help the process by making all share dealing electronic and essentially paperless. Although you are still entitled to have a paper certificate and your own name on the company register, it will generally be easier and cheaper not to do so. Once settlement is cut to three days, it will be difficult to return a certificate in time for a sale and brokers may also make an extra charge to cover the additional cost of handling paper.

An alternative is to become a sponsored member of Crest, whereby a broker runs a Crest account for you. This will cost £20 a year plus whatever charge the broker makes. The advantage is that you remain on the share register, but the cost could prove too high if you deal only occasionally.

The most common route for private investors is likely to be the use of nominee accounts. These are accounts in the name of a nominee company, which holds shares on the investor's behalf while he remains the beneficial owner. They are already used in a number of situations, such as for discretionary broking services and personal equity plans.

Nominee accounts are certainly convenient, but do have some drawbacks. You may lose out on share perks, since the shares are not registered in your own name, and you will have to make arrangements with your broker if you want to receive copies of annual reports or go to shareholders' meetings. This may involve a cost, on top of any fee charged for running the nominee account.

Another effect is that margin trading may become more

popular. This is a facility whereby the stockbroker gives credit to settle share purchases, using existing shares held in a nominee account as security. This is not just a convenient way of making settlements but also allows you to 'gear' your portfolio, by borrowing against it to buy more shares. The disadvantage is that, if the market crashes, the value of shares held as security could end up being worth less than the credit given.

For this reason, stockbrokers are likely to lend only against blue chip shares and will need to monitor portfolios closely. Currently there are no regulations on margin trading but, given the potential risks, rules may be introduced if it becomes widespread.

The Alternative Investment Market

The Alternative Investment Market (AIM) was launched in June 1995 as a replacement for the Unlisted Securities Market. As the name implies, it offers an alternative market-place for companies that are too small or not yet ready to seek a main stock market listing.

To join, companies will have to supply a prospectus, background details on all directors, details of promoters, names and holdings of major shareholders, a working capital statement and a risk warning.

They will also need to have a 'nominated adviser' and a 'nominated broker'. The former must be chosen from a Stock Exchange register and will, in effect, be the company's mentor for the market, ensuring it meets the AIM rules. The broker will be responsible for providing information to the market and for matching prospective buyers and sellers of the company's shares if there is no market-maker.

For investors, AIM shares generally carry more risk than the main market. This is partly because the companies are likely to be smaller and have less of a business track record on which their prospects can be judged, but also because the market itself is likely to attract far fewer buyers and sellers – the institutions, which dominate trading, naturally prefer the main market where deals can be much larger. Where there is no market-maker, deals will be on a matched basis, which means you could find yourself stuck with shares for which there is no buyer available.

There are, however, tax benefits. Capital gains tax can be deferred on the profit from selling an asset if the proceeds are reinvested in qualifying AIM shares, while any transfer of AIM shares will avoid capital gains tax if it is at cost value rather than market value. Some shares will also qualify under the Enterprise Investment Scheme (see Chapter 12), which offers up-front income tax relief and capital gains tax relief on sales. Finally, AIM companies may be eligible investments for venture capital trusts, which offer their investors similar benefits to the Enterprise Investment Scheme, plus tax-free dividends.

Market indices

Movements in the stock market are generally measured with reference to an index. For the UK market, there are two that are principally used: the FT-SE Actuaries All-Share index and the FT-SE 100 index – known colloquially as 'Footsie'.

The All-Share index does not in fact cover all shares quoted on the market, but the 850 or so that it does cover account for around 96 per cent of the total market capitalisation. Consequently, it gives the most representative overall picture.

The Footsie, which was begun at the start of 1984, covers the top 100 companies by size. The prices are calculated every minute during the trading day, so it gives immediate feedback to dealers on what is happening.

Although share price movements, and those of unit trusts, investment trusts and so on, are often measured in relation to the All-Share or the Footsie, there are various other indices covering particular sectors, such as smaller companies or individual industries. These can be more relevant for judging the performance of an individual share or specialist trust. For example, smaller companies are unlikely to follow the same pattern as the large companies represented by the Footsie index; if the smaller companies sector is booming, a share that is performing only in line with the Footsie is probably doing relatively badly.

Lump-Sum Investment

Stocktrade – Trading on Technology

In 1986 The Stock Exchange rules on single capacity and standard commission rates were abolished.

The moves which were designed to enhance liquidity and boost London's standing as an international trading centre paved the way for the introduction of modern technology and removed the requirement to trade from a pitch on the market floor.

The privatisation issues which swelled bargain numbers generated a demand for low cost dealing services and the execution only broker emerged to take his part as a major force on the broking scene.

The concept was by no means revolutionary. After all, why pay for something you neither want nor need? Prior to 1986 brokers were bound by the rules to charge the same rates, but post 1986 rates were open to negotiation. Today Execution Only dealing rates are frequently less than half the advisory rates and in many instances are capped with maximums only marginally above advisory minimums.

Stocktrade has developed the use of computer technology to provide a quality focused integrated dealing and settlement system. Conceived to provide a standard format for all 1200 U.K. branches of a leading bank, the service combines the most desirable facets of traditional dealing expertise with the advantages of computer functionality to generate a fast, efficient and friendly dealing and settlement system. What separates Stocktrade from many other Execution Only brokers is the fact that once telephone contact has been established, the dealer can immediately provide the caller with the touch price ruling in the market and assuming the caller wishes to proceed, a confirmed deal. Unlike many of its competitors, Stocktrade has a direct link with the market via its Trade system which means there are no delays in dealing. You receive not just the price at which you have dealt, but also the net amount on your contract note, before putting the 'phone down. Traditional dealing skills ensures that improved prices are obtained wherever possible.

Both purchases and sales are normally settled automatically, sales by BAC's payment enabling cleared funds to be paid into the appropriate designated account. Purchases are settled by direct debit or credit transfer although both sales and purchases can be settled by cheque if required.

Stocktrade can also offer a direct computer link via 'Infotrade' which provides a price feed, company information, a portfolio valuation system, which updates at the time of dealing, and an on-line dealing service, for those who wish to combine a small amount of computer literacy with an enthusiasm for managing their own affairs.

Finally, quality of service delivery is at the heart of our mission, a preoccupation which took us to the top of the independent Compeer study of 19 Execution Only brokers, for settlement day deliveries of stock, a statistic which means we deal and pay up on time! And the rates? We charge £15 minimum, 0.75% and a maximum of £60 for our standard private client service. Fund Management clients deal at 0.3%.

Equities

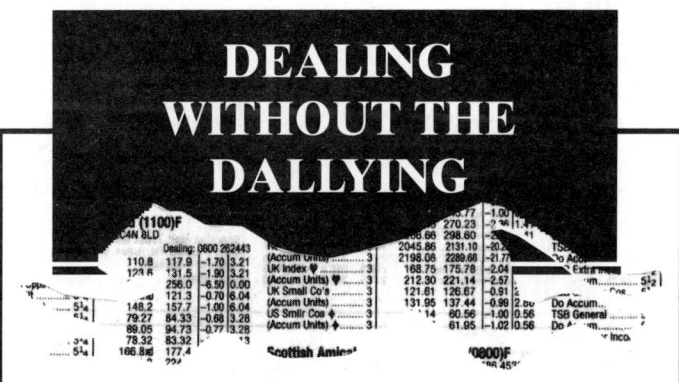

Stocktrade specialises in execution-only stockbroking. We have a strong team, who provide a fast, friendly and efficient service, ideal for people in the know. We like to think we're the best at what we do.

Telephone and Postal Dealing
Commission structure from £12 minimum to
£60 / £100 maximum, tiered to service level

•

Customised Dealing Services
for Private Clients, Companies, Banks, Institutions, Solicitors,
Self Invested and Self Administered Pension Plans

•

Live Telephone Dealing

•

Bed & Breakfast transactions
Maximum commission charge £35 up to £50,000
(over £50,000 by negotiation)

Contact
John Frame or Mike Graham
Tel : 0131 529 0144

STOCKTRADE
The Scottish Execution Only Stockbroker

STOCKTRADE, A division of Brewin Dolphin Bell Lawrie Ltd A member of the London Stock Exchange and regulated by The Securities and Futures Authority Ltd Registered Office: 5 Giltspur Street, London, EC1A 9BD. Registered in England No. 2135876

Lump-Sum Investment

Private investors

Until quite recently, private investors were very much in decline in terms of their representation in the stock market. Meanwhile, the institutions saw a steady and substantial increase in the funds under their control and took on a heavily dominant position.

While there is still a heavy imbalance in favour of institutions, the private investor has staged a comeback. Currently, in 1996, there are about 10 million people who own shares, compared to around a quarter of that in the early 1980s. This is partly owing to an increase in inheritances following on from the growth in home ownership. People who already have a basic portfolio of investments and are then presented with a 'windfall' of, say, £50,000 to £100,000, are quite likely to give some thought to equities. Another factor has been the growth in company share option schemes for employees. But there is no doubt that a major influence has been the privatisation programme.

This is something of a mixed blessing. It has certainly brought about wider share ownership but, one could argue, of the wrong kind. Out of the 10 million shareholders, only a quarter or so hold shares in more than three companies and only some 300,000 are active dealers in shares. Many simply hang on to the few shares they bought, either for the incentives attached, or because they have virtually forgotten they have them.

Perhaps more dangerous was the reputation privatisation issues acquired as 'get rich quick' schemes. Priced to be enticing, the earlier issues in particular gave opportunities to make immediate attractive profits – and many buyers made the most of it, selling the shares as soon as they had the letters of allocation. While there is nothing wrong in making a quick profit, anyone who thought the principle could be extended to other shares, with the same degree – or lack – of risk, is likely to have been severely disappointed.

For quick, convenient and seven days a week, phone

Equities

On a more positive note, privatisations have boosted the growth of dealing services aimed at smaller investors. A number of these simply deal without offering any advice, which may not be suitable for the stock market beginner, but they have contributed to the general opening up of the stock market to a wider circle of people and the more user-friendly approach now being adopted by stockbrokers. If privatisations have helped to dispel some of the fear and mystique that surrounded equities, that is a step in the right direction; the next stage is to learn a little more about the rest of the market.

Ordinary shares

To begin at the beginning, an ordinary share represents a stake in the ownership of a company. In theory, it also confers the right to have a say in how the company is run, at least to the extent of having a vote at the annual general meeting. In practice, of course, most private investors do not have enough shares for their vote to count for much and many do not even bother to go to the meeting; nevertheless, the right exists.

Shareholders are also entitled to a portion of the company's profits, paid out in the form of dividends. As a rule, some of the profits will be kept back to be reinvested in the company itself for future growth. The remainder are distributed at so much per share; the more shares you hold, the larger the total dividend.

In return for these rewards, you take on a risk. Should the worst happen and the company be forced into liquidation, the ordinary shareholder is last in line for getting any of his money back. As a rule, though, you can only lose as much as you put in – you will not be called upon to make good anyone else's losses. This is because companies listed on the Stock Exchange have

cost-effective sharedealing, ShareLink on 0121 200 2242.

limited liability – hence the term PLC, or public limited company.

An exception is if the shares have been issued partly paid, as several privatisation issues have. This means that at the time you buy the shares, you pay only part of their price, with subsequent calls being made for the rest of the money. In this case, if the company incurs debts it cannot meet, you could be required to pay over the outstanding balance on the shares you hold. The majority of shares, though, are dealt in on a fully paid basis, so your maximum loss is equal to your investment.

With luck, the worst case will not happen and the company will stay in business, but you still stand to lose a part of your investment if the share price falls. Equally, of course, you will make a profit if it rises. So what factors make a share price move?

The short answer is supply and demand for the shares. Quite simply, if demand outstrips supply – if there are more willing buyers than willing sellers – the price will move up; in the opposite case it will move down. So the next question is, what affects supply and demand?

In the first place, all shares are influenced by what might be termed national events: the general economy and the political situation. Increasingly, these days, they are also affected by international events; one country's exports are another's imports, so a recession in the latter country means they will buy less, restricting export growth in the former.

There are further influences at sector or industry level; again, there are trade factors, and also strikes, which can have a knock-on effect if the striking company or industry is a major supplier to another.

Then you come down to the particular company, and what drives demand here is quite simply the expectation of profit. For individual investors, the anticipated profit may be in the form of capital growth – the expectation that the share price will increase. But what lies behind such an increase is the profit made by the company, translated into rising dividends: it is the income potential that ultimately underpins the share price.

Anticipation also plays an important part in determining share prices. An obvious example is a general election, where the market may react in advance to what people think is the likely

Equities

outcome. This is referred to as discounting an event – if it happens as expected, there will be little further movement, but if expectations are confounded, it could produce a violent swing.

But while it is perfectly in order to act on guesswork, it is illegal to engage in insider dealing, which amounts to taking advantage of unpublished information that may affect share prices.

Dividends

Dividends are generally paid twice a year, the first payment being the 'interim' dividend and the second the 'final' dividend, paid at the company's year-end. The amount is generally expressed in terms of pence per share, net of basic rate tax; this can be reclaimed by a non-taxpayer, while higher rate taxpayers must pay the difference.

As explained above, dividends underpin the share price and anticipation comes into play. Hence the price will often move ahead of the declaration and, if it fails to live up to expectations, the price can fall back, even though the dividend itself may have increased since the last declaration.

The yield on a share is the gross dividend divided by the share price. The average yield on UK shares is generally around 3 to 4 per cent; as interest rates creep up, this does not look particularly enticing. But what shares also offer is the prospect of growing income and, given inflation, this is a valuable asset.

Yields do, of course, vary, both between companies and between sectors. Broadly speaking, sectors with lower growth prospects will tend to have higher yields. For individual shares, the yield will obviously rise if the share price falls, while the dividend is maintained; the key question then is why the share price has fallen. It may be owing to 'technical' or short-term factors and, indeed, unit trusts in both the Income and Recovery sectors tend to look for just this type of share, which offers capital growth prospects and good income in the meantime. But it may be that profits, and dividends, are expected to fall in the future, so a share cannot be judged by its yield alone.

As mentioned, companies do not usually pay out all their profits as dividends, but retain some for future use. In this case, the dividend is said to be fully 'covered'. Equally, though, they

Lump-Sum Investment

could call upon these reserves to boost dividends in a year when earnings have been low, in which case the payment would be uncovered. Some degree of smoothing from year to year is perfectly acceptable, but a fully covered dividend is always more reassuring.

An alternative to cash dividends is a 'scrip' dividend, where the company offers the option of additional shares instead of money. In some cases, the value can be much higher, and if you are looking for cash, you can simply sell the extra shares. Of course, there will be dealing costs, but you may still come out ahead, and companies may also offer a buy-back scheme, which will cut the costs for small investors.

In principle, you cannot lose on this type of offer, but you do need to take care over the capital gains tax implications; if you have already used up the annual exempt allowance, you will be faced with a tax bill, although in the longer term it could reduce the liability on your remaining holdings in the shares. Scrip dividends are also treated by the Inland Revenue as having paid 20 per cent income tax which cannot be reclaimed. If you are in any doubt, you should seek independent advice.

Price/Earnings ratio

Besides the dividend, another means of judging shares is by the price/earnings ratio, or p/e for short. This is calculated as the share price divided by earnings per share and the result shows how many years it would take the company to earn enough to match the share price, if both remained unchanged.

In practice, the p/e ratio is used as a measure of the 'cheapness' of shares – the lower the ratio, the cheaper the share, relative to the company's earnings potential. But it has to be viewed in context. Average ratios vary between sectors, and are also affected by the economy in general – high inflation should lead to lower p/e ratios, since future dividends will be worth much less in real terms than the share price you have to pay now.

Also, while a high ratio means a share is relatively expensive, and should be viewed with caution, a low ratio is not always a reason to rush in and buy. It could be that the share price is low for good reason, because the market does not rate its prospects.

Equities

If you plan to invest overseas, you should bear in mind that p/e ratios may be on a quite different level to those in the UK. In fact, the UK has a relatively low average compared to markets worldwide, while Japan's is notoriously high.

How to buy and sell

It is no longer necessary to have a family stockbroker to gain access to the stock market. As mentioned above, the combination of Big Bang and privatisation issues has boosted the growth of new dealing services, often with low or no minimum investment requirement, while stockbrokers have been opening their doors to newcomers with a more obvious welcome than was once the case. Some larger companies have also become involved in share dealing services, particularly where they offer corporate personal equity plans that may include the shares of other companies.

Banks have also expanded the range of dealing services they offer. National Westminster, for example, has a computer-based 'Touchscreen' service that offers instant dealing. It was initially developed in response to privatisation issues but, at the time of writing, it can now be used to deal in 500 different shares and is available in around 300 branches across the country, for both customers and non-customers.

Several banks also provide postal and telephone dealing services, the latter generally confined to existing customers, while the former are open to anyone. For the most part, these are purely dealing services, though occasional advice may be given.

If you want more comprehensive advice, a bank may have its own associated stockbroker service, but you may be just as well off choosing a broker for yourself. The Association of Private Client Investment Managers and Stockbrokers (Apcims) pro-

---

Sharedealing made simple.
Phone ShareLink on 0121 200 2242.

duces a brochure that includes a directory of its members, outlining in brief the services they offer.

But there was a setback for private investors on 1 January 1996 when the Stock Exchange decided to abolish the rule that at least 25 per cent of new share issues had to be set aside for retail investors. Floating companies can now decide the proportion for themselves – or place all shares with institutions.

However, a couple of brokers have responded by setting up new services that provide information on forthcoming new issues and a way of participating.

Another way for smaller investors to play a more active role in the stock market is through an investment club, of which there are now more than 1000 in the UK. ProShare, an organisation dedicated to promoting wider share ownership, offers a matching service to put people in touch with existing clubs or with each other if they want to start a new club. It also publishes a manual on setting up and running a club.

Computer software for investment tracking

Advances in computer technology in the last few years have put investment software within the budget of the individual investor. At the same time, the range of products on offer has also expanded so that there is now a wide variety of software available for general portfolio management, charting or both. The increasing popularity of Microsoft Windows has inevitably made its presence felt as well. Though there are still programs that can run without it, they are increasingly in the minority. A Windows program typically provides a better graphic display than one that runs under DOS (Microsoft's Disk Operating System) but it usually also requires a more powerful computer. If your budget is limited, there is nothing wrong with using one of the perfectly competent DOS programs still available on an older machine.

One of the first things to consider is where to obtain the raw material upon which to base your decisions – your data. If you have a small or inactive portfolio, copying information manually from a newspaper into your software is easy enough. This quickly becomes tedious as a portfolio becomes larger, so most investment programs these days allow you to enter data automatically

OVER BREAKFAST, CONSULT 500 LEADING INVESTORS.

Market Data Centre's stock of over 800 investment books, journals and videos could help you make better informed investment decisions.

Apply now for a free catalogue containing details of these books and the latest investment software.

Please call **0800 413 775** for further information.

MARKET DATA CENTRE LTD
19–21 GREAT TOWER STREET,
LONDON EC3R 5AQ
TEL: 0171 522 0094
FAX: 0171 522 0095

1995/96

from your modem (if you are getting it from a bulletin board or the Internet) or Teletext (if you have a text card fitted to your computer). The seriously enthusiastic, who like to monitor their investments throughout the day will probably want a real time data feed such as Market Eye or Tenfore.

As one might expect, the middle ground of the investment software market is rather crowded. Apart from a number of British companies, there is also a significant US presence. Investors looking just for charting software could do worse than look at products from Equis, Omega or Market Arts. They are all visually attractive but are obviously aimed primarily at the American market. In terms of features they represent excellent value for money, but do have a strong bias toward technical analysis (basing investment decisions on previous price activity rather than company profit performance or yield). In addition, they generally place far less emphasis on portfolio management than their British competitors. The UK software companies offer a pretty broad spread of products, so it is important to be very clear what you are actually looking for. Just asking for 'investment software' is also asking for trouble. If you always base your buy and sell decisions on the quality of company management or gross profits, there is little point paying for a charting program with a large number of irrelevant features.

Of the British companies Indexia comes the closest to the US approach, with its products focused mainly on technical analysis, although portfolio management is certainly not excluded. The range extends from Intro, which is aimed at the small or novice investor, to Indexia II Plus which incorporates an impressive range of analytical and charting tools. All the products are compatible with each other, so moving up the product range does not involve a new learning process each time. Though the software is not Windows based, it still produces clear charts and is quick in operation.

Updata Softwares take a slightly different approach with its program Invest. The software has rather less emphasis on technical analysis and more on information management. It has been designed to run in conjunction with a Teletext card, though it will accept information from other sources as well. The program runs under Windows and is therefore able to support

Equities

DDE (Dynamic Data Exchange). Invest uses this to share information with other Windows programs. This is particularly handy for portfolio management, as you can have your existing holdings (or possible acquisitions) laid out in a spreadsheet for analysis and continually updated by the DDE link. Those who have a Teletext card can also build their own choice of database with Invest using the free information supplied.

Synergy Softwares aim to provide an integrated solution to investment tracking with its STAR system. This provides the user with charting, analysis and data in one package. Data is retrieved from Synergy's own bulletin board in compressed form (to reduce call costs) and then distributed automatically to the database files. The portfolio management facilities allow the creation of up to 60 separate portfolios and a range of reports to be generated on each. A capital gains tax module is also available which will automatically calculate any chargeable gain (allowing for RPI indexation) on any portfolio.

Pricetrack is an inexpensive program based around a set of spreadsheets that follows a similarly integrated approach on a subscription basis. The subscription covers the data and any software upgrades with customers having the choice of either weekly or monthly updates on floppy disk. The information provided includes not only prices but also fundamental data such as dividends, annual results etc. The program is split into three modules which cover database manipulation/graphing, reports (such as company results) and portfolio management. The focus of the program is to allow you to monitor the performance of your own portfolio as well as screen the markets for future investment opportunities.

Winfolio DF 4.0 from Mann Made Software offers a similar set of features but also incorporates an automatic long-term investment method. Originally developed for unit trust investment, it has now been extended to cover equities, bonds and PEPs as well and accepts data from Prestel, Teletext or manual entry. It offers simple but visually attractive charting and allows you to simulate buy/sell decisions as well as including basic portfolio management.

Apart from the companies already mentioned there are now several firms who specialise in distributing a range of investment software from various developers. Market Data Centre is an agent for nine software companies and also stocks an enormous range of books on the subject of investment and analysis. It usually has several of its packages installed on computer so customers have the opportunity to see a range of products in action when trying to decide what to buy. Trendline Systems stocks a range of American software as does Comcare. Both companies can arrange demonstrations of products.

Synergy Software (STAR) Tel: 01582 424282
Indexia (Intro, Indexia II and Indexia II Plus) Tel: 01442 878015
Updata (Invest) Tel: 0181 874 4747
Pricetrack Tel: 01275 472306
Mann Made Software (Winfolio DF 4.0) Tel: 01204 385159
Market Data Centre Tel: 0171 522 0094
Trendline Tel: 01707 644874
Comcare Tel: 0161 902 0330

Finding a broker

When it comes to choosing a broker, the first step is to make sure what type of service you want. As regards share dealing, there are three options, as follows:

1. *Execution-only.* This is essentially for dealing only, with no advice given, although company reports or recommendations may be available. Some brokers may be prepared to accept 'limit' orders, under which you specify a maximum buying or minimum selling price; others may only be prepared to deal 'at best' – the best price that can be readily obtained on the market.
2. *Advisory.* This is offered by the majority of brokers and may cover individual share purchases and sales or provide a

---

**One call is all it takes.
Phone ShareLink on 0121 200 2242.**

Equities

Fidelity Stockbroking Service

Why pay for advice you don't need?

Deal Size (UK Securities)	Avg. Traditional Stockbroker Commission*	Fidelity Commission	Avg. Savings per deal
£5,000	£98	£50	49%
£15,000	£218	£70	68%
£40,000	£349	£95	73%

- Up to 73% savings on commission
- Free Designated Nominee
- 0800 Callfree trading number
- Options Trading
- New issues service
- Self-Select PEP

The Fidelity Stockbroking Service offers the independent investor everything a traditional stockbroker provides – except the advice – at substantial savings. Just compare commission levels above.

Fidelity's trading expertise in handling large orders means that we are often able to negotiate better prices for our customers than those publicly quoted on The London Stock Exchange.

For active investors there's Stockbroking PLUS which offers a linked Money Market Account, trading on world markets and unique frequent dealing commission credits.

In addition we now offer extensive savings on commission and charges with our Options Trading and Self-Select PEP services. What's more, you have the reassurance of the Fidelity name – one of the leading and most respected stockbroking and fund management groups in the world. We offer more, by charging less.

Callfree 0800 222190
9am - 6pm (Mon-Fri) 10am - 4pm (Sat & Sun) Fax 01737 830360 anytime

To: Fidelity Brokerage Services, FREEPOST KT4392, TADWORTH, Surrey KT20 6BR. Please send me a brochure and application for Fidelity's:
Stockbroking Service ☐   New Self-Select PEP ☐   Options Trading ☐

Mr/Mrs/Miss(please print) _____
Address _____
_____ Postcode _____

Fidelity Brokerage

Based on a September 1994 Fidelity survey of advisory commissions of 10 leading stockbroking firms. This advertisement is issued by Fidelity Brokerage Services, member of The London Stock Exchange and The SFA.

We cut commission – not service.

comprehensive portfolio service. At the outset, the broker will discuss with you your needs and desires, without obligation; thereafter you will be consulted before any transaction can take place and you can also initiate consultations or deals.
3. *Discretionary.* In this case, you hand over all responsibility to the broker, although there will be an initial discussion to sort out your aims, attitude to risk and so on. You will also be kept informed of all transactions, as well as receiving regular valuations and reviews.

In addition to these dealing services, stockbrokers may also offer a comprehensive financial planning package. This would include, for example, advice on cash management, school fees planning, retirement planning, life assurance and tax planning.

One other facility is a nominee service, under which the broker (or a third party, such as a bank) will hold certificates on your behalf, in the name of the nominee company. This can save you having to get involved with any paperwork, as the broker will be able to handle it all, but it does mean you can miss out on any perks, because the shares will not be registered in your own name.

The majority of stockbrokers are regulated by the Securities and Futures Authority, through which they are authorised on an individual basis to give advice. Clients are eligible for the Investors Compensation Scheme in the event of default, and brokers generally also carry professional indemnity insurance against fraud and negligence.

Costs

The stockbroker's charges will usually be in the form of commission on dealing, though where there are additional financial planning services there may be an annual fee. The level of commission charged will vary from firm to firm, but will generally depend on three factors:

1. *The type of service:* execution-only dealing is usually cheaper than advisory or discretionary facilities.
2. *The location of the broker:* provincial brokers are usually

Equities

somewhat cheaper than their London counterparts by virtue of having lower overheads.
3. *The size of the deal:* the scale of charges reduces for larger transactions and there is usually a minimum charge at the bottom end.

On top of the commission, you will also be liable to stamp duty at 0.5 per cent. Examples of charges are shown in Table 5.1.

You may be able to deal within specified price limits, or at the best available price in the market that day. Once the order has been executed, you will receive a contract note from the broker, showing the price of the shares and the dealing costs. Settlement will follow within five working days of the transaction.

Table 5.1 *The costs of buying shares*

£1000-worth	
Stockbroker's commission	£22.00
Stamp duty at 0.5%	5.00
Total	£27.00
£10,000-worth	
Stockbroker's commission	£133.50
Stamp duty at 0.5%	50.00
Total	£183.50
£25,000-worth	
Stockbroker's commission	£263.50
Stamp duty at 0.5%	125.00
Total	£388.50

Shares in a portfolio

The minimum portfolio size specified by stockbrokers varies considerably, from firm to firm and depending on what type of service you want. Equally, different brokers will vary in their views on what constitutes a sensible minimum, regardless of what they might be prepared to accept – some will say around £25,000, others anything up to £100,000.

Lump-Sum Investment

Chiefly, it depends on your circumstances and the amount of risk you are prepared to accept. The points to bear in mind are first, that small deals cost relatively more than larger ones, as Table 5.1 shows, and second, that to achieve a spread of risk you should think in terms of holding 10 to 15 shares. If you were to put £5000 into each of 10 holdings, that would mean a portfolio of £50,000; if you then add in 'safety' money in alternative investments, you can begin to see why some advisers think in terms of six figures.

If you are only investing the odd few thousand, you will be restricted to the UK and only a small number of shares at that, whereas a unit trust, for instance, could give you a stake in a worldwide spread of holdings.

Having said that, there is nothing to stop you going directly into equities with any amount to invest. The so-called 'Super Sid' investor would usually be in the £5000 to £20,000 bracket and stockbrokers are generally prepared to accept smaller sums than they used to, particularly as they might now see only the equity portion of a larger portfolio, whereas in the past they tended to be given charge of all a client's investments. The only 'rule' is to appreciate the risks involved, and the same is true of speculation; as the saying goes, if you don't know whether you are a speculator or an investor, the stock market is an expensive place to find out.

There are, of course, a host of such sayings, many of them contradictory, and there is no guaranteed formula for investment success. If you plan to be a middle of the road, long-term investor, the best attributes are probably moderation and patience: don't expect to get rich overnight and don't hold out for even bigger profits at the risk of losing what you already have. Few people ever manage to buy at the very bottom of the market and sell at the very top; if you can come somewhere close, you should find ample rewards.

One other point on portfolio organisation is that it is worth considering using a personal equity plan for the first £6000, the maximum investment that is allowed per year in an ordinary plan (a further £3000 can be put into a single company plan). The advantage is that all income and capital gains arising from the investment are tax free. Against this have to be set the plan charges; for unit trust-based plans, there are usually no charges

---

The INSPIRE Foundation
(Integrated Spinal Rehabilitation)

*****

We receive neither National nor Local Government funding

Perhaps your Company could help us to continue underwriting this very worthwhile work in support of persons who have sustained spinal cord injuries

*****

Please telephone 01722-336262 Ext 2465   Registered Charity No 296284

---

other than those on the trusts themselves, so if you are investing in trusts as well as equities, you may do better to use the PEP allowance for the former. PEPs are discussed in detail in Chapter 9.

Other ways to play the market

Warrants

Buying shares is not the only means of investing in the equity market. An alternative is to buy warrants, which may be available on the shares of trading companies and investment trusts.

A warrant conveys the right to buy a share in a company at some future time. The price is fixed at the outset and known as the 'exercise price', and the option may be taken up on specified 'exercise dates'. These may be a particular day, or a set of dates, each year up to a final date when the option lapses.

Buying the share would be worth while if the exercise price plus the original cost of the warrant add up to less than the current market price of the share, although if you plan to sell the

Lump-Sum Investment

share for a quick profit you would also have to take your sale costs into account. If there is no opportunity for profit, the right to buy need not be taken up, but the warrant will lapse without value once the final exercise date has passed.

Like shares, warrants are traded on the Stock Exchange so can be bought as investments in their own right with no intention of taking up the exercise rights. The price of a warrant is generally much lower than the price of its related share, but will move in line with it, giving you exposure to the share's fortunes for a lower outlay.

But, by the same token, warrants are much more volatile, and therefore riskier, than the shares themselves. If, for example, the share price rises by 50p, the warrant price will rise by a similar amount, but the lower starting-point means the proportionate rise will be much greater. Equally, the effect of any fall in the share price will be enhanced. This is called the 'gearing' on the warrant, which is measured as the share price divided by the warrant price.

A high level of gearing offers high potential rewards but also greater risk. The other factors involved are the remaining lifespan, up to the final exercise date, and the premium, which is the excess of the exercise price plus the cost of the warrant over the current market price of the share. The longer the lifespan, the higher the premium may be, as there is more time for the share price to rise high enough for the warrant to generate a profit.

Assuming the risk is acceptable, warrants can be suitable for higher rate taxpayers as they do not pay any dividends. Hence there will be no liability to income tax; profits will be taxed as capital gains, which can be offset by the annual £6300 exempt allowance.

Options

Futures and options contracts both come under the generic heading of derivatives – a family of financial instruments that allow a number of techniques, both to increase and decrease risk. But while futures are out of the price range of the ordinary investor, options can be very useful. They are traded through the London International Financial Futures and Options Exchange (Liffe) and there are a number of stockbrokers who will deal in them on behalf of private clients. You can go to one of them for just this service alone, even if your main portfolio is handled by a different firm.

The options used by private investors are based on either individual shares or an index. In the former case, a standard contract covers 1000 shares in a particular company, while index options are based on the value of the FT-SE 100 index. In either case, there are two types of option: 'calls' and 'puts'.

Take the case of an equity option. Here, the buyer of a call option has the right to buy a quantity of shares, at a specified price, at any time between now and the expiry date, which can be up to nine months away. A put option confers a similar right to sell shares. The buyer of the option is not obliged to take it up, but if he chooses to, the seller must honour it; either way, the seller gets to keep the cost of the option, which is known as the 'premium'.

Suppose you expect a share price to rise. Instead of buying the share itself, you can buy a call option, which will cost a lot less. If the price does then rise - above the price specified in the option, plus the premium you paid for it - you have two choices. First, you can exercise the option, then sell the shares for a profit. Alternatively, you can sell the option, for a higher premium than you paid, making a smaller profit but for a much lower outlay than if you had bought the actual shares.

Put options can be used as insurance if you believe that the price of a share you hold will go down. If it does fall, you can exercise the option and thereby limit your losses. If the price rises instead, you can simply let the option lapse and perhaps recoup its cost by selling the shares at a profit.

You can also sell, or write, options, but unless you are prepared to take on a heavy risk you should only do so if you have the shares to sell or the money to buy. Suppose, for example, that you hold shares whose price looks likely to remain rather flat. You can then write a call option against them. If your predictions are correct, the buyer of the option will probably not want to exercise it, so you have gained the premium for no outlay. If the share price rises and the option is exercised, you will lose out on the price rise, but you still keep the premium, so you will be better off than if you had sold the shares at the original market price.

Lump-Sum Investment

As with equities, dealing services in options can be on an execution-only, discretionary or advisory basis. For the beginner, an advisory service is probably best, as it allows you to build up a knowledge of the market. Commission scales tend to start somewhat higher than those on equities, but again, it will vary from firm to firm, so it is worth shopping around. A list of firms that deal in options can be obtained from Liffe.

One other possibility is to bet on the index, which can be done through a couple of organisations. The effect is similar to using an option, but losses are not automatically limited – you have to decide to close the bet if the index is moving against you. Winnings are also tax free, as the betting tax will be paid by the company and included in the quoted price spreads.

Other types of share

As well as ordinary shares there are other types that investors may consider.

Preference shares carry the entitlement to a fixed dividend each year. Most of them are 'cumulative', which means that if the dividend is missed one year, it would have to be made up later if the company resumes dividends on its ordinary shares. Preference shares also take priority over ordinary shares if the company is wound up. Currently, with interest rates at low levels, the income from preference shares looks attractive but, as with any shares, the capital value is not guaranteed.

Convertible stocks are securities which carry a fixed dividend plus the option to convert them into ordinary stock, at a set price, at some fixed time in the future. They also rank ahead of ordinary shares in the event of liquidation. Again, the yields look attractive when interest rates are low, and there is also the chance of making a profit from the conversion.

Debentures are loans to a company that are secured on a

**One call is all it takes.
Phone ShareLink on 0121 200 2242.**

specific asset, such as property. The yield is fixed and there is a stated redemption date when the loan will be repaid.

Stock market terms

Most readers will no doubt have come across stock market jargon, at least to some extent, but this is a reminder of the more common terms.

Bear: someone who believes the market will fall
Blue chip: companies regarded as high quality and the most safe – said to be named after the highest value chip in poker
Bull: someone who believes the market will rise
Nominee account: a facility whereby shares are held on behalf of an investor in a company's name
Partly-paid: an issue of shares on which only part of the price is paid up-front
Rights issue: the offer of new shares in a company to existing shareholders at a price below the current market price
Scrip issue: a free issue of shares to existing shareholders
Stag: someone who buys a new issue in the hope of selling immediately for a quick profit

Where to find out more

A directory of private client stockbrokers, listing their services, can be obtained from the Association of Private Client Investment Managers and Stockbrokers, 112 Middlesex Street, London E1 7HY; tel 0171 247 7080.

A free information pack and a list of brokers dealing in traded options can be obtained from Liffe, Cannon Bridge, London EC4R 3XX; tel 0171 623 0444.

Cut through the jargon with ShareLink. For a free booklet phone 0121 200 2242.

INVESTING A LUMP SUM

Deciding how best to invest a cash lump sum may sound easy – until you have to do it in practice.

Depending on how large your lump sum actually is, you should consider seeking professional financial advice. But whether you decide on this route or prefer to do it yourself, it is in your best interests to learn the basic ground rules of investment – before you even start to consider specific financial products.

Rule number one is to clearly define your objective. In particular, do you need to use your capital to generate income now, possibly because you are retired and your pension is inadequate? Or, do you want your capital to grow either with a view to turning it into income later on, or to fund a large item of expenditure such as your children's education?

It is vital that you clearly set your objective at the outset as this will determine what types of investments match your requirements.

Rule number two is to decide the level of risk you are prepared to accept, or indeed, can afford to take. The major risk is that your capital may reduce in value because the markets you have invested in fall. As a general rule of thumb, the lower the risk, the lower the potential rewards, but the greater security of your capital. The higher the risk, then the greater the potential rewards, but the less secure is your capital.

Rule number three is to decide how much money you can prudently afford to invest. In other words, keep a part of your capital on one side to meet an emergency. The longer you can keep your money invested, then the better are the potential rewards but the greater the potential penalties for getting at it at short notice.

Rule number four is do not put all your eggs in one basket. The professionals will always spread their risks and so should you.

Rule number five is do not be swayed by tax efficiency alone. How a particular investment relates to your specific tax situation is a significant factor. But the overall suitability of an investment to your circumstances is more important.

Having absorbed the basic rules, you are ready to consider your investment options. Ideally, whether your objective is income now or capital growth, you should look to spread your investments. By doing this, you can mix your investments to further balance risk against reward.

At the safe end of the spectrum, your options include National Savings products. These effectively fall into two categories, those which provide income and those dedicated to growth. Then there is the myriad of ordinary deposit and term accounts offered which can give monthly interest if that is your priority.

But when interest rates are relatively low, the returns on such vehicles can be pedestrian. Without sacrificing safety, better options might be the guaranteed income and growth bonds and the guaranteed stockmarket bonds offered by life assurance companies.

The former are well established products and guarantee a specific level of income or growth together with the return of your capital at the end of a predetermined term.

The latter are a new breed of product which, in general terms, offer the potential for stockmarket-linked performance on top of specific guarantees relating to income, growth and capital invested.

You should be sure you understand exactly what type of product you are interested in and, in the case of stockmarket bonds, whether the capital you get back has been reduced by any income paid out. The other point to note is that the guarantees may operate *only* if you keep your money invested for the whole term of the bond, which could be up to give or six years.

Moving up the risk spectrum, there are lump sum or single premium investment bonds offered by life assurance companies which can provide either an income or capital growth. Here, you can invest in a range of funds managed by the life company, and while the value of your capital is not guaranteed, you can select the funds to closely match your own particular risk profile. Such bonds do not have a fixed term, but realistically, they should be considered as medium to long term investments perhaps for five years or more.

Those interested solely in income should also consider Government stock or Gilts which have a fixed life and pay a taxable income twice a year. Gilts have a "nominal" value and providing they are held to maturity, this is the amount you will get back. But because they are traded on the markets, the price of gilts changes daily and their current value, or how much they cost to buy, can be more or less than their nominal value.

Also for income seekers is a new type of Personal Equity Plan or PEP, which invests in corporate bonds, that is the loan stock issued by companies listed on the stockmarket. A PEP allows you to take all income and capital gains entirely free of tax at any time, but the value of your capital is not guaranteed and can rise or fall with the stockmarkets.

At the riskiest end of the investment spectrum, the main option is some form of share-based investment, preferably such pooled or collective investments as unit or investment trusts bound up in the tax efficient shelter of a Personal Equity Plan (PEP).

Investment and unit trusts can provide either income or growth or a combination of the two. You can invest up to £6,000 a year in a PEP and while you are free to cash it in at any time, the value of your capital can rise and fall with the stockmarkets and is not guaranteed.

Author: Ian Harper, Corporate Communications Manager

Equities

DO YOU WANT INCOME OR CAPITAL GROWTH?

GENERAL ACCIDENT LIFE'S INVESTMENT PRODUCTS ARE TAILOR MADE TO SUIT YOUR NEEDS

Investing a lump sum can be a lot more difficult than you think - you've got the money but what's the best thing to do with it?

General Accident Life can help you to make the right choice.

Our lump sum investment products have plenty to offer you.

- **Flexibility** - the contract can be tailored to suit YOUR needs
- **Choice** of income or growth generating products
- **Table topping** financial strength
- **Competitive** range of investment contracts

General Accident Life offers an extensive range of competitive products that cover all your needs.

If you would like further information or advice about General Accident Life's Investment products, please phone Free on 0500 100 200.

General Accident

General Accident Life Assurance Limited
Registered in England No 226742
2 Rougier Street York YO1 1HR
Regulated by the Personal Investment Authority

Lump-Sum Investment

Other useful telephone numbers are:

The Stock Exchange: 0171 588 2355
The Securities and Futures Authority: 0171 378 9000.
ProShare: 0171 600 0948

6

Unit Trusts and Offshore Funds (1)

Unit trusts, offshore funds, investment trusts and life assurance products all have a common characteristic: they pool investors' money into a large fund, so that smaller investors can participate in a broad spread of assets that they could never achieve by their own means. The concept was set out in the prospectus of the very first investment trust to be launched, in 1868, and it is still quoted by that trust in its literature today: 'We intend to provide the investor of moderate means with the same advantages as large capitalists in diminishing the risks ... by spreading investment over a number of stocks.'

The primary advantage of collective investments, as they are known, is this reduction of risk. If you hold only one share and it crashes, you lose everything, but if you have a stake in a portfolio, one failure will be cushioned by other successes. There are also other plus points which will emerge over the next few chapters, such as professional investment management, ready access to overseas markets and certain tax benefits – particularly through personal equity plans, which are discussed in Chapter 9.

Unit trust investments can start from as little as £500 for a lump sum and there is no set maximum. As mentioned in the last chapter, many people would consider £25,000 to be the working minimum for a direct investment into the stock market, but investors with up to £100,000 available may find that the range and scope of collective investments will amply satisfy their requirements. Larger investors may also find them useful to add

Lump-Sum Investment

The "Offshore" Advantage

Anyone who is living, working or retired in a foreign country should consider offshore banking, primarily because of the tax advantages which may be available. By holding their wealth offshore, expatriates could a avoid paying tax unnecessarily on interest earned or on capital gains and, in the case of foreign-domiciled customers, reduce or avoid UK inheritance tax. Interest offshore is paid gross and, because of the way in which the JK Revenue calculates tax liabilities, this could be worth more than gross interest earned in "onshore" locations such as the UK.

The financial advantages of offshore banking are the obvious attraction. However, when you become an expatriate your needs change. For a start you can't pop into your local branch to discuss things. Simple transactions such as bill payments need to be considered and, for example, it may be difficult for banks at home to deal with overseas queries.

Choosing the right bank can make all the difference to making your money work harder for you. Lloyds Bank is the only UK high street bank that provides a unique Club service for expatriates from dedicated offshore centres. The specially-trained staff provide Members with up-to-date information on savings and investment and can help to make living and working abroad a rewarding experience.

Tax efficiency, specialist expertise and a personal relationship with a dedicated Club Executive and supporting team are just a few things Members can expect from the Lloyds Bank Overseas Club.

Foreign nationals who live and work in the UK but prefer to bank "onshore" in the UK, are catered for by Lloyds Bank at a designated centre at Waterloo Place in London. The staff are trained to provide help and information on special banking services for foreign nationals and have access to specialised financial advice to help you make the most of your earnings.

For further details of Lloyds Bank in the UK, phone Waterloo Place on 0171 839 2099.

Maintaining long-distance relationships.

Lloyds Bank maintains a long-distance relationship with its, customers through the regular Club magazine "Shoreline". This provides articles informing Members of changes in world markets, country profiles, changes in tax laws, property, health and education.

A visiting programme is designed to promote stronger relationships and provides feedback to improve service. Staff from the Lloyds Bank Offshore Centres in Jersey and the Isle of Man visit their Members on a regular basis with frequent visits to the main countries where Members live – in every continent of the world.

A new 24-hour telephone banking service will be available to Club Members from summer 1996. It will then be possible to obtain information and carry out transactions on accounts 24 hours a day. It is already possible to give payment instructions by telephone or fax using a code system which is free to Club Members.

LLOYDS BANK OFFERS A COMPLETE RANGE OF OFFSHORE SERVICES.

The Overseas Club

The Overseas Club offers its Members an offshore cheque account, paying good interest, and their own personal Club Executive and supporting team Club Members also benefit from access to investment management services, help and information on UK tax, information on management of UK property and much more.

Investment Expertise

Investment products and investment management are provided by Lloyds Private Banking. Advice is available on funds structured for higher income, for savings and capital growth on unit trusts, investment trusts, equities, bonds, pensions, insurances – a wide range of options for investment, savings, financial planning protection.

The investment teams seek widespread international diversification through the principal markets and major currencies. Lloyds Bank has a well-known policy of risk limitation requiring only high-quality companies and institutions to be considered. The Bank's experience and international outlook can help protect against political and geographical disruption.

Private Banking

Clients with over £100,000 can elect a full one-to-one banking relationship with their specially-selected Account Manager. The aim is to a build a long-term relationship, one based on trust and understanding.

For further details of Lloyds Bank Offshore see the advertisement on page ? or call +44 (0) 1624 638104.

Issued by Lloyds Bank Plc, which is regulated by the Personal Investment Authority and IMRO for investment business. Rules and regulations made under the Financial Services Act 1986 for the protection of investors, including the investors Compensation Scheme, do not apply to the investment business of Lloyds Bank Plc and its subsidiaries carried out from offices outside the United Kingdom.

Investment advice may be provided by Lloyds Bank Insurance Services (Life and Pensions) Limited, Lloyds Private Banking (Channel Islands) Limited or Lloyds Private Banking (Isle of Man) Limited.

Advice on general insurance is provided by Lloyds Bank Insurance Service Limited.

Isle of Man offices of Lloyds Bank Plc, Private Banking (Isle of Man) Limited and Lloyds Bank Insurance Service (Life and Pensions) Limited are registered with the Isle of Man Financial Supervision Commission, the former two companies for banking and investment business, the latter company for investment business only. Lloyds Bank Plc is licensed under the Banking Supervision (Bailiwick of Guernsey) Law 1994.

Deposits made with an offshore branch of Lloyds Bank Plc are not covered by the Deposit Protection Scheme under the UK Banking Act 1987 (as amended).

Deposits made with an Isle of Man office of Lloyds Bank Plc are covered by the Depositors Compension Scheme contained in the I.O.M. Banking Business (Compensation of Depositors) Regulations 1991.

Advertisement feature

Paid in US dollars?

This new card gives you real independence

New from Lloyds Bank for US dollar earners

An interest-bearing offshore cheque account with payment card

If you want an offshore account in the Channel Islands or Isle of Man with a British bank, you don't have to have it in sterling. If you're earning US dollars it makes sense to open a Lloyds Bank US Dollar Offshore Cheque Account. You'll have a cheque book, earn higher interest the higher your balance and now you can also have a VISA payment card.

This means you have the freedom to shop all over the world where you see the VISA or Delta sign and settle your bill in dollars.

So there's no need to go to a US-based bank to get a dollar card.

The Lloyds Bank US Dollar Offshore Cheque Account can be opened with a deposit of just $2,000 and has tiered interest rates which means higher balances earn higher rates.

THE BENEFITS

- No need to change your dollar earnings into sterling.
- VISA payment card to make purchases in local currency.
- Ability to make cash withdrawals with your card in local currency through thousands of cash dispensers around the world.
- Increasing rates of interest, the larger your balance.
- Possible tax advantages of an offshore account.
- Political stability of the Channel Islands and Isle of Man.
- The comfort of dealing with one of Britain's largest banks.

AVAILABLE NOW

If you want the best of both worlds - a dollar account and VISA card with a trusted British bank in an offshore location - telephone or fax and we'll send you full details and an application form straight away.

Lloyds Bank Offshore Centre:

Phone
+44 (0)1624 638104

Fax
+44 (0)1624 638181

Alternatively write to:
Lloyds Bank Offshore Centre, PO Box 12, Douglas, Isle of Man, British Isles IM99 1SS.

There is a modest annual fee of US$50 (US$25 for Overseas Club Members). Deposits made with overseas offices of Lloyds Bank Plc are not covered by the Deposit Protection Scheme under the UK Banking Act 1987 (as amended). Deposits made with an Isle of Man office of Lloyds Bank Plc are covered by the Depositors Compensation Scheme contained in the I.O.M. Banking Business (Compensation of Depositors) Regulations 1991. Isle of Man offices of Lloyds Bank Plc are registered with the Isle of Man Financial Supervision Commission for banking and investment business. Lloyds Bank Plc, Registered Office: 71 Lombard Street, London EC3P 3BS, England.

DTC96

BRINGING THE PERSONAL TOUCH TO OFFSHORE BANKING

an overseas content to their holdings, even where they are investing directly in UK equities.

The growth in the unit trust industry over the last decade has been substantial. In 1984 there were 102 companies, running 687 trusts, which had a total value of £11.7 billion. At the end of 1995, there were 160 companies, operating 1633 trusts, with a total value of funds under management of £112.6 billion. These trusts span a huge variety of geographical and industrial specialisations, from broad-based UK General funds to Asian Smaller Markets or International Technology. Investment choice is examined in the next chapter.

The size of companies, and the number of trusts they run, vary considerably: the top 10 alone account for almost £52 billion of funds under management and the top 20 for over £70 billion, as shown in Table 6.1. Most companies are members of the Association of Unit Trusts and Investment Funds, which can supply a range of information and contact details.

Unit trust regulations

A unit trust is subject to a trust deed, which lays down the terms under which it operates, for example, where and how it will invest, the calculation of unit prices and the charges it may levy. The money in the fund is held on behalf of investors by trustees, generally a bank or insurance company, who are responsible for ensuring that the managers conform to the rules laid down in the trust deed.

The regulation and authorisation of unit trusts is in the hands of the Securities and Investments Board, which lays down rules on what investments are available to a unit trust. The bulk of the portfolio will normally be invested in quoted shares or gilts, but up to 10 per cent may be in unquoted securities, including up to 5 per cent in other unit trusts, and up to 5 per cent may be invested in warrants. Trusts may also make use of traded options and futures contracts for the purposes of efficient fund management, but these must be covered by holdings of cash or near cash, such as government securities.

To ensure that a trust preserves an adequate spread of risk – which, after all, is a prime objective – not more than 5 per cent of

Table 6.1 *Top 20 unit trust groups by funds under management*

Group	Funds under management (£m)
Schroder	9847.5
M&G	8240.1
Gartmore	5666.9
Mercury	5000.7
Perpetual	4656.4
Barclays Unicorn	4224.5
Fidelity	3656.8
Allied Dunbar	3580.4
Standard Life Trust Management	3543.0
Save & Prosper	3387.6
Friends Provident	2646.2
Prudential	2367.0
Morgan Grenfell	2041.0
Fleming Select	1801.7
Hill Samuel	1747.6
Henderson	1702.9
Abbey	1682.6
Legal & General	1670.6
Norwich Union	1649.9

Source: Association of Unit Trusts and Investment Funds, February 1996

the portfolio can normally be held in the shares of any one company. However, provided the total of 5 per cent plus holdings does not itself exceed 40 per cent of the portfolio, an individual holding may go up to 10 per cent. This means that if one share suddenly shoots up in value, it will not have to be immediately sold. In practice, a trust would normally have upwards of 40 different holdings, depending on its size, so it is likely to be well within the limits.

The other main rule is that a trust cannot hold more than 10 per cent of any one company's issued share capital. This is to ensure that a trust does not build up a controlling stake in a company, which could undermine its basic objectives.

Charges

There are two types of charge levied by unit trust managers: the initial charge and the annual charge. The level of these will be specified in the trust deed and the managers cannot raise the charges above that level without getting permission from the unit holders. For this reason, the levels stipulated are sometimes higher than the charges that are actually applied; this gives the managers the flexibility to make an increase at a future date without the bother of seeking permission.

In recent years there has been a tendency for charges to rise, so trusts that have been in existence for many years may carry lower charges than those more recently launched, unless the managers have sought permission for an increase. These days, the typical initial charge is between 5 and 6 per cent. Some gilt trusts have a lower charge, around 3 per cent, and cash trusts also have a very small or zero charge, while the specialist overseas trusts tend to carry the highest fees.

Out of this initial charge, the managers pay commission to intermediaries who sell the trusts for them. The usual amount of commission is 3 per cent, with the rest of the charge going towards the managers' costs, such as advertising. But if you buy direct from the managers rather than through an intermediary, the 3 per cent allowed for commission will still be charged and simply kept by the managers. Sometimes, however, the managers may make a special discount offer. Introductory discounts, of 1 per cent or possibly more for large investments, are quite common during the launch period of new trusts.

The annual charge is commonly between 1 and 2 per cent, though again cash trusts generally have a lower charge, around 0.5 per cent, while specialist trusts are likely to be at the top end of the scale.

In most cases, the annual fee is taken out of the trust's income, but some trusts now charge it to the capital account instead. This is done to maximise the income that can be paid out, but investors should bear in mind that it will reduce the capital growth from the trust and may ultimately lead to a lower total return. Opponents of the idea have also argued that it is not tax-effective: investors stand to receive relatively higher income and lower

Unit Trusts and Offshore Funds (1)

capital gains, whereas most will be liable to tax on the former and not the latter.

While it may seem best to go for trusts with the lowest charges, performance can be a more important factor in determining the investment return. Obviously, the higher the charges, the better the performance needs to be for the same result, but over longer periods, differences in performance – as the next chapter will show – can be more than large enough to wipe out the effects of a higher charge.

Normally you should think of holding on to unit trusts for at least a medium-term period, say three to five years. If you buy and sell more frequently, the initial charge on each purchase could start to eat into your returns. However, if you do plan to be an active investor, this effect can be lessened by sticking with one management group.

Most managers offer a discount on switches between their own trusts, as an incentive to investors to keep their money within the group. The amount varies from 1 per cent to as much as 4 per cent, which means switching can be done at very little cost.

Bid and offer

If you look at unit trust prices in the newspaper you will see that there are two quoted, the 'offer' price and the 'bid' price. The offer is what you pay to buy units, while the bid is what you get when you sell. The difference between them is usually greater than the quoted initial charge of 5 to 6 per cent, because the calculations are based on complex rules laid down by the regulatory authorities.

To start with, a trust must have a creation price and a cancellation price. The creation price is based on the value of the shares in the trust's portfolio (valued at their offer price, which is the price at which they could be bought on the market), plus stockbroker's commission and stamp duty. To that is added any cash held by the trust plus accumulated income from dividends and interest payments, and the whole lot is then divided by the total number of units in existence.

The cancellation price is almost a mirror image, being the value of the shares held in the portfolio at their bid price, less the stockbroker's commission, plus cash and accumulated income, again divided by the total number of units.

The full offer price that the managers can charge when selling units then becomes the creation price plus the initial charge. The full bid price, which is the minimum at which the managers can buy back units, is equal to the cancellation price.

The difference between these two is called the full spread and can be as much as 10 or 11 per cent. In practice, of course, few people would be prepared to buy an investment that would immediately drop 11 per cent in value, so the managers normally quote prices somewhere between the two extremes. The 'dealing' spread, which is the difference between the two quoted prices, is typically around 6 or 7 per cent. An illustration of the various prices is shown in Table 6.2.

When a trust is in demand, with new money coming in, the managers are likely to be buying more shares for the portfolio, so the quoted prices will move towards the top end of the range to reflect the costs of this. In this case the trust is said to be on an 'offer basis'.

Correspondingly, when more people are selling the trust than buying it, the managers may need to sell shares to meet the redemptions. The prices will then move towards the bottom end of the range and the trust is said to be on a 'bid basis'.

These price movements within the permitted range stem from the aim to be fair to all investors, particularly those who continue to hold units. For example, if sellers were given too high a price, it would dilute the value of the trust for the remaining unit holders.

As long as you buy and sell on roughly the same basis, it makes little difference where the prices are within the range. But if you buy when the trust is on an offer basis and sell when it is on a bid basis, you will effectively suffer the full spread.

Generally, managers will not move abruptly from one to the other, but will try to anticipate the trend of demand – whether the market is rising or falling – and move gradually over several days. But a very large order can force a sharper movement, so it is possible that the price can move against you quite suddenly.

There have been proposals, not as yet carried through, to allow certain variations in unit trust pricing. One in particular is the

Table 6.2 Price calculations

Maximum offer price = creation price + initial charge	106.00p	
		⎫
Minimum offer price = minimum bid price + dealing spread	102.67p	6% initial charge — Offer price range ⎬ 9.75% full spread
Creation price = offer value of shares + commission + stamp duty + cash + accumulated income, divided by number of units in issue	100.00p	⎭ 6.25% dealing spread
Maximum bid price = maximum offer price − dealing spread	99.37p	Bid price range
Minimum bid price/cancellation price = bid value of shares − commission + cash + accumulated income, divided by number of units in issue	96.25p	

Lump-Sum Investment

option to replace part or all of the initial charge by an 'exit fee' which would be applied if units were sold within a given period from purchase. The argument in favour of this is that more money would be invested up front, while the trust can still recoup its costs if investors switch in and out quickly. Exit fees are already in use on some personal equity plans (see Chapter 9).

Different types of unit

Unit trusts may offer either or both of two types of unit: accumulation and distribution. Accumulation units are designed to reinvest any income earned by the trust with a corresponding increase in the unit price. Distribution, or income, units, instead pay out the income, usually twice a year, although some pay quarterly or annually.

The difference is simply a matter of convenience. Trusts that have the sole aim of producing capital growth, and those that invest in certain overseas markets, have a very low yield – in the case of Japan, it may be virtually zero. To pay out to every unit holder twice a year could cost more than the income itself, so it is easier to accumulate it into the fund. The managers will, however, send out information on the income that has been accumulated as investors will have to declare it for tax.

Distribution units are used by trusts that are designed for income or a combination of income and growth. Payments are made net of basic rate tax. Some trusts offer to reinvest the income in further units, but this will usually mean paying the initial charge each time. If you do not want the income, and there is a choice available, accumulation units should prove more cost-effective.

When you buy distribution units in a trust, the price will include an allowance for any income that has accrued since the last payment date. So when you receive the next distribution, part of it will represent the income earned since you invested, while the rest is in effect a return of the extra amount you paid for the units. For tax purposes, this portion – known as an 'equalisation payment' – counts as capital; it is not liable for income tax, but will be deducted from the purchase price in calculating any capital gains tax liability.

Please Help these Sick, Dying and Traumatized Children

Children in Distress

Children in Distress is a Christian Charity, founded in 1990, for the relief of suffering of the children of Eastern Europe.

In March 1992, a newly constructed 100-bed Children's Hospice in Cernavoda, Romania was opened, offering these sick and dying children love, comfort and peace as they approached the end of their shortened, love-starved existence. In September 1994, a residential school for HIV-infected children was opened on the site.

In 1993, construction began on a 100-bed specialist hospital – St Luke's Children's Hospital/Hospice in Saranda, Albania. This hospital will provide urgently needed medical and nursing care. It is due to open at the end of 1995.

Each facility is staffed by a combination of British nurses and doctors, working alongside and training a similar number of Romanian and Albanian staff.

CHILDREN IN DISTRESS

We ask you to help us bring to reality the vision of a world where children do not have to suffer unnecessary pain and distress nor cry in vain; a world where they can be loved and treasured, healed and restored. We believe that this world can come into being when we as Christians join hands and hearts and voices in prayer and in rich self-giving.

Will you join with us by supporting God's world of healing and love:

In Romania where at Cernavoda St. Laurence Children's Hospice is loving into life over 75 children and soon will double its potential and has opened a small residential school for AID's infected children.

In Albania where St. Luke's Children's Hospice and Hospital is working in the town of Saranda.

If you would like to help us in the vital work by making a donation, taking out a covenant or by remembering us in your will, please contact

The Director, Rev. Dr. John Walmsley at
Children in Distress,
Unit 2/1, Thirsk Industrial Park,
York Road, Thirsk, N. Yorks YO7 3BX
Tel: 01845 526272. Fax: 01845 526291

Funds of funds

A few years ago, a new type of unit trust was introduced, referred to as a 'fund of funds'. This is a kind of 'super trust' which invests across the range of the group's other trusts and thereby acts as a managed fund.

Initially, the concept attracted a fair degree of scepticism and even now only a third or so of the management groups offer such a trust. The advantage claimed is that it offers the equivalent of an investment management service for relatively small sums. For smaller investors, highly specialised trusts can be too risky, as performance is very volatile and timing – when to buy and sell – is crucial. Through the fund of funds, the investor can obtain a stake in these specialist trusts at lower risk, because the portfolio is spread over a range of trusts, and the manager makes the decisions on his behalf.

One drawback is that the fund of funds is limited by the other trusts run by the group. Obviously, it would not be worth while unless the range of trusts it can invest in is fairly broad. But even then it may not be possible to get the best mix, because the individual trusts have their own objectives which may not fit with the overview of the fund of funds. For example, the investment strategy of the Japan trust, which is focused solely on that market, might not be the best approach for the Japanese portion of the fund of funds, which takes a global view. And, of course, if the Japan trust happens to be performing badly, the fund of funds manager has the difficult choice of whether to invest in a poor fund or not to be in Japan at all.

So far, the performance of the funds of funds does not suggest that they have any particular advantage over ordinary international trusts, which also take a global view and are not limited in their investment choices.

Cash trusts

Cash, or money market, trusts are a more recent innovation, born out of uncertain stock market conditions. Unlike the normal run of unit trusts, cash trusts do not involve any risk to your capital, because they invest in fixed capital instruments. In most cases

Unit Trusts and Offshore Funds (1)

St Anne's Shelter & Housing Action

St Anne's Shelter & Housing Action works with single homeless people; people with alcohol problems; people with learning disabilities and people with mental health problems. St Anne's has over eighty group homes, registered care homes, nursing homes and supported housing schemes; two day centres; two hostels for homeless people; this country's first detoxification centre for drunkenness offenders; and an adult placement scheme for people with learning disabilities and volunteer befriending schemes. St Anne's has a reputation for innovation in social care and responsiveness to client needs. It is currently developing its range of services for homeless young people, and is embarking on a new project to provide supported housing linked to supported employment for homeless young people to mark twenty five years of caring in the community.

- day support, accommodation and specialist projects for homeless people.
- small registered care homes and nursing homes for people with learning disabilities.
- small registered care homes for people with mental health problems.
- services geared to individual needs aiming to promote independence, skills and choice for residents.
- a range of supported housing.

Head Office: 6 St Mark's Avenue, Leeds LS2 9BN.
Tel: 0113 2435151. Fax: 0113 2451526

25 years caring in the community

---

they carry no initial charge and the annual charge is generally only 0.5 per cent.

The aim is to provide a temporary refuge for investors who want to sell holdings in equity trusts when the stock market is falling. The managers benefit because the money stays with the group, while investors may also benefit because they will qualify for any switching discount the group offers if they later go back into an equity trust.

Cash trusts can also provide a higher income than bank or building society deposit accounts. By pooling investors' money into one large fund, the trust can secure top rates of interest on the money market, while the minimum individual investment is generally only £1000 or less. But one drawback is that there is currently no standardised method for calculating the yield on these trusts; companies may quote net or gross of expenses, and a simple or compound rate. A set formula is being considered, but meanwhile, investors should be wary of anything that looks substantially better than its rivals.

Lump-Sum Investment

A few cash trusts provide a cheque-book facility for larger investments, so that you can have instant access to your money. Otherwise, if you want to sell, managers are obliged to issue a cheque within 24 hours of receiving the necessary documentation.

Index trusts

While most trusts are actively managed, index-tracking trusts take a passive line. The aim is to track the movement in one or another stock market index: there are index trusts based on the UK, the US, Europe, Japan, South East Asia and worldwide. One way of doing this is to buy holdings in every stock that is included in the index, but for the US, for example, this would be impossible, as there are just too many. Instead, the trust will aim for a representative sample in appropriate portions. Generally, trusts do not expect to be spot on every time, but will set a target margin of error.

Not surprisingly, the concept has both its supporters and its critics. On the downside, it does not seem much of an achievement simply to match the index, especially as investors will do slightly worse than that when charges are taken into account. It is also worth remembering that a tracker trust will follow the index downwards as well as upwards, while traditional trusts have the option to go partly into cash to avoid the worst of a fall.

However, supporters point out that many trusts consistently underperform their relevant index; over longer periods, the average performance of funds in any one sector may well be below the index for that market. So while an index trust is never likely to be top of its sector in the performance tables, it is never likely to be bottom either. Index trusts can also operate on low charges and have been prominent in recent price competition, particularly with newcomers to the unit trust market.

Futures and options trusts

These are a fairly recent development in the unit trust world and there are currently only around 35 available. The use of futures and options contracts had previously been regarded as potentially too risky for unit trusts – some people felt that if high risk trusts

Unit Trusts and Offshore Funds (1)

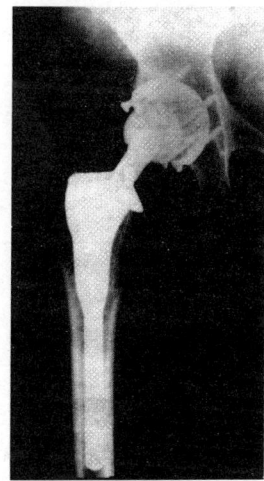

How would you feel at 50 to be told that you were **not old enough** for a hip replacement?

This could mean pain for another 10 or more of your active years.

Of the 50,000 hip replacements carried out each year in the United Kingdom, 13% are revisions – **why?** Because they loosen.

This X-ray shows a hip replacement developed by the Furlong Research Foundation which is expected to last your natural lifetime. **Age is now irrelevant.**

Please help us by donations, convenants and bequests so that we can continue to help you.

Furlong Research Foundation
Lister House, 11-12 Wimpole Street,
London W1M 7AB
Tel: 0171 436 1919   Fax: 0171 636 4351

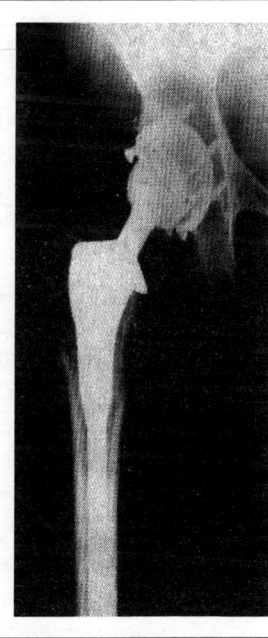

How would you feel at 50 to be told that you were **not old enough** for a hip replacement?

This could mean pain for another 10 or more of your active years.

Of the 50,000 hip replacements carried out each year in the United Kingdom, 13% are revisions – **why?** Because they loosen.

This X-ray shows a hip replacement developed by the Furlong Research Foundation which is expected to last your natural lifetime. **Age is now irrelevant.**

Please help us by donations, convenants and bequests so that we can continue to help you.

Furlong Research Foundation, Lister House,
11-12 Wimpole Street, London W1M 7AB
Tel: 0171 436 1919   Fax: 0171 636 4351

were allowed, it would affect the general reputation unit trusts had of being relatively safe and thereby discourage investors altogether.

One type uses futures contracts to match the performance of an index. Buying futures is cheaper than buying each individual share, so most of the trust's money can be kept in cash, earning interest, which is paid out as income distributions. The trust tracks only the capital value of the index, ignoring share dividends, but with the interest, the total return should be roughly equivalent.

These are called 'bull' funds and are designed for investors who think the market will rise. There are also 'bear' funds, designed for those who think it will fall, which produce the exact opposite of the index movement: when it falls, the trust price rises by an equivalent amount.

Geared futures and options trusts involve higher risk with the potential for greater reward. For example, a 'two times geared' trust would give double exposure: if the index rises by 10 per cent, the trust price will rise by 20 per cent, but falls will also be doubled. However, as with any unit trust, your loss is limited to your initial investment.

A third type uses futures and options in a hedging role to reduce risk. The effect is that when the market is falling, the value of the fund should fall by less than the index, so that losses are cut, while in a flat market returns should be enhanced. In rising markets, however, the fund may underperform the index, so some growth potential may be sacrificed in return for the protection against a fall.

A unit trust recently launched at the time of writing uses 'put' options to guarantee that investors will never lose more than 5 per cent of their initial investment. Each year it sets a minimum selling price for units which depends on whether the stock market has gone up or down. If the unit price has risen by 10 per cent or more over the year, the minimum price will be set at 5 per cent below the current unit value, locking in the gains that have been made. If, on the other hand, the market has fallen, the selling price will be set at 95 per cent of the previous minimum. Unlike other guaranteed funds, investors can sell their holdings at any time and still take advantage of the guaranteed minimum price.

The mechanics of futures and options contracts are described more fully in Chapter 5.

Warrant trusts

Spring 1994 saw the launch of the first unit trust to invest in warrants. These may be issued by trading companies, investment trusts and offshore companies and it is intended that the unit trust will hold a mix of all three.

The mechanics of warrants are explained in Chapter 5. The main point to bear in mind is that the price of a warrant is generally much less than that of its related share, but price movements of the two are broadly in line. This means that the proportionate movement in the warrant price will be much greater: if the share price rises, the gain on the warrant can be several times as much, but losses will be similarly magnified.

Because of this volatility, the unit trust should be considered a relatively high risk investment, although the risk is tempered to some extent by the spread of holdings and the facility to switch heavily into cash if the market is unattractive.

Unit trusts and tax

The income earned by a unit trust may be of two types, technically known as 'franked' and 'unfranked'. Income deriving from dividends on UK equities is franked, which means it is regarded as being tax paid and the trust has no further liability.

Other income, for example, from dividends on foreign shares or interest on cash deposits, is unfranked and the trust will have to pay corporation tax on it. In the 1993 Budget, the basic rate of income tax on dividends was reduced from 25 per cent to 20 per cent; during the 1993/94 tax year, trusts had to pay a transitional corporation tax rate of 22.5 per cent but from April 1994 the rate has dropped to 20 per cent.

Phone ShareLink for a PEP talk on 0121 233 9955.

Lump-Sum Investment

Dividends from the unit trust are paid, or reinvested, net of basic rate tax and the investor receives a tax credit for the amount paid. Basic rate taxpayers have no further income tax liability, while non-taxpayers can reclaim the tax credit at the new rate of 20 per cent. Higher rate taxpayers, however, must pay the difference between the tax credit and their 40 per cent liability, in other words, 20 per cent.

As to capital gains tax, the unit trust has no liability on its dealings. Any profits you make when you sell may be liable, but only if your total profits from all relevant investments exceed the annual exempt allowance, which for the 1996/97 tax year is £6300.

Special facilities for the investor

Share exchange schemes
Unit trust groups run various schemes designed to encourage investors to buy their units. Most groups offer 'share exchange' schemes for people who want to sell direct holdings in shares to invest in unit trusts instead. This has become increasingly popular for privatisation issues.

There will always be a cost advantage to the investor. Occasionally the managers may want to keep your shares for their own trusts, in which case they may pay you the offer price for the shares, or a mid-market price, rather than the bid price less selling expenses which you would receive if you sold them privately. Otherwise, you will be paid the bid price but the managers will either bear the sale costs themselves or offer a discount.

Regular savings schemes
As well as accepting lump sums, many unit trust groups offer regular savings schemes, starting from a minimum of around £50 a month. As a rule there are no penalties for stopping or taking money out, and lump sums can also be added in at any time. Income would not normally be paid out, as the administration would be too complex, so trusts which offer accumulation units are preferable.

Even if you have a lump sum to invest, it can be better to 'drip-feed' it into a trust over a period rather than put it all in at once. This is due to a phenomenon known as pound-cost averaging.

Unit Trusts and Offshore Funds (1)

The argument is fairly straightforward: if you invest a bit at a time, you will benefit from times when the price falls because the same amount of money will buy more units. With a fluctuating price, the average cost of units over a period will be less than their average price. On the other hand, if you buy all at one go, the price could be at a peak or a trough, so timing becomes all-important – and few people can be confident of getting it right.

Table 6.3 gives an example of the mechanics of pound-cost averaging, using large price swings to clarify the effect.

Schemes for a regular income

Only a small number of trusts pay a monthly income, but many groups now offer monthly income portfolio schemes. Most trusts pay out dividends two or four times a year, so by packaging together three or six trusts with different distribution dates, a scheme can produce monthly payments.

The trusts in a package may not all pay out on the same day of every month and, more particularly, are not likely to pay the same amount. A refinement is to incorporate a deposit account in the scheme which will collect all the dividends and then pay out level amounts each month.

There are two drawbacks to packaged schemes offered by unit trust groups. First, you are restricted to the trusts of that group, which may not all perform well. Second, the trusts included in the package may not be ideal for your requirements. Several schemes include a gilt or fixed interest trust, which can boost the income

Table 6.3 *Pound-cost averaging*

Month of purchase	Unit price	Number of units bought for £50
1	100p	50
2	80p	63
3	125p	40
4	90p	56
5	85p	59
6	110p	45
Average price	98.3p	313 units bought for £300; average price paid: 95.8p

Lump-Sum Investment

level at the outset but provides little opportunity for capital growth and thereby rising income over time.

The alternative is to put together your own package, choosing the type of trusts you want from different groups. Several professional advisers run schemes of this type or can assemble one to match your particular needs. In some cases you can choose the level of income you want, but you need to remember that if you choose a level higher than the trusts are actually paying out, units would have to be cashed in to make up the difference. Over time this would make progressive inroads into your capital, so you would do better to settle for a lower income to start with and hope capital growth will boost it.

Keeping track of your investment

Generally, managers revalue at least once a day and prices are quoted in both *The Financial Times* and *The Daily Telegraph*. However, most groups now deal on a 'forward pricing' basis, which means that the deal is carried out at the price set by the next valuation. The remainder use 'historic pricing', which means the price used is that of the most recent valuation, but they must deal at a forward price if it is requested and will also move to forward pricing in certain circumstances, for example, if there is a large movement in the market.

So the prices published in newspapers are not necessarily what you will be quoted if you sell that day, but unless a very large deal has just gone through there is unlikely to be a substantial difference from one valuation to the next. *The Financial Times* indicates whether dealing is on a forward or historic basis, and also shows the cancellation price, so you can see whether a trust is on a bid or offer basis.

Another source of information is the manager's report on a trust, which is usually sent out to unit holders twice a year. Among other things, this will list details of the trust's holdings and any changes made since the previous report; it will also give a commentary on performance and how this ties in with the markets in which the trust invests. Although the information will be somewhat out of date by the time you receive it, it does provide a guide to the general strategy being followed.

Unit Trusts and Offshore Funds (1)

How to invest

Investments can be made through an intermediary, such as a bank, stockbroker or financial adviser, or you can deal directly with the unit trust group by telephone or post. Advertisements in the national press may also carry a coupon form for buying units.

Initially you will receive a contract note, which gives details of the amount invested, the price and the number of units bought, and subsequently you will be sent the certificate. To sell, you can simply send the certificate to the group and a cheque will be issued within a few days.

Some professional advisers provide unit trust portfolio management services, usually for a minimum sum of £10,000 or so. These are looked at in Chapter 7.

Offshore funds

'Offshore' is a slightly misleading term, conjuring up visions of exotic islands where the very rich go to escape the rigours of taxation. Offshore funds can, indeed, be based in places such as Bermuda and the Cayman Islands, but the more prosaic definition is simply a location that is outside the UK mainland. The traditional bases for funds that might attract UK investors are Jersey, Guernsey and the Isle of Man, but the development of EU regulations has made Luxembourg a popular choice – the Channel Islands and the Isle of Man are outside the European Union (EU) – and more recently Dublin has established an offshore centre.

Offshore funds are collective investments but can take various forms; they may be open-ended, like unit trusts, or closed-ended, like investment trusts. The exact structure and legal framework will depend on where they are based.

Regulation

Moves to allow cross-border dealing in collective investments within the EU have resulted in an array of rules and jargon. For a start, European funds are often referred to by the French acronyms 'SICAV' and 'SICAF'. The former are open-ended funds, which means the size is unrestricted and will increase or decrease according to demand and supply; the latter are closed-ended, which means they have a fixed amount of capital.

Lump-Sum Investment

Portman Channel Islands Limited is a wholly owned subsidiary of Portman Building Society, the UK's 12th largest Building Society, with assets in excess of £3 billion. The Society operates throughout the South of England with a network of over a hundred branches.

Portman Channel Islands Limited, established on the Island of Alderney, within the Bailiwick of Guernsey, was the first Building Society subsidiary to open on the island. It was only in 1990 that an amendment to the UK Building Societies Act permitted the setting up of offshore subsidiaries and, since then, sizeable deposits have been attracted. The finance industry within Alderney is licenced and regulated by the Guernsey Financial Services Commission.

Portman Building Society has given an Undertaking agreeing to discharge the liabilities of Portman Channel Islands Limited insofar as the Company is unable to discharge them out of its own assets and while the Company remains a subsidiary of the Society. This effectively guarantees deposits with Portman Channel Islands Limited. As Portman Channel Islands Limited is registered outside the UK, the company is registered under The Banking Supervision (Bailiwick of Guernsey) Law, 1994, as amended. Building Societies are regulated by the Building Societies Commission and the regulations extend to a Society's offshore subsidiary.

Portman Channel Islands Limited offers a range of deposit accounts with varying terms to satisfy depositors' requirements. With relatively low initial investment required and no minimum limit on further investment where available, coupled with the ability to transact business using a system of confidential passwords, the Company will meet your offshore savings needs. Interest is paid gross and it is up to the depositor to make any required declaration to the tax authorities.

A one year Fixed Rate Bond is also available, paying a fixed and guaranteed rate of 6% for deposits of only £500+.

Portman Channel Islands also offers a special facility by which depositors can give instructions over the telephone or fax, and this has proved very popular, especially with expatriate customers, who want to avoid postal delays. The telephone line is open from 9am to 5pm UK time with an answerphone operating at all other times. The fax line is open 24 hours a day.

Withdrawals are effected on the date of the instruction provided this is received by 2.30pm UK time for cheques by post and interbank transfer or noon for telegraphic transfers to UK banks.

There are no charges on the accounts offered by Portman Channel Islands other than for telegraphic transfers. The accounts are operated in Sterling but foreign currency cheques are accepted and the Sterling equivalent will be credited.

Obviously, all transactions are fully confidential and, recognising that this is of importance to its customers, Portman Channel Islands has its own completely independent computer system. However, it is necessary that identification of new customers is obtained to comply with guidelines laid down for the prevention of money laundering.

The Board of Directors of the Company draws on the knowledge of the professional skills available within the Islands with legal and accountancy support of non-executive directors from Alderney, Guernsey and Jersey. The importance of Portman Channel Islands Limited to its parent, Portman Building Society, is demonstrated by the appointment of its Vice-Chairman, Operations Director and Group Finance Director as its representatives on the Board.

For further information about Portman Channel Islands and its range of investment accounts, please contact Sara Fisher, Managing Director on (UK) 01481 822747 (fax (UK) 01481 822160) or write to Ollivier Court, Alderney, Channel Islands.

Unit Trusts and Offshore Funds (1)

Get on the right investment tack with Portman Channel Islands.

Race away to riches with three exciting offshore investment opportunities from Portman Channel Islands. Designed for both short and long term saving, these accounts offer excellent rates of interest plus the investment flexibility you may require.

GOLD PLUS ACCOUNT - 6.10% GROSS P.A.

Monthly interest option available at 5.75% gross p.a. Minimum deposit £5,000. Penalty free withdrawals with only 90 days notice.

GOLD BOND ACCOUNT - 6.75% GROSS P.A.

Rate fixed and guaranteed for 5 years. Monthly interest option available at 6.50% gross p.a. Minimum deposit £5,000.

INSTANT GOLD ACCOUNT - 5.50% GROSS P.A.

Instant access with no penalties. Monthly interest option available at 5.15% gross p.a. Minimum deposit £5,000.

To chart your best investment course, call us now on Alderney (01481) 822747/8. Or fax Alderney (01481) 822160 for further details.

Portman Building Society (PBS) has given an Undertaking agreeing to discharge the liabilities of Portman Channel Islands Ltd (PCIL) in so far as PCIL is unable to discharge them out of its own assets and while PCIL remains a subsidiary of PBS. This effectively guarantees that your deposits with PCIL are secure. (The Undertaking will cease to have effect if PCIL ceases to be a subsidiary of PBS). Annual interest paid on 1st January. Gold Bond interest cannot be added and no further transactions permitted during the fixed term. Gold Plus Account and Instant Gold interest rates are variable. Rates correct at time of going to press. Interest is paid gross, and it is the account holder's responsibility to advise the appropriate tax authorities of interest received. Portman Channel Islands has its principal place of business at Ollivier Court, Ollivier Street, St Anne, Alderney, Channel Islands. Deposits made with Portman Channel Islands Ltd. are not covered by the Deposit Protection Scheme under the UK Banking Act 1987. However, the Company is licensed under the Banking Supervision (Bailiwick of Guernsey) Law 1994 as amended. Portman Channel Islands registered office: PO Box 20, St Peter Port, Guernsey, Channel Islands. Registered in Guernsey Number 25871, Portman Channel Islands Ltd. is a wholly owned subsidiary of Portman Building Society. The most recent audited accounts of Portman Channel Islands Ltd. are available on request. Portman Channel Islands Ltd. is not registered under the Banking Business (Jersey) Law 1991. The paid up capital and reserves of the Company exceed £6 million.

Open-ended funds can apply for the status of UCITS (Undertakings for Collective Investment in Transferable Securities), which is granted by the regulatory authority in the country of origin. The main UCITS rules are drafted by the EU, but stipulations on how and where a fund may invest come under local regulations and may vary from country to country. At the time of writing, cash funds and funds of funds cannot qualify as UCITS, but the EU directive is being amended to encompass them. Once a fund has UCITS status, it can be freely marketed throughout member states, subject to marketing rules laid down by each individual country.

The Financial Times lists offshore funds as being one of three types: SIB recognised, Regulated and Other. The first category refers to funds that have been approved by the Securities and Investments Board, which means that they may be freely marketed in the UK, in the same way as unit trusts. Funds with UCITS status get this approval more or less automatically.

Funds based outside the EU can also apply for SIB recognition if their country of origin has 'designated territory' status. This is granted by the SIB to countries where the local regulations and compensation scheme arrangements are deemed to be of similar standard to those applying in the UK. From the investor's point of view, if a fund is SIB recognised, it is not too important where it is based, as it will be subject to much the same level of regulation as UK funds.

Regulated funds are those that are authorised under local regulations but have not obtained SIB recognition. This does not necessarily mean that they are less well regulated; it may simply be that the managers are not looking to attract UK investors or, in the case of European funds, that they wish to invest outside the limits of the UCITS rules. These funds can still be sold to UK investors, but only through private placements; they cannot use direct advertising or mailing.

Some countries allow funds to be set up and operated without coming under regulation. These are listed in *The Financial Times* under the heading of 'Other Offshore Funds' and are often aimed at institutional rather than private investors.

Taxation

For a UK investor, offshore funds are subject to one of two tax regimes. The fund may have 'distributor' status, in which case it must pay out at least 85 per cent of its income, which is paid gross but is subject to tax at the investor's normal rate. Any capital gains made on selling out of the fund will be liable to capital gains tax, subject to the usual annual exempt allowance.

Alternatively, the fund may be of the 'accumulator' type, which means all income is rolled up within the fund. No income tax is payable while you are invested, but when you come to sell, all gains are liable to income tax, whether they derive from income or capital growth.

Which of the two is preferable depends on your circumstances. If you are a higher rate taxpayer now, but expect to drop down to basic rate in future, then with an accumulator fund you can defer the tax bill to that point. Alternatively, if you are looking for capital growth, a distributor fund would mean a small tax bill each year, but the bulk of the return would be in capital gains, against which you have the annual tax-exempt allowance (£6300 for the 1996/97 tax year).

The problem with distributor status is that it is only granted for a year at a time, and in retrospect. Although the income distribution rule is fairly easy to comply with, there is another rule that bans 'trading'; this is designed to prevent funds cheating by turning income into capital gains, but the wording is rather vague and funds have occasionally been caught out. If you cash in your holding and distributor status is then refused, you can face an unexpected income tax bill.

Some years ago, when income tax went up to 60 per cent against a capital gains tax rate of 30 per cent, this was a severe penalty. Now that the two rates have been equalised, it is less drastic, but there is still a disadvantage because of the exempt allowance for capital gains tax.

Pros and cons

With so many onshore unit trusts and other funds available, the obvious question is, why look offshore? Originally these funds were primarily aimed at those who were non-resident for tax purposes and could therefore gain a tax advantage; there were few attractions for the UK investor. But the developments in EU regulations, combined with certain restrictions on UK-based unit trusts, have meant that a number of companies are now finding that an offshore base presents greater opportunities.

The major feature that is driving the UK unit trust companies to set up offshore is the facility to pay dividends gross. This is particularly attractive for funds that focus on producing income, such as bond funds and, in future, cash funds. Although the income is ultimately taxable in the hands of a UK investor, there may be cash flow advantages in gross payments, and for non-taxpayers it saves the trouble of reclaiming tax paid.

Another issue is investment flexibility: offshore funds can invest in areas that are not available to unit trusts, such as currencies and commodities. Even where the investments are of the same type, the restrictions may be fewer or non-existent. For example, a unit trust may invest only up to 10 per cent of its portfolio, in total, in countries that are not on the SIB's list of recognised stock exchanges. A Dublin-based UCITS fund, on the other hand, could put up to 10 per cent in each of these countries, and some may be wholly unrestricted.

A potential drawback is that, even if a fund is SIB recognised, it does not come under the UK compensation scheme. In some cases, the local regulations may in fact offer a higher degree of protection, but some areas do not operate any compensation scheme. You should always check that the fund assets are held by an independent custodian and, for preference, stick to those run by a well-known name.

Offshore funds are often based on a single price, to which the front-end fee is added, rather than having a bid/offer spread like unit trusts, so they may be slightly cheaper to buy into. Annual charges, on the other hand, may be rather higher than for onshore trusts because, in addition to the management charge, the fund may have to meet the fees of the auditor and the custodian or trustee.

Umbrella funds

Umbrella funds, the first of which appeared in 1984, technically consist of a single overall fund which comprises several different sub-funds or share classes. One of the main advantages for some time was that investors could switch their holdings between the different sub-funds without being liable to capital gains tax, which would only arise when they sold out of the whole fund. Unfortunately, this loophole has since been closed and CGT now arises on all switches, just as it would if you moved from one unit trust to another run by the same group.

However, there may still be an advantage in cost terms, as the initial fee will be waived for switches between sub-funds. Some companies also run a parallel portfolio management service, which will look after your investments within the fund and make appropriate switches, but there is an extra charge for this. The main drawback of umbrella funds is that you are committing yourself to just one company, which may not have the best performing funds across the full range.

Another point to watch out for is whether the fund intends to apply for distributor status. This is granted to the umbrella fund as a unit, which means each separate sub-fund must comply with the regulations. If one fails, the fund as a whole fails, which has tax repercussions for the investor as outlined above.

How to invest
As mentioned, funds that have obtained SIB recognition can be freely marketed in the same way as unit trusts, but others can only advertise indirectly, by offering to send out a prospectus. In either case, but particularly the latter, it is probably worth while consulting a professional adviser.

Open-ended investment companies

While unit trusts with UCITS status can theoretically be sold throughout the EU, in practice they are not attractive to Europeans, who prefer the single price and the tax structure of a SICAV. As a result, several UK companies have set up offshore operations, mainly in Luxembourg and Dublin, to run SICAVs. But as SICAVs can be sold in the UK, and the range of funds offered generally parallels the groups' unit trusts, some are questioning whether there is a need to run two separate operations.

Obviously, it would be a considerable loss to the UK investment industry if management groups abandoned unit trusts in favour of offshore SICAVs. A solution that has been proposed is to allow SICAV-style funds, currently referred to as open-ended investment companies (OEICs), to be operated from and sold in the UK.

At the time of writing, details of how OEICs will operate have not been finalised, but it seems likely that they will be similar to unit trusts except in two main respects. Firstly, they will have a single price, with separate dealing charges. Second, they have the flexibility to have more than one class of share, and different classes can each have their own charging structure to cater for different types of investor. As companies, they will also have boards of directors and annual general meetings of shareholders.

The main beneficiaries of OEICs are likely to be the management groups themselves, as they will be able to develop a single product range that can be sold throughout Europe, from a UK base instead of offshore. For the investor there may be little material gain over unit trusts – which may eventually come to be replaced altogether – although charges may be more flexible and this may also allow simplified umbrella funds.

Where to find out more

The Association of Unit Trusts and Investment Funds produces general performance figures and other statistical data, but does not offer advice or recommendation on individual trusts or management groups. It runs the Unit Trust Information Service, which can provide an introductory booklet, a unit trust user's handbook and a directory of trusts, and can be contacted on 0181 207 1361 or by writing to 65 Kingsway, London WC2B 6TD. The groups themselves also have a range of literature on their own products.

The *Unit Trust Yearbook* is published annually by Financial Times Business Enterprises and contains details of both management groups and all unit trusts available.

Unit trust prices are quoted in daily newspapers such as *The Daily Telegraph* and *The Financial Times*; *The Financial Times* also publishes the prices of offshore funds.

Unit Trusts and Offshore Funds (1)

Give him a future

Remember the RSPCA in your will

By including the Royal Society for the Prevention of Cruelty to Animals in your will now, you'll be helping us to save thousands of animals from the horror of cruelty.

The RSPCA rescue hundreds of distressed and abandoned animals, like the one pictured here, every single day. Nursing them back to health and finding them new homes costs a great deal of money.

A bequest in your will is the best way you can help us to continue our vital work.

If you'd like a free copy of our straightforward booklet on making a will, supporting the fight against animal cruelty and the correct wording of your will, please write to, or telephone:

Linda Norgrove, Head of Legacy Dept., RSPCA, FREEPOST, HORSHAM, West Sussex RH12 1ZA. 01403 264181

Registered Charity No. 219099

THE RSPCA RECEIVES NO GOVERNMENT FUNDING

7
Unit Trusts and Offshore Funds (2): The Investment Choice

In recent years there has been a degree of consolidation in the unit trust market, which has slightly reduced the number of companies operating in this field. Nevertheless, the number of trusts has continued to grow steadily, as Table 7.1 shows. With well over 1600 available, it is difficult to know where to start,

Table 7.1 *Authorised unit trusts*

Year	Number of trusts	Number of companies
1981	529	93
1982	553	99
1983	630	91
1984	687	102
1985	806	110
1986	964	121
1987	1137	139
1988	1255	153
1989	1379	162
1990	1407	154
1991	1400	157
1992	1456	151
1993	1528	156
1994	1559	162
1995	1633	160

Source: Association of Unit Trusts and Investment Funds

Unit Trusts and Offshore Funds (2): The Investment Choice

especially as many have similar aims and specialisations. The best way is probably to decide first what type of trust you are after, and then to choose between the different management groups offering that type.

On the most basic approach, trusts can be divided into four types:

1. Trusts whose primary objective is to produce income;
2. Trusts whose primary objective is to produce capital growth, either with a general portfolio or specialising in a particular country or sector;
3. Trusts that aim to provide a mix between income and growth;
4. Cash trusts.

The first three of these groups may invest in the UK or overseas (or, in the case of international trusts, both). The fourth type is in a sense a sub-section of the first, since the aim is income, but cash trusts differ from others in that they do not involve any capital risk.

Unit trust categories

Looking in more detail, the Association of Unit Trusts and Investment Funds sets out 23 separate categories of trust for the purpose of making performance comparisons. These are grouped under eight headings, as follows.

UK funds
All trusts with at least 80 per cent of their investments in the UK.

UK Growth and Income
Trusts with at least 80 per cent of their assets in UK equities, which aim to produce a combination of income and growth. These trusts must also aim to have a yield of between 80 and 110 per cent of the yield of the FT-SE-A All Share Index.

UK Equity Income
Trusts which invest at least 80 per cent of their assets in UK

Lump-Sum Investment

equities and which aim to have a yield of more than 110 per cent of the yield of the All Share Index.

UK Growth
Trusts which invest at least 80 per cent of their assets in UK equities and have a primary objective of achieving capital growth.

UK Smaller Companies
Trusts which invest at least 80 per cent of their assets in the shares of companies which form part of the Hoare Govett UK Smaller Companies Extended Index.

UK Gilt & Fixed Interest
Trusts which invest at least 80 per cent of their assets in UK gilts and fixed interest securities.

UK Equity and Bond
Trusts which invest at least 80 per cent of their assets in the UK but have less than 80 per cent in either UK equities or UK gilts and fixed interest securities.

International
Trusts with a portfolio that is less than 80 per cent invested in any one geographical area (with the exception of the International Fixed Interest sector).

International Income
Trusts which invest at least 80 per cent of their assets in equities and which aim to achieve a yield above 110 per cent of the yield of the FT-Actuaries World Index.

International Growth
Trusts which invest at least 80 per cent of their assets in equities and which have a primary objective of capital growth.

International Fixed Interest
Trusts which invest at least 80 per cent of their assets in fixed interest stocks. This includes all such trusts, regardless of whether they have more than 80 per cent in a particular

Unit Trusts and Offshore Funds (2): The Investment Choice

geographic sector, unless it is the UK, in which case they come under the UK heading.

International Equity Bond
Trusts which have less than 80 per cent of their assets in either equities or fixed interest securities.

Japan
Trusts which invest at least 80 per cent of their assets in Japanese securities.

Far East

Including Japan
Trusts which invest at least 80 per cent of their assets in Far Eastern securities including a Japanese content that is less than 80 per cent.

Excluding Japan
Trusts which invest at least 80 per cent of their assets in Far Eastern securities but exclude any Japanese content.

Australasia
Trusts which invest at least 80 per cent of their assets in Australian or New Zealand securities.

North America
Trusts which invest at least 80 per cent of their assets in North American securities.

Europe
Trusts which invest at least 80 per cent of their assets in European securities, including the UK, but not exceeding 80 per cent in the UK.

Specialist
Trusts which invest their assets in a specialist area, regardless of any geographical specialisation they may also have.

Lump-Sum Investment

Commodity & Energy
Trusts which invest at least 80 per cent of their assets in commodity or energy securities.

Financial & Property
Trusts which invest at least 80 per cent of their assets in financial or property securities.

Investment Trust Units
Trusts which are able to invest only in the shares of investment trust companies.

Fund of Funds
Trusts which are able to invest only in other authorised unit trust schemes.

Money Market
Trusts which invest at least 80 per cent of their assets in money market instruments.

Convertibles
Trusts which invest at least 60 per cent of their assets in convertible stocks.

In addition, there are exempt trusts and personal pension trusts. Neither are relevant to the ordinary investor; exempt trusts are available only to tax-exempt institutions, such as pension funds and charities, while personal pension trusts are for use only with pension contracts (see Chapter 11).

Table 7.2 shows some past performance results for each of the categories outlined above. These figures, which are compiled on a regular basis by the Association of Unit Trusts and Investment Funds, show the realisation value of £1000 invested over various time periods in the median fund in each sector – the middle one in the performance rankings, rather than the average.

Past performance, as the saying goes, is not necessarily a guide to the future; as the table demonstrates, different sectors may come to the fore over different periods. It is also important, in looking at figures of this type, to check exactly what they purport

Unit Trusts and Offshore Funds (2): The Investment Choice

Table 7.2 *Past performance of unit trusts*

Sector	Average value of £1000 invested		
	5 years	10 years	15 years
UK Growth and Income	1602	2759	9080
UK Equity Income	1562	2881	9439
UK Growth	1679	2745	8248
UK Smaller Companies	1883	2892	8736
UK Equity and Bond	1663	3230	10,542
Uk Equity and Bond Income	1486	2495	6750
UK Gilt & Fixed Interest	1426	1945	3698
International Income	1777	2510	—
International Equity and Bond	1615	2452	5543
International Fixed Interest	1516	1907	4138
International Growth	1757	2648	6888
Japan	1248	2267	8437
Far East including Japan	1851	3657	8111
Far East excluding Japan	2522	6196	10,756
Australasia	2112	3348	3087
North America	2189	2866	7708
Europe	1888	2906	12,487
Commodity & Energy	2354	3016	3214
Financial & Property	1722	2440	6761
Investment Trust Units	1767	2992	8586
Convertibles	1524	1993	3808
Money Market	1282	—	—
Fund of Funds	1609	2548	—
Building Society Higher Rate	1216	1796	1861
FT-SE-A All Share Index	1829	3190	9849

Note: A gap indicates that no trusts have been in existence that long. All figures are on an offer to bid basis, with net income reinvested. Figures as at 1 April 1996.

Source: Association of Unit Trusts and Investment Funds

to show. Unit trusts are usually shown on an 'offer to bid' basis, which reflects the cash-in value if you had bought and sold on the respective dates. Alternatively, figures may be on an 'offer to offer' basis; this takes out the effect of the price spread and the initial charge, but can give an idea of what the manager has achieved. Statistics are also generally quoted with net income reinvested, which compounds the capital growth; if you are investing to earn income to spend, then obviously the capital return will be rather less.

Also shown in the table, for the purposes of comparison, are the results of £1000 invested in a building society higher interest account and the equivalent figures for the FT-SE-A All Share Index. Index comparisons should be treated with caution, as an index does not include dealing costs or the charges encountered with a trust. In the case of an overseas trust, there are also currency considerations; the return in sterling terms may vary significantly from the market trend shown by the index.

Investment aims

The first step in deciding where to put your money is to determine whether you are looking for income or capital growth. The two are not necessarily mutually exclusive; while trusts that go all out for capital growth will not produce any income to speak of, there are others that combine both objectives. Similarly, the strategies pursued by equity income trusts can often produce good growth, even where that is a secondary aim.

Income trusts

If you are looking for income, you need to bear in mind that investing in equities will not provide you with very high income at the outset. Even so-called 'high income' trusts may yield only around 5 per cent gross which, at the time of writing, beats a building society but not by much.

The advantage of investing in equities, however, is that they should produce some capital appreciation and a rising income over time, while a building society deposit will be static in value and the income will rise and fall with interest rates.

The income comparison is illustrated in Table 7.3, which shows the gross annual income paid by an equity income trust and a building society higher rate account over a ten-year period. The building society provided higher income for the first six

Unit Trusts and Offshore Funds (2): The Investment Choice

Table 7.3 *Annual income from an equity income trust compared with a building society higher rate account*

£1000 invested 1 April 1986

	Annual income		
Year	Unit equity income (£)	Corporate bond trust (£)	Building society (£)
1	55	95	78
2	61	94	76
3	78	106	82
4	84	107	114
5	94	107	133
6	97	101	111
7	91	94	85
8	83	84	57
9	84	88	54
10	89	87	55

Note: Figures relate to the annual gross income paid by the average UK equity income unit trust, the average corporate bond and the gross interest from a building society seven-day notice account with a minimum balance of £2500, 1 April 1986–1 April 1996.

Source: Association of Unit Trusts and Investment Funds

years, but was then overtaken by the trust, which would also have grown in capital value. The table also shows the gross annual income from a corporate bond trust, which beats the building society after just two years.

It is possible to get a higher initial income from a unit trust by choosing one of the specialist types: those investing in gilts and fixed interest securities, convertibles or preference shares. These can offer a starting yield of around 6 to 8 per cent gross. But again, with these trusts there is much less potential for capital growth on the assets, hence the income return is less likely to improve over time.

In general, there is a limit to the amount of genuine income that can be produced, and to go above that level will entail some sacrifice of capital or capital growth potential. A couple of trusts launched in 1993 were specifically designed to convert future capital growth into current income, by the use of options. The

HIGH YIELDS NEED NOT ERODE CAPITAL

Investors are often warned of the consequences of income investments in terms of reduced capital return. But there is no immutable law which says these type of investments are bound to undermine capital; indeed, collective income investments which aim for above-average income range widely in their yields, underlying investment portfolio and investment objective.

Conventional income finds typically consist of debt instruments such as gilts (ie government debt) or corporate bonds. Gilts are low risk because they have fixed maturities and, since the IOU is from the government, there is almost no risk of the original investment not being paid. The drawback to gilts is that because this final repayment – the redemption price - is always known, price anomalies, and therefore opportunities to realise gains are limited. The market is always pricing in inflation and expected changes in interest rates: higher rates are bad news because they mean capital losses for existing gilts investors.

Funds which invest in corporate bonds have only slightly more scope. These bonds work just like gilts, save that they are issued by companies. Such is their credit standing that major UK companies can issue bonds at fractions of a percentage point above the equivalent gilt. Corporate bonds can usually point to preservation of capital as a realistic aim, though.

Perhaps the most interesting category of funds are those which deal in hybrid bond and equity instruments. Convertibles are issued like bonds with a fixed interest coupon, but can convert into equities under a pre-specified formula. This "equity kicker" is an interesting feature, especially on smaller company issues which often escape the notice of large funds, and are under-researched and even mis-priced.

Convertibles necessarily pay a higher yield than that on mainstream issues yet a rising equity price will provide them with the capital uplift that gilts find hard to achieve. Only when the market is falling will convertibles be affected. On the whole, they fall less slowly than equities and only in very harsh conditions will they appear unsuitable.

A convertibles funds will anyway often have supporting components made up of preference shares, loans, debentures and similar bonds. A skilled manager will weight these various elements in a fund to accent positive/defensive characteristics as market conditions dictate. Investors should be aware that the manager's fee they pay is for real expertise in a technically complex market; those who choose bond funds are often charged for passive management and could as well buy a single issue in the market for a similar kind of overall return.

In general, convertibles possess more risk than a gilt fund but inherent flexibility provides superior opportunities. A good convertibles fund should offer the best gross yields in the 6%-10% range commonly available on income vehicles over the past couple of years. It should also be among the best capital performers, providing appreciation well above today's low inflation. For investors who don't want the income, a convertibles fund can also make a persuasive investment if the income is reinvested and allowed to compound.

Unit Trusts and Offshore Funds (2): The Investment Choice

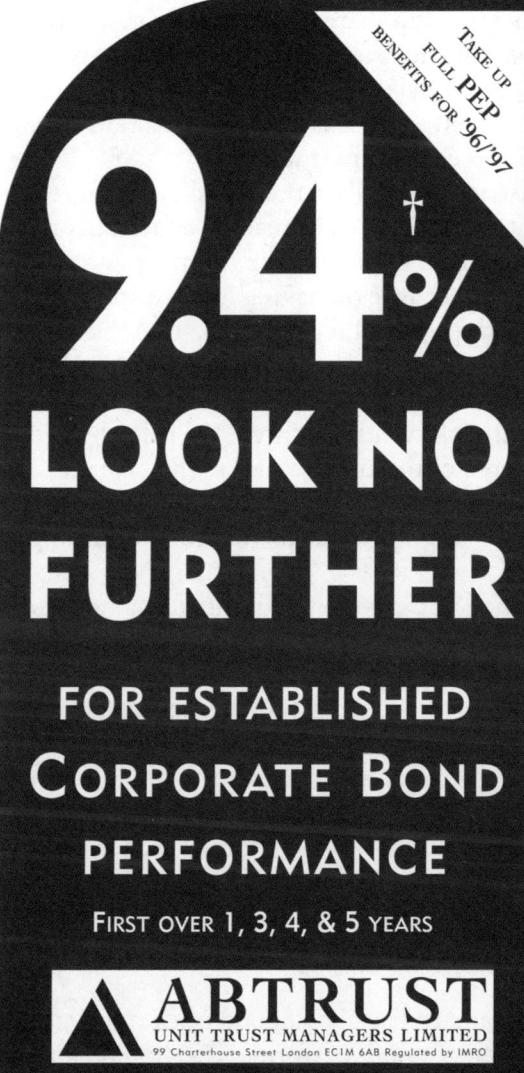

Lump-Sum Investment

trusts invest mainly in blue chip shares and special loan securities, which produce a reasonable base yield, and then also write options, on which a premium is earned. The premium boosts the level of income, but the effect of the options is that any capital growth above 4 or 5 per cent is given up.

Options are also used to limit falls in the capital value, but there is no capital guarantee and in certain market conditions there could be a progressive drop. Of course, this is true of any trust, but with these there is less chance of making it up again in future, since the capital growth potential is restricted. There is also no guarantee on the income: one trust reduced its level from 10 per cent net to 9 per cent.

Even with equity trusts the yield can differ. As a rule, the higher the target yield, the greater the constraints on the manager and the more growth prospects may have to be sacrificed. So trusts with a more modest pay-out now may prove more rewarding in the long run.

But the pursuit of income can work to advantage on the growth side. The yield on a share moves broadly in inverse relationship to its price – if the price falls and the dividend remains the same, it will represent a higher yield. So it may then become an attractive holding for an income unit trust. If the share price subsequently recovers, it will bring a boost to the capital growth on the trust. Of course, as the price rises, the yield will fall, so the manager will sooner or later have to sell in favour of another higher yielding stock. But although he may then miss out on further growth prospects, he equally avoids the danger of hanging on too long and seeing the share price fall back again, so it can turn out to be a useful discipline.

To a large extent, then, if a trust has a good track record for its dividend payments, the capital performance should also be satisfactory. Although past results cannot be relied upon, a consistent dividend history is a fair indication of a manager's ability, as these trusts have a fairly broad range of investment possibilities and are therefore less dominated by market movements than a more specialised vehicle such as a commodity trust.

So the starting-point for choosing an income trust is to weigh up your needs for income today as against income in the future. If you are looking for immediate high income over a short time-span, a fixed interest or preference trust may be suitable. If you are prepared to settle for less now to have more in the future, then think about an equity-based trust or one with mixed holdings. In the latter case, check out the proportions held in ordinary shares as against preference shares or fixed interest securities; again, the higher the content of ordinary equities, the better should be the prospects of a rising income. Another important point is the level of annual management charge. This will normally be paid for out of the trust's income, so the higher the charge, the less will be left to distribute to unit holders.

If the trust is fairly new, you can only go by its portfolio structure and the charges. If it has a track record, you can also check the dividend history; ideally, payments should at least have kept pace with inflation. Finally, check the capital growth; although this may not be your top priority it will underpin the income return.

Overseas income trusts
The bulk of trusts focusing on income are invested in the UK, but there are a growing number based on overseas markets. Some of these invest in particular geographical areas, such as North America or Europe, while others are international in scope. These latter trusts are classified under two sector headings, equity income and fixed interest, which have the same characteristics as the equivalent UK trusts.

The overseas equity income trusts tend to have lower yields than their UK counterparts because the stock markets themselves have lower yields, and the management charge may also be higher, which will detract from the return. You should also bear in mind the currency factor, which can add to the degree of risk involved.

Special schemes
As mentioned in Chapter 6, there are a number of schemes available that are designed to produce a monthly income by packaging together trusts with different pay-out dates. If you are looking for regular income, a package has the advantage over an individual monthly-paying trust – of which there are around a dozen – that a spread of investments gives a spread of risk. There

will, of course, be a higher minimum investment than for a single trust.

Set packages have the drawback that there may be little or no choice of which trusts are included, which means there may be a higher fixed interest content than you would like, and also commit you to one management group. The alternative is to put together your own package from among all the income trusts available. If you are prepared to manage with uneven payments, so much the better; aiming to get a similar level of payment on the same day each month will restrict the choice and may mean a sacrifice of overall performance.

Generalist trusts

As mentioned, income and growth are not mutually exclusive targets, as there are a number of trusts which offer elements of both, either through a combination of higher and lower yielding equities, or through a mixture of equities with fixed interest securities.

These generalist trusts are often regarded as the plain vanilla of the industry, worthy but dull. Most groups have one, and some even have more than one, but they are rarely likely to be the subject of eye-catching advertisements. The yield is generally in the region of 3 per cent gross and they are expected to show steady, rather than spectacular, performance.

Equity and Bond funds are those that mix equities with fixed interest stocks and have less than 80 per cent in either. The yield can be rather higher than on general funds, depending on the mix of holdings; the greater the proportion of fixed interest securities, the higher the yield but, as mentioned in the last section, this entails lower growth prospects. Most of these trusts, however, steer a middle course between the two in the same way as Growth and Income trusts.

Although they may never top the performance listings, Table 7.4 shows that the returns are not to be scorned. Certain specialist sectors may well do better, but others will do a lot worse, so unless you have confidence in your powers of selection, or sufficient money to put together a range of specialist holdings, a generalist trust can be a good home for a first investment. Equally, if you are building up a portfolio, a general trust can

Unit Trusts and Offshore Funds (2): The Investment Choice

Table 7.4 *Past performance of General and Balanced funds*

Sector	Average value of £1000 invested		
	5 years	10 years	15 years
UK Growth and Income	1602	2759	9080
UK Equity and Bond	1663	3230	10,542
International Equity and Bond	1615	2452	5543

Note: Figures are on an offer to bid basis, with net income reinvested, as at 1 April 1996.

Source: Association of Unit Trusts and Investment Funds

form a stable core, from which you can venture into higher risk holdings.

Growth trusts

By far the majority of unit trusts available are designed to produce capital growth. They comprise a large variety of types, from broadly based international trusts to those specialising in a particular geographical area, such as the UK or Japan, and those concentrating on a particular industry or market sector. Given this huge range, it is impossible to make generalisations and not easy to set about making a choice. At any one time, different markets will be in the ascendancy, and the time-scale you have in mind for your investment will also have a bearing on where the best prospects lie. However, it is possible to narrow down the choice by considering the following alternatives.

UK versus overseas
Many UK investors naturally incline towards the home market, and there are arguments to support this. For one thing, the returns from a unit trust are in sterling, so if you invest in an overseas trust you are exposed to a currency risk on top of the market risk. Some trusts aim to offset this by using 'hedging' techniques, but that in itself can have certain risks as well as costs.

Second, the stock market will respond to and reflect general factors in the economy, which may be appropriate since your other financial arrangements will be subject to similar influences.

Lump-Sum Investment

On the other hand, the major world economies move very much in line with each other anyway.

Also, any investment in a single market, even one the size of the UK, has limitations in terms of choice of stocks and spread of risk. If you are planning to build up a portfolio of any size, or you already have other UK investments, you should think of spreading your investments further afield for better balance.

International versus single country
If you decide to look abroad, you have the choice between single country trusts and those that maintain a global spread. Single country trusts range from those based on large markets, such as the US, to much more specialised types; for example, trusts focused on Switzerland or Thailand.

The same arguments apply to investing in a single overseas market as to investing in the UK: there is less spread of risk. This is particularly true in the smaller markets, where there may be a limited number of stocks available. There may also be problems or delays in buying and selling which can affect performance and add to the risk. For investors seeking to build an international portfolio, perhaps mainly through direct equity holdings, these trusts can offer convenient access to smaller markets; otherwise they give the chance of high rewards if you are prepared to accept high risk. The more cautious investor, on the other hand, will do better with an international trust or a selection of those based on the larger world markets.

General versus specialised
As well as trusts with a geographical specialisation, there are others which focus on a particular industry or market sector. These may operate on a global basis, such as an international technology trust, or within one particular market, such as a Japanese Smaller Companies trust.

Like trusts with a geographical specialisation, these carry a higher degree of risk than a general or international trust. But whereas you could build a collection of holdings in different countries, it would not be feasible to cover every type of industry. Hence the attraction is less to create a market balance among your investments than to inject a higher risk/higher reward

Unit Trusts and Offshore Funds (2): The Investment Choice

element. Smaller companies, for example, are much more volatile than larger ones; they rise faster, but can also fall faster. Similarly, recovery and special situations trusts seek to take advantage of stocks that are under-priced; if the expected improvement occurs, all well and good, but it depends on how well the manager makes his selections. Industry-specific trusts can be even more dramatic; gold trusts, for example, had a phenomenal run in 1980, but subsequently spent a long period in the wilderness.

Management style

Once you have decided where to invest, you then face the choice of management group. Again, there are no easy answers: no one investment strategy is proved to be right or wrong. However, there are certain considerations which may help to sort out what accords with your own views or needs.

Active versus passive
Some managers take a very active approach, turning over the portfolio regularly in the search for value, while others operate on a longer term view. The former may have greater potential – if the manager gets it right – but the dealing costs will be higher and results may be more volatile.

Top down versus bottom up
This refers to the stock-picking approach of the manager. Some start from the top: country first (in the case of an international trust), then industry, then the specific share. Others build up from the bottom, choosing shares they think are attractive, with perhaps overall proportions for sectors or countries.

House style
Some management groups have an overall 'house style' within which the managers of individual trusts operate; this may be simply a matter of the risk/reward approach they adopt or may go further, in that, for example, if particular industries are favoured at a given time, they are represented across the range of trusts. In other cases, each trust manager operates at a very individual level. A house style may impose constraints, but the

Unit Trusts and Offshore Funds (2): The Investment Choice

individual approach could lead to a change of fortune, or at any rate of philosophy, if one manager leaves and another takes over.

Hedging and liquidity
Where a trust invests overseas, the returns – which are expressed in sterling, of course – will be affected by exchange rate movements as well as market trends. In some cases the manager may 'hedge' part of the portfolio to neutralise the currency effects; this can – if it works – protect against losses, although it also means missing out on favourable movements and there is a cost involved. Others take the view that if you buy the market, you also buy the currency, and that the two should not be artificially separated.

Similar views are taken on liquidity. Some managers will move out into cash if the market is falling, while others believe it is up to the investor to decide by staying in or selling out of the trust. Obviously, switching out and perhaps buying back in later would mean the investor faced a new front-end charge, but if the trust goes into cash and subsequently reinvests there will be dealing costs, and there could be a loss if the timing is not judged accurately.

Size of fund
There is a theory that a small trust will tend to outperform a larger one. This has some logic, in that a small trust is more flexible and can therefore respond more quickly to changes in the market – assuming the manager interprets the trend correctly. Large funds operating in a small market may also be hampered by a limited choice of stocks.

Small trusts will obviously tend to hold fewer stocks, but larger ones also vary in whether they are widespread or concentrated. The fewer the holdings in the portfolio, the higher the risk/reward ratio, as a gain or loss in any one holding will have a greater proportional influence.

Location
Some groups run their overseas trusts entirely from a UK base, while others have local offices in the major markets. Naturally there is much debate over which is better: the objective view from

Lump-Sum Investment

a distance or the 'feel' gained by being on the spot. In fact, those operating from the UK will normally make regular visits to the country and may also liaise with local brokers for information and – particularly in smaller markets – for dealing. Given the sophistication of global communications, one suspects there is not a great deal of difference, and certainly performance results do not point to either approach being consistently more successful.

New launches

One other theory on the relative merits of different trusts is that new launches will do well. This can depend on the reason for the launch and its timing. Some are 'bandwagon' products, investing in a market that is currently rising, in which case they are likely to look good to start with, particularly as they have new money to spend on the most attractive shares, while older trusts in the same market may be stuck with shares that have gone out of fashion.

The ideal timing, of course, is to launch just before a market goes up, to get the full benefit of the rise, but (aside from the difficulty of correctly predicting market movements) it is harder to attract money into a sector that is currently looking dull.

Are you an active investor?

One important question to consider before choosing a trust is whether you plan to monitor and alter your investment actively or simply want to invest and forget about it. In the latter case, you are likely to do best by sticking to fairly general trusts; the more specialist offerings are more volatile and need to be kept under supervision.

If you expect to be active and switch your holdings around between different trusts, this should influence your choice of management group. Of course, you are not bound to stick with

---

For more flexible tax free investment phone ShareLink PEPs on 0121 233 9955.

Unit Trusts and Offshore Funds (2): The Investment Choice

IS BUILDING THEIR FUTURE WORTH THE INVESMENT?

THE BOYS' BRIGADE
BELIEVES THE ANSWER IS
YES!

THE BOYS BRIGADE encourages youngsters for life in THE FAMILY, THE WORKPLACE AND THE WIDER COMMUNITY

Thousands of volunteers work tirelessly to encourage and train tens of thousands of young people to take a proud place in tomorrow's society. From the suburbs to inner cities and deprived rural areas the BB welcomes boys of all backgrounds and makes a positive difference to their lives and the life of their communities.

<u>YOU CAN HELP US</u>
An investment in the Boys' Brigade is an an investment in
THE FUTURE

I am interested in knowing more of the work of the Boys' Brigade
Name: _____ Tel No: _____
Address: _____

Ch. Reg. No. 305969

The Boys' Brigade, Felden Lodge, Felden Lane, Hemel Hempstead, Herts, HP3 0BL

171

the same group and there are drawbacks to doing so: no one group is going to top the performance tables with every trust it runs. But against that there is the advantage that switches from one trust to another within the same group attract a discount on the front-end charge, which can significantly cut the costs of active investment. So you should look for a group – or perhaps two or three – which have a wide range of funds and offer a good switching discount.

Portfolio management services
If you would like your investments to be actively managed, but lack the time or knowledge to do it yourself, there are a number of advisers who offer portfolio management services. These may be run on a discretionary or an advisory basis. In the first case, you would set out your basic aims, such as income or capital growth and the amount of risk you are prepared to accept, and the adviser would do the rest; you would be kept informed of changes to the portfolio and receive regular valuations, but would not be consulted on each deal.

With an advisory service, the adviser would consult you (and vice versa) before any change was made. The minimum for a discretionary service starts at about £10,000; for an advisory service it is likely to be higher, because of the extra work involved. Charging systems vary; the adviser may operate on the commissions he gets on each trust purchase, but it can be more efficient for both sides to rebate commission and charge an annual management fee.

Broker unit trusts
An alternative to a discretionary management service is a broker unit trust, offered by a number of professional advisers (not necessarily brokers). Often an adviser might be running a large number of individual portfolios on a discretionary basis and making similar investments and changes for each. By setting up a broker unit trust he can consolidate these portfolios into one fund, with a single transaction when he buys or sells, thus considerably reducing the administration.

The trust may invest directly into securities or through a range of unit trusts in a similar way to a fund of funds. In either case, it

Ostriches in Britain?

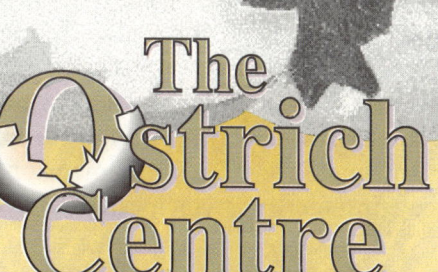

The Ostrich Centre is different ....

.....We keep your Birds at our Purpose Built Breeding Centre in South Wales, so you can visit your investment at any time!

Your Ostrich can return you up to 70% profit per year, for up to 25 years ... and that's guaranteed!

Investments range from £1490 to £13900, our prices include full livery and insurance for your birds at our Centre.

We welcome Private buyers, with various packages available, including staged payments!

Over the next 10 years Europe and more so the UK, is going to experience a massive growth in the Ostrich Industry, it is currently growing faster than any other.

The Ostrich Centre aims to be at the forefront, by becoming the largest UK providers of Ostrich produce.

The Ostrich Centre, Garrod Avenue, Dunvant, Swansea, West Glamorgan. SA2 7XD
Telephone ; 01792 291100   Fax ; 01792 291111

Simply fill in the details below and return to us for your FREE full colour brochure, and details of how you can become an Ostrich Owner!

Name (Mr.,Mrs., Miss.,)
....

Address
....
....
....

Telephone No
....

must have a defined investment objective and strategy and will be governed by the same regulations as an ordinary unit trust. Funds are normally valued daily and the prices are published in national newspapers.

The advantage for the investor is that his money is professionally managed, without the need for him to get involved in each transaction, but he still has access to the fund manager and a degree of personal service that he obviously would not get from the manager of an ordinary unit trust. There is, however, an extra layer of charges, as the adviser will charge a management fee, which needs to be weighed up against the 'added value' in terms of improved performance.

Offshore funds

For the UK investor, the appeal of offshore funds lies largely in the fact that they can offer investment in areas that are not open to onshore unit trusts, in particular, currencies and commodities.

Currency funds can be based on sterling or foreign currencies. Sterling funds can be deposit-based, offering the benefits of wholesale money market rates on short-term deposits, or invested in fixed interest securities, which gives the prospect of capital gains – or a combination of both. Foreign currency funds operate in a similar way, but have the added dimension of exchange rate movements against sterling, which can generate capital gains or losses.

Some companies offer a range of funds based on different individual currencies, with free switching between them. As a rule, though, single currency funds are high risk; markets move fast and timing is crucial to the end result. Unless you have a particular reason for wanting exposure to a certain currency, or have a large amount to invest that can be spread over several funds, you may be better off with a managed currency fund or a management service linked to a range of funds.

Commodity funds are also not for the faint-hearted. Where onshore unit trusts invest only in the shares of commodity-linked companies, offshore funds may additionally use commodity futures contracts or invest directly into the commodities themselves. The outlay required and the risk involved are rather less

Unit Trusts and Offshore Funds (2): The Investment Choice

"Thank you Cinnamon Trust, I'm over 80 and I can still enjoy the love of my pet."

THE CINNAMON TRUST

The specialist Charity for elderly and terminally ill people and their companion animals.

National pet fostering when owners face a spell in hospital or hospice.

Help at home for housebound owners e.g. walking the dog.

National register of pet friendly care homes, nursing homes and sheltered housing.

A safe and happy future assured for pets who outlive their owners, no matter what their age.

The Cinnamon Trust   Registered Charity No. 293399
Poldarves, Trescowe, Penzance, Cornwall TR20 9RX.

The Cinnamon Trust

The Cinnamon Trust is the only specialist national charity which seeks to relieve the problems, and sometimes injustices, faced by elderly and terminally ill people and their pets.

Often in these later years, illness and infirmity mitigate against the companionship of a pet – just at the time when such a relationship is most rewarding and beneficial. Often, anxiety over the long-term future of a much loved pet prevents a life-long owner replacing a decease pet.

The Trust runs a nationwide pet fostering service for elderly and terminally ill owners who face a temporary spell in hospital or hospice. Through its established network of over 1400 volunteers, the Trust provides help for these owners in their own homes when difficulties arise – walking the dog for example.

It is not widely known that there are residential homes, nursing homes and sheltered housing for the elderly that are pet friendly and the iniquitous practice of parting owner and pet when the former becomes too frail to stay at home continues. Through its 'Pet Friendly Care Homes' register, the Trust is able to refer owners in this predicament.

The Cinnamon Trust also provides loving permanent care for companion animals whose owners have died. The first of what will be a countryside series of home from home sanctuaries has already been established at Poldarves in Cornwall.

The Trust which now enters its second decade of active service is funded entirely by voluntary contributions.

Lump-Sum Investment

than if you undertook the same investments on your own behalf – you can only lose the money you put into the fund, whereas with direct investment you could be committed for further sums – but unless you are an inveterate gambler, this type of investment should only be considered within larger portfolios and then only for a small proportion.

Points to watch for with offshore funds are the level of charges, which may be smaller initially but larger annually than onshore funds, and the tax status. As explained in Chapter 6, offshore funds may have distributor or accumulator status. In the first case, at least 85 per cent of the fund's income must be distributed and will be taxed at the appropriate income tax rate in the hands of the investor, while capital gains will come under the standard CGT rules. In the second case, all income is rolled up within the fund and no tax is due while you remain invested, but when you sell out, all profits will be taxed as income at your highest rate.

With foreign currency funds, for example, most of the benefits come from capital gains, so distributor status is advantageous; when you sell, you can make use of the annual CGT exempt allowance before you need pay any tax. With sterling funds that generate interest, accumulator status allows the tax bill to be deferred, which will be a benefit if your tax rate is likely to fall in the future.

8

Investment Trusts

Investment trusts are not trusts, but companies. Their aim in life is to invest their capital somewhere else – in other company shares, in fixed interest securities and the like. Investors who buy investment trust shares are, therefore, getting a 'slice of the action' of a whole portfolio of shares for the price of one. In this respect, they are similar to unit trusts (with which they are often compared and contrasted) and certainly their basic reason for existing is identical: to provide the small investor with a spread of risk for a modest outlay.

This spread of risk is legally insisted upon by the fact that, to qualify for the tax treatment described below, investment trusts cannot invest more than 15 per cent of their assets in any one security, meaning a theoretical minimum portfolio of at least seven. In practice, trusts are likely to have anything between 40 and 200 holdings. The exceptions to this rule are the shares of other investment trust companies, which themselves will automatically provide a spread of risk. They must also distribute at least 85 per cent of the income they receive from their investments to their shareholders.

The taxation position
Investment trusts are similar to unit trusts in that liability to tax on any gains they make belongs to the shareholder, rather than the company itself. This means shareholders can realise up to £6300 of gains (in the 1996/97 tax year) before being liable to tax.

On the income side, dividends from other companies in which

Lump-Sum Investment

Go by Post to get the most
– How postal accounts offer better rates than most bank and building society savings accounts

Ask yourself two questions:
1. What is the interest rate that I am paying on my mortgage?
2. What is the interest rate I am being paid on my savings in the bank/building society?

I would bet that the first figure is much higher than the second.

This is how banks and building societies make their money – by charging mortgage holders more than they pay savers. This is not new. However, in recent years, savers have felt increasingly unhappy about the rates they are paid on their savings. They often find that they may put their money into an account which is paying attractive rates only to find out later that they have fallen behind the market again.

The problem has been increased by the recent falls in interest rates – good news if you are looking for a mortgage but not good news if you want to see your savings grow.

So, how can you maximise the rates you are paid on your bank or building society savings?

Contrary to what you might think, the larger high street banks or building societies do not necessarily offer savers the best interest rates. Better rates are often offered by smaller building societies and particularly by postal accounts run by building societies.

Postal savings accounts are the same as any bank or building society savings account, except they do not go into the branch to pay in or withdraw money. Because such accounts are run by post and telephone, rather than through a branch network, the societies that run them are able to keep costs down and can afford to offer savers a higher return on their money First National Building Society, Ireland's oldest and largest building society, has just launched its own Postal Account Service. Like many such services it offers a range of accounts, including an instant access account and accounts that pay better interest rates the longer the notice period for withdrawal of money – 30, 60 or 90 days (money can be withdrawn sooner from these accounts, although interest will be lost). The minimum investment level is £500. In addition, First National has launched a two year postal bond account offering a guaranteed and fixed rate.

Because First National is not supporting a branch network in the UK, it is able to offer savers competitive rates on all its accounts and a friendly and efficient service from its central processing point in Epsom. First National's aim is to offer top rates across all notice periods and investment bands.

So, if you find you have your money tucked away in accounts which are not paying you top rates of interest, you might consider a postal account. With the option of instant access and notice periods, savers can make the decision as to how 'liquid' they need their savings to be. Savers should look at where their money is now and consider consolidating their savings somewhere where they are likely to get a better rate and a rate that will not fall the minute they turn around.

For further information contact First National Building Society on Freephone 0800 558844.

OUR TWO YEAR POSTAL BOND ACCOUNT
the place to look for more interest

Why spend time searching the high street for a top rate of interest, when the solution is to be found somewhat closer to home?

Our Two Year Postal Bond Account pays 6.25% gross p.a., and you will also enjoy all the convenience of dealing direct with one of the longest established building societies in the UK or Ireland: First National Building Society.

WHY WE PAY MORE INTEREST

We can afford to be more generous with our interest rates because, by providing you with a direct service, we don't have the expense of operating a network of high street branches in the UK.

LOOK HOW MUCH YOU CAN EARN

Our Two Year Postal Bond guarantees you a return of 6.25% gross p.a. - regardless of what happens to interest rates. You can invest in a First National Two year Postal Bond Account with as little as £1000.

For full details call us free on

0800 558844

9.30am - 5.30pm Monday to Friday

Registered In Ireland

First National Building Society offers the protection afforded by the Building Societies Investor Protection Scheme established under the Building Societies Act 1986.

TO OPEN YOUR 2 YEAR POSTAL BOND ACCOUNT RETURN THIS COUPON TODAY

Please complete this coupon and return it to: FNBS, FREEPOST SEA 0652, Epsom, Surrey, KT18 5BR. There is no need for a stamp as we pay the postage.

To open your Two Year Postal Bond please complete this coupon fully and return it with your personal cheque and two original utility bills * (not more than three months old). These will be returned to you. Please note we are unable to open your Postal Bond without Utility Bills.

Name:
Address:

I would like to open a 2 year Postal Bond ☐
I would like my interest paid: annually ☐

or at Maturity ☐ and enclose a cheque for £............ payable to First National Building Society and crossed "Account Payee Only".

AX01

☐ Please send me more information

Postcode
Telephone Number: (Home)
(Work)

Gross rate shown is the annual contractual rate of interest payable not taking account of the deduction of income tax at the basic rate. Interest will be paid net of basic rate of income tax (which may be reclaimed by non- tax payers) OR, subject to the required certification, gross. Only UK residents may apply to open an account. *Utility bills include Gas, Electricity, Water or Phone also acceptable Bank/Credit Card/Mortgage Statements and Council Tax Bill.

the trust invests are paid net of basic rate tax to the holders of the investment trust shares. Non-taxpayers can reclaim the tax; higher rate taxpayers will have to pay more.

Do investment trusts have a unique selling point? The answer is yes, they have several, some of which may be attractive to investors, others possibly offputting.

The share price and the discount

The major difference between investment trusts and unit trusts is that the former are 'closed-ended' funds of money while the latter are 'open-ended'. Unit trusts expand and contract according to the demand for them; if demand outstrips supply, new units are created; if supply exceeds demand, units are cancelled. Investment trusts, on the other hand, have a fixed number of shares.

This difference in structure has a practical effect on prices. The price of units in a unit trust is directly related to the value of its underlying investments, while the share price of an investment trust moves up and down according to the demand for it – just like the share prices of other quoted companies.

In fact, if you totted up the value of holdings in an investment trust's portfolio and divided by the number of shares in existence, the result (known as the net asset value) is almost certain to be different from the share price. Occasionally, the share price is higher, in which case it is said to be at a premium. More commonly, it is lower, which is described as a discount. At the time of writing, the average discount for all investment trusts was 9 per cent.

Why should the share price stand at a discount? One reason is technical. As a going concern, the investment trust's portfolio is valued at mid-market prices – halfway between bid and offer; but if it were to be liquidated or taken over, the valuation would move to the lower bid basis and there would also be professional costs involved in winding it up. However, the major part of the discount is explained by supply and demand. If the shares of a trust are in demand, the discount will narrow or the price may even move to a premium; if the trust is out of favour, the discount will widen.

There is some debate over whether the discount is a benefit or a drawback. The argument in its favour is that it means you are buying a stake in more shares than you are paying for. For example, if the discount stands at 10 per cent, then every £90 you invest in the trust effectively represents £100-worth of the shares in its portfolio. On the other hand, if the discount is still the same when you come to sell, you will lose the 10 per cent again.

The discount can be thought of as an extra layer of risk – or reward. At one level you have the opportunity to gain or lose with movements in the value of the underlying portfolio. On top of that, you will gain if the discount narrows between the time you buy and sell, and lose if it widens. Broadly speaking, if the market is rising and the value of the portfolio is going up, the trust is likely to be in greater demand and the discount will narrow, so you gain twice over. Conversely, when the market is falling, demand drops off, the discount widens and you lose twice over.

While you should be cautious about buying a trust that is already on a very low discount – the expectation being that it will widen – it would be wrong to place too much emphasis on the discount. The manager's ability to produce good performance is likely to be a much larger factor in the investment return.

One other point about the discount is that if it gets too large the trust can become vulnerable to a takeover. An institution can offer an attractive price to shareholders while still leaving plenty of scope to make profits for itself. A case a few years ago was the Globe investment trust, which was standing at a 20 per cent discount when it was taken over by Coal Board Pension Funds.

In practice, though, discounts have narrowed considerably in recent years – only ten years ago, discounts of 20 or 30 per cent were not uncommon. Savings schemes and personal equity plans have led to higher and more consistent demand from private investors, which has helped to bring discounts down and should continue to do so.

Gearing
The 'magnifying' effect of the discount is itself a form of gearing. But investment trusts can go one better than that: unlike unit trusts, they can borrow money to invest, alongside the shareholders' funds. If, for example, you can borrow money at 10 per cent, and invest it in something that goes up 50 per cent in a year,

Lump-Sum Investment

then you have magnified the profits. (Needless to say, if the stock you are investing in goes *down*, you will have magnified your losses.) An example of how gearing can work in your favour is shown in Table 8.1. In this case, the borrowing is in the form of a debenture stock.

Charges
Unlike unit trusts, investment trusts do not have an initial charge as such, though there are dealing costs when you buy shares just as there are with the shares of other companies. There is also an annual management charge, which tends to vary across the different categories: general trusts carry a charge of around 0.3 per cent of the asset value, while on specialist trusts it can be as much as 1 per cent. Newer launches have also tended to have higher charges than the older established trusts, but even so, they compare well with unit trusts.

Investment characteristics

The closed-ended structure of an investment trust, mentioned above, influences the management style as well as the share price.

Table 8.1 *Gearing on an investment trust*

Capital structure of trust:
4,000,000 5% debenture stock	£4,000,000	
6,000,000 £1 ordinary shares	£6,000,000	
	£10,000,000	

Assume the portfolio doubles in value over five years and that the debenture stock is repaid at the end of that time. The effect is as follows:

	Year 1	Year 5
Value of portfolio	£10,000,000	£20,000,000
Less debenture stock	£4,000,000	£4,000,000
Assets attributable to 6,000,000 ordinary shares	£6,000,000	£16,000,000
Net asset value per ordinary share	£1	£2.67

Thus, while the portfolio has increased by 100 per cent, the assets attributable to each ordinary share have increased by 167 per cent (from £1 to £2.67).

A lasting and living memorial to your generosity

ALMSWORTH COMMON, EXMOOR. PHOTOGRAPHY BY BRIAN HARRIS FOR CPRE

The English countryside has been the delight of countless generations – yet this very heart of our national heritage is constantly under threat from damaging development.

Working at national and local level since 1926, CPRE has played a major part in the creation and protection of National Parks, the provision of Green Belts around cities and in establishing firm planning controls. Important contributions are also being made to agricultural, forestry, water and transport policies and hedgerow protection. CPRE's success is based on solid research, constructive ideas and reasoned argument.

CPRE is ever-vigilant but its work as a small but cost-effective charity is totally dependent on public support. By making a bequest or a donation to CPRE, you can help to ensure that England's Green and Pleasant Land is enjoyed by future generations. Remember, a legacy to a registered charity like CPRE is exempt from Inheritance Tax.

If you would like further information about remembering CPRE in a will, write to David Conder, Room 14, Council for the Protection of Rural England, Warwick House, 25 Buckingham Palace Road London SW1W 0PP

PATRON HM THE QUEEN
PRESIDENT JONATHAN DIMBLEBY

REGISTERED CHARITY NUMBER 233179

Lump-Sum Investment

While the unit trust manager must accommodate new money coming in or demands for units to be redeemed, the investment trust manager is working with a fixed pool of assets, regardless of how shares are being bought or sold.

As with the discount, the closed fund has its supporters and its critics. In a rising market, new money attracted into a unit trust can be used to snap up good opportunities, while the investment trust manager may not be able to move so fast. But in a falling market, a unit trust may have to sell its better holdings to meet redemptions, while the investment trust is insulated.

This insulation allows the investment trust manager to make more speculative decisions. Indeed, investment trusts do not have the same restrictions on their holdings as unit trusts – they can invest in unquoted shares and the smaller stock markets around the world that are not yet approved for unit trusts. Obviously these can be more risky, but, with no redemptions to worry about, the manager can afford to take a long-term view.

Investment range

From the start, investment trusts had an international outlook. Many were set up in Scotland, which had a long history of looking abroad for opportunities. This is still reflected in today's trusts, which currently number over 330.

One of the problems in classifying investment trusts is that their investment scope is generally much more loosely defined than is the case with unit trusts. Another difficulty for investors is that the older trusts, in particular, often have names that have little to do with their aims: Scottish Mortgage, for instance, is an international general trust with no particular focus on either Scotland or mortgages.

Some guidance is given by the categorisation used by the Association of Investment Trust Companies (AITC). This divides trusts into 20 different sectors, as shown in Table 8.2. In most cases, the definition is that a trust has at least 80 per cent of its assets in the particular sector, but in the case of Smaller Companies the minimum is 50 per cent and for Venture and Development Capital, it is simply 'a significant proportion' in unquoted companies. International trusts have the broadest

Table 8.2 *Investment trust categories and average performance*

Comparative return to investor of £100 invested over various periods, adjusted to include income reinvested and exchange rate movements on overseas trusts

Sector	1 yr	3 yrs	5 yrs	10 yrs
International: General	127.4	147.0	208.0	397.5
International: Capital Growth	129.0	159.0	215.3	361.8
International: Income Growth	124.7	126.9	181.5	336.3
UK: General	123.7	145.3	185.3	302.7
UK: Capital Growth	131.9	161.4	192.1	416.8
UK: Income Growth	122.4	135.7	183.7	391.5
High Income	108.7	124.4	157.5	256.5
North America	118.8	128.5	226.5	277.7
Far East: Excluding Japan	119.6	160.3	278.6	861.4
Far East: Including Japan	125.1	169.0	228.4	486.0
Japan	120.2	155.8	152.7	323.1
Property	97.3	154.7	107.5	147.5
Continental Europe	123.8	158.7	175.8	306.5
Pan Europe	121.5	148.3	198.1	382.4
Commodity & Energy	112.1	84.4	93.4	—
Emerging Markets	125.4	132.5	260.7	—
Closed-End Funds	113.5	141.3	157.9	639.1
Smaller Companies	121.5	140.6	185.0	295.2
Venture & Development Capital	124.9	177.5	231.0	345.3
Split Capital*	—	—	—	—
FT-SE-A All-Share Index	127.7	144.5	188.5	338.0
MSCI World Index (£)	127.8	144.7	198.0	304.1
Standard & Poors Composite	138.1	142.8	242.5	338.7
Retail Price Index (previous month)	102.9	108.9	115.4	156.1

Note: Investment trust figures are based on size-weighted average.
* Performance figures not applicable.

Source: Association of Investment Trust Companies, 29 February 1996

definition, of having less than 80 per cent of assets in any one geographical area, and split capital trusts are the most complicated type, with various different share classes.

The variation in scope between trusts within the same category means that performance comparisons are not necessarily on a like

Lump-Sum Investment

with like basis, but to give a general guide to investment returns, Table 8.2 shows the average for each sector, plus a few key indices, over periods to the end of February 1996.

How to invest

Investment trust shares can be bought through a stockbroker, bank or other authorised dealer. When a new trust is launched, the company must publish a prospectus in at least one newspaper. In some cases, a full prospectus is published, including a coupon to apply for shares; otherwise there will be a contact address given from which you can obtain the full prospectus and an application form.

If you have only a small amount to invest, the minimum commission charged by stockbrokers would be disproportionately high and a much cheaper route is through a savings scheme, of which there are currently 51 available. The first scheme was launched in 1984 and the concept has proved highly successful at attracting private investors into investment trusts.

Despite the name, savings schemes can be used for lump sums as well as regular investments. The minimum can be as little as £20 a month or £250 for a lump sum. Dealing costs are very small – usually 1 per cent or less – because investors' money is pooled within the scheme to buy shares in bulk. In some cases this means that dealing takes place only once a month, so it is a good idea to find out when the deadline is. This and other information on savings schemes can be obtained from the AITC.

Share exchange schemes
As with unit trusts, several companies offer share exchange schemes through which you can swap holdings of equities for investment trust shares. The company will sell the shares on your behalf and may either bear the selling costs itself or offer a special

---

Phone ShareLink for a PEP talk on 0121 233 9955.

discounted charge. The charge for buying into the investment trust will normally be at the low savings scheme rate, but may be waived altogether.

Keeping track of prices

Investment trust prices are published daily in newspapers such as *The Daily Telegraph* and *The Financial Times*. The Association of Investment Trust Companies publishes a monthly information service, usually around the third week of the month. This gives two sets of performance figures: the total return on £100 invested as measured by the trust's net asset value – which gives an idea of what the manager has achieved in isolation from share price movements; and the share price total return on £100. In each case figures are over one, three, five and ten years. It also gives a host of statistical data, including the geographical spread of trusts, the total value of assets, the share price, the net asset value, the discount, the gearing potential, the gross yield and the annual growth in dividends as measured over five years. In addition there is information on savings schemes and personal equity plans and a contact list of names and addresses for the management groups.

Variations on a theme

Limited life trusts

Whatever the so-called 'advantages' of the discount, some companies have seen it as a drawback, and they have decided to get round it by offering 'limited life' trusts. These either have a fixed redemption date, at which point the company will be wound up and its assets realised at full market value, or a series of dates – perhaps once a year – at which shareholders have the option to vote for the winding-up of the company.

Either strategy has the advantage that the discount is unlikely to stray up too far; there can be a drawback, however, in that it means fund managers cannot be as far-sighted in their investment policy as they would with an ordinary investment trust.

Split capital trusts

Split capital trusts started out in the 1960s with the aim of accommodating two types of investor within the one trust: those who were seeking high and growing income, but had little or no interest in capital growth; and those seeking capital growth, with no desire for income. This was achieved by having two classes of share: income and capital. More recently the concept has been expanded and split capital trusts may now also include zero dividend preference shares, stepped preference shares and highly geared ordinary shares. All split capital trusts have a fixed lifespan, although shares can be bought and sold at any time.

The original type of income shares offer high income during the life of the trust and a fixed redemption price when it is wound up. The nearer the trust is to its winding-up date, the nearer the share price is likely to get to its redemption value, but meanwhile it may stand above that, reflecting expectations of future income. So if you hold the shares to redemption there may be a capital loss.

A newer type of income share may get a proportion of the assets at winding-up, on top of the fixed redemption price, but only after other classes of share have taken their entitlements. In contrast, 'annuity income' shares have only a nominal redemption value, perhaps as little as 1p, so there is a built-in capital loss, but meanwhile they receive all the income generated from the trust's portfolio. Finally, highly geared ordinary shares, which are found in 'hybrid' trusts paired with zero preference shares, have no fixed redemption price but receive the surplus assets after the zeros have been paid off, and meanwhile receive all the trust's income.

Income shares are suitable for investors seeking high and rising income, particularly if they are non-taxpayers or can hold the shares tax-free within a personal equity plan. The highly geared ordinary shares are better suited to experienced investors who are prepared to accept a capital risk in return for potentially high rewards.

Capital shares normally receive no dividends during the life of the trust, but at winding-up they get all the remaining assets after the prior claims of preference and income shares have been met. There is thus a risk involved, but the chance of very good returns. Zero dividend preference shares, on the other hand, have a fixed redemption value and take top priority at winding-up. The return is not guaranteed, as the trust will have to generate sufficient

Investment Trusts

FOR A FAST
01274 736 736
DEAL, DIAL

EXECUTION-ONLY TELEPHONE SHAREDEALING

- Low cost - from only £9. Standard Rate: 0.8% commission up to £5,000, 0.1% thereafter
- Convenient - call from anywhere to buy or sell
- Quick - most deals can be confirmed immediately
- Call - for an information pack today

YORKSHIRE BUILDING SOCIETY'S SHARE DEALING SERVICE

YorkSHARE Limited, a member of the London Stock Exchange, is regulated by the Securities and Futures Authority and is a subsidiary of Yorkshire Building Society.

assets to meet the liability, but the risk is very low.

Stepped preference shares offer a combination of income and capital returns, with a fixed redemption value and a fixed rate of annual dividend growth. As with zeros, the returns are not guaranteed, but the risk is small.

Split capital trusts offer a lot of potential for investors who have specific capital or income needs, or are prepared to take on higher risk for potentially high returns. However, because of their complex structure it is important to be sure exactly what each type of share's entitlement is, and what the likelihood is of its being met – for example, what growth rate the trust will have to achieve between now and the winding-up date to repay the various classes of share.

Warrants

Around 159 trusts now have warrants available and new launches sometimes offer a free warrant for every so many shares you buy. A warrant is not itself a share, but gives you the right to buy a share at a fixed price at some point in the future.

The terms, which are set when the warrant is issued, specify the 'exercise price', at which the future share can be bought, and the 'exercise date', on which the option can be taken up. This may be a particular day, or a period between two dates, each year up to the final exercise date. There is no obligation to buy at any point and obviously it will only be worth while if the exercise price, plus the original price of the warrant, compares favourably with the current price of the share.

Of course, once the final expiry date has passed, the warrant becomes worthless. But during their life warrants can be bought and sold just like the shares themselves, so warrants can be bought as investments in their own right, with the intention of selling at a profit, rather than exercising the right to buy shares.

The warrant price is generally much lower than the share price, but its movements are proportionately greater. This is known as the gearing, the level of which is measured as the share price divided by the warrant price. The higher the gearing, the greater are the potential risks and rewards of the warrant. Two other features to look for in choosing a warrant are the premium – the amount by which the warrant price plus its exercise price exceeds the current price of the underlying share – and its remaining lifespan, up to the final exercise date. The longer the lifespan, the higher the acceptable premium: there will be more time for the share price to increase and represent a profit over the exercise price.

One other point to bear in mind is that warrants do not entitle the holder to any dividends. This means there will be no income tax liability, while capital gains will come within the annual £6000 capital gains tax allowance. The exceptions are subscription shares, which do pay an annual dividend, but currently there are only a couple of trusts which issue these.

Lloyd's trusts

The well-publicised losses of Lloyd's insurance market led, in October 1994, to a new approach to attracting capital: allowing investment by limited liability companies. This engendered the launch of a new family of investment trust.

Lloyd's trusts invest primarily in equities, gilts, bonds or some mix of these. As with ordinary investment trusts, the shares can be bought and sold on the stock market and some of the trusts qualify as holdings for a personal equity plan. In addition, the trusts will use their portfolios to underwrite Lloyd's syndicates, which they may do to a limit of twice the capital involved.

In theory, then, investors' money will work twice over. The underyling portfolio will generate dividends, and offer the potential for capital appreciation, in the ordinary way. On top of that, a proportion of any underwriting profits will be passed on to the shareholder. However, because Lloyd's accounts take three years to complete, these profits would only come through in dividends in the fourth year from launch, which means 1997.

The downside is that there are also two ways of losing money. The underlying portfolio may fall in value, while any underwriting losses that are sustained will have to be met by selling assets. But the risk is mitigated by the fact that there will be a time limit on claims for the contracts underwritten, which is not the case for existing Lloyd's Names, and also because, with limited liability, you can never lose more than you invest.

At the time of writing there are a dozen such trusts. The

majority are fairly small and not very frequently traded, hence there has been no significant movement in share prices to indicate whether the concept is a successful one or not. Information and analysis have also been scarce, partly because it would involve analysing all the underlying Lloyd's syndicates to which the trusts are exposed, which is a highly specialist and lengthy procedure.

The decision on which syndicates to support is obviously a major factor in the potential investment return. The larger trusts have tended to spread themselves across the market, while some of the smaller ones have taken a more specialist approach. To some extent this selectivity can be an advantage; while a large spread should in theory reduce risk, in practice it also reduces choice and makes monitoring more difficult.

Costs are also a consideration. Fees and commission have to be paid to Lloyd's, Lloyd's members' agents and other advisers to the trust, as well as the trust manager, all of which will reduce the returns for investors.

So even if you are prepared for the risks – which means being prepared to lose your entire investment – picking a trust is not straightforward. One way around this is a 'fund of funds', which invests in a selection of the trusts available. Otherwise, you should certainly consider taking professional advice.

Venture capital trusts

Venture capital trusts (VCTs) were first announced in the 1993 Autumn Budget, but there then followed a year of consultation before details were given in the 1994 Budget. The first trusts were launched in 1995.

There were already a number of investment trusts which specialise in the venture and development capital sector. What is different about the new ones is that, in return for meeting specific investment criteria, they will offer considerable tax concessions.

For investments of up to £100,000 a year, there is front-end income tax relief of 20 per cent if you subscribe at launch, no tax on dividends and no capital gains tax on sale profits. There is also rollover relief – capital gains tax on profits from other assets will be deferred if the proceeds are reinvested in a VCT, although it will have to be paid when the VCT shares are sold, unless the money is further reinvested into another VCT. The criterion for all these concessions is that the VCT shares must be held for at least five years.

For its part, the VCT must, within three years of being set up, have 70 per cent of its holdings in qualifying companies – broadly, unquoted trading companies with a capitalisation of less than £10 million. Investment into any one company must be no more than £1 million to be included in this 70 per cent. Investments may include loans, with a minimum term of five years, but at least half the portfolio must be in ordinary shares.

Venture capital is by its nature a risky area – many new ventures quickly bite the dust. On the other hand, VCTs spread the risk, as they invest in a selection of companies, and can invest up to 30% of their portfolios outside the venture capital sector – in blue chip shares, say, which would significantly reduce the overall risk. Moreover, the tax reliefs are attractive, although in exchange you are locked in for five years.

There are three main points to consider if you are thinking of investing in a VCT. Firstly, you should look at where it is investing. There can be considerable differences between seedcorn investment, where money is put into companies at a very early stage of their development, and expansion finance, which covers a later stage. The latter tends to be less 'exciting': the potential returns are smaller, but the risk level is also lower. Secondly, you should look at the management group's track record in the sector, as experience is even more crucial here than in other investment areas. Finally, there are the charges. These are likely to be higher than for the average investment trust, because of the quantity of research needed into each company the trust invests in, although the US practice of charging performance fees seems unlikely to catch on in the UK.

Housing Investment Trusts

Housing Investment Trusts were introduced in the 1995 Budget as a way of stimulating investment in private rented housing. By way of encouragement, they will be able to pay corporation tax at the smaller companies rate of 24 per cent and will be exempt from capital gains tax.

Lump-Sum Investment

Properties can be acquired from 1 April 1996 and must be unlet or let under assured shorthold tenancies. Thereafter they must be let on assured tenancies. There is a maximum property value of £125,000 in London and £85,000 elsewhere.

At the time of writing, trusts have yet to be launched, but it is expected that they could produce an income of 5 to 6 per cent a year. This is based on current yields on residential property of 10 to 12 per cent, less the costs of management and maintenance. There are also prospects for capital growth. The trusts are likely to appeal mainly to institutions, but private investors may also be attracted – if only in the hope of avenging past losses in the housing market!

Lifestyle products

Until recently, investment trusts were viewed purely as vehicles for investment or saving as an end in itself. But in practice, as discussed in Chapter 1, many people have a specific reason for saving – perhaps their children's future or their own retirement. Some investment trust groups are now responding to this by designing 'lifestyle' products that serve a particular purpose.

This has been prompted in part by new rules, introduced in January 1995, for the disclosure of charges on financial products. This tends to be a disadvantage to insurance companies, whose products have traditionally involved 'front-end loading' of charges, in contrast to investment trusts and unit trusts, which take a flat charge from each investment. As a result, investment trust companies have seen opportunities to compete in new areas.

Pension plans are one example. The plans are underwritten by insurance companies, as they must be administered by an authorised pension provider, but the underlying investment is into investment trusts. The advantages over insurance companies' own plans are that costs tend to be lower and charges are not front-end loaded, which means contributions are generally more flexible – they can be altered, or stopped and restarted, without incurring penalties.

PEP mortgages, discussed further in the next chapter, are another opportunity that investment trusts are starting to take up, while one company has launched a children's savings plan

THE ROYAL NAVY SUBMARINE MUSEUM
(Registered Charity No. 277960)
Haslar Jetty Road
Gosport
Hampshire
PO12 2AS
01705 510354

The Royal Navy Submarine Museum is a Charitable Trust, whose major aim is to provide financial support to ex-submariners and their families in need. As a Memorial Museum, it serves to illustrate the contribution made by the Submarine Service to the nation's security since its inception in 1901, and the sacrifice made by its officers and men in peace and war. Its aspirations over the next five years, as well as maintaining its charitable contributions, include the conservation and restoration of *Holland 1* (the Royal Navy's first Submarine), building an extension to the current Museum to provide an additional gallery and waterside cafe, developing disabled facilities, and building a new HQ to house its valuable written and photographic archive. Funding for these projects can only be achieved through donations and grants.

that takes advantage of the child's own tax allowances. As the effects of charges disclosure work through, and competition throughout the financial services industry increases, more such developments are likely.

Where to find out more

The primary source of information is the Association of Investment Trust Companies, Durrant House, 8-13 Chiswell Street, London EC1Y 4YY. The Association produces a free information pack which provides a booklet on buying investment trust shares plus details of all trusts, savings schemes, personal equity plans and the addresses of the management groups. In addition, it publishes free fact-sheets on subjects such as personal equity plans, school fees, investing for income, investing for children, split capital trusts and warrants.

For more comprehensive coverage, the AITC offers a monthly information service, which includes statistical data on the trusts, performance figures and a list of contacts for the management

Lump-Sum Investment

groups. Subscriptions are available on a full monthly basis, at a cost of £35 a year, or quarterly, for £20 a year.

For more details, there is an enquiry line on: 0171 431 5222.

9

Personal Equity Plans

Personal equity plans (PEPs) were first announced in the 1986 Budget and came into being at the beginning of 1987. The aim was to encourage wider share ownership through tax advantages: all profits within a PEP were free of capital gains tax and all dividends, so long as they were reinvested in the plan, were free of income tax.

However, in the early days PEPs had little appeal to ordinary investors. A plan had to be held for a full calendar year to qualify for the tax benefits, but a more significant drawback was that the annual investment limit was only £2400. This meant that in practice the tax advantages were worth very little, particularly as few people pay capital gains tax anyway.

Another problem was that, for people who had no other equity investments, £2400 was too small an amount to get a proper spread of individual holdings and even packaged schemes had to be fairly basic to keep the administration charges at a reasonable level. Unit trusts and investment trusts, which can provide a wide spread for a small sum of money, could be included in plans, but only up to a limit of £420 or 25 per cent of the total investment.

So PEPs initially had little interest except for larger investors as a tax shelter for a small portion of their portfolios. But there was a surge in popularity in 1989, when the investment limit was increased to £4800 and in 1990, when it was raised again to £6000. By this time, the rule on holding a plan for a calendar year had been removed, and half the total limit could be put into qualifying unit and investment trusts. Further improvements followed: in 1991, single company PEPs were introduced, with a

Lump-Sum Investment

separate investment limit of £3000, and the scope of plans was widened from UK shares to those quoted in EU countries; in 1992, the £3000 ceiling was removed from qualifying unit and investment trusts, allowing the full £6000 to be invested in these vehicles; and in 1994, the Chancellor introduced a new brand of PEPs investing in corporate bonds.

PEP rules

The investment limits apply to a tax year, rather than a calendar year, and for 1996/97 they remain at £6000 for a general PEP plus a further £3000 in a single company PEP. Plans can be taken out by anyone over 18, and husbands and wives each have their own investment allowance. All profits made within a plan are free of capital gains tax and dividends can now be paid out to the investor free of income tax as well as accumulated tax-free within the plan.

Following the 1993 Budget, the income tax 'rebate' on dividends earned within a PEP dropped from 25 per cent to 20 per cent. This was because the income tax rate charged on dividends was reduced to 20 per cent, so the amount that could be reclaimed fell accordingly. From April 1996, the same applies to interest payments on cash held in a plan.

For basic rate taxpayers, this has had the effect of making PEPs a little less worth while than before. If you hold shares or trusts within a PEP, you are saving only 20 per cent in tax on the dividends, compared with holding the same investments directly. So where the PEP involves extra charges, the benefits may be marginal or even completely outweighed.

Conversely, for higher rate taxpayers, the PEP advantage is slightly greater than before. If you hold shares directly, you receive dividends together with a tax credit that can be set against your income tax liability. For basic rate taxpayers, this tax credit exactly matches the liability, but higher rate taxpayers have to pay the difference between the value of the tax credit and their tax rate of 40 per cent. As the tax credit is now worth only 20 per cent instead of 25 per cent, the extra tax due has gone up from 15 per cent to 20 per cent. So there is a greater benefit to be had from holding investments free of tax within a PEP.

Personal Equity Plans

The traditional equity-based PEPs may invest in authorised shares, unit trusts, investment trusts or any combination of these. Shares must be quoted in an EU country, while to be fully qualifying, unit trusts and investment trusts must be at least 50 per cent invested in EU shares. Trusts which do not qualify under this rule can still be included in PEPs, but only up to a limit of £1500.

The newer corporate bond PEPs may invest in fixed rate bonds issued in sterling by companies incorporated in the UK, with a minimum term to redemption of five years. They may also include preference shares and convertibles.

PEPs must be run by a registered scheme manager and you are restricted to one scheme manager a year for a general PEP, although if you have a single company PEP as well, that can be with a different manager. There is also nothing to stop you choosing another manager in subsequent years. Plan managers include banks, building societies, unit trust groups, investment trust companies, stockbrokers and independent financial advisers.

There are now around 1200 different PEPs generally available, as well as plans run by some institutions specifically for their own clients. These can be divided into six different categories.

Types of plan

Managed PEPs

Managed PEPs are the largest category and the easiest option, particularly if you are making your first foray into the stock market. Essentially, all you need do is hand over your money and the plan manager will make all the investment decisions on your behalf. Some plans invest only in shares, others only in unit or investment trusts and others again in a combination of these.

The minimum for a lump-sum investment can be as little as £500, though some managers will only accept the full £6000. On the whole, plans that include shares are likely to require a larger investment than those based only on unit or investment trusts.

They may also involve higher charges. Some plans carry an initial charge as well as an annual management fee, and on top of these there are dealing charges for buying and selling shares and

Lump-Sum Investment

PEPS – Past, Present and Future

The rise of Personal Equity Plans (PEPs)
It has been ten years since the then Chancellor, Nigel Lawson, first mentioned PEPs in his Budget speech in 1986 and according to the Inland Revenue, there is now over £22 billion invested in them*.

So, what are PEPs and what makes them so valuable?
A PEP, short for Personal Equity Plan, is one of the most flexible and sensible ways of savings there is, with very few possible drawbacks.

PEPs allow everyone over 18 to invest in the stock market TAX FREE. In the past, many people have reasoned 'I pay tax on my income. If I save my income and do well with those savings I have to pay tax again'. This is no longer true. Investing in PEPs has removed the great disincentive to save as any capital gains you make or income you receive is entirely free from tax – you do not even have to declare your PEP on your tax return.

Each year you can put up to £6,000 into a 'general' PEP and your partner can too. You can build a tax free investment over which you have complete control. You can take money out either as a tax free lump sum or as regular tax free income.

The wide choice of PEPs means that they can meet a wide range of financial planning objectives. PEPs can compliment personal planning by providing high levels of tax free income providing extra income in your retirement, to pay off a mortgage or to meet school or university fees for example. Unlike many other tax efficient investments there is no fixed period for which you must hold your PEP which means you can have easy access to your money whenever you need to.

Important reasons for investing in a PEP
- Your investment is tax free from day one
- You can invest in a PEP by monthly payments, by lump sum or a combination of the two
- PEPs are a long term investment, so offer you considerable potential for capital growth and/or a rising tax free income
- PEPs have relatively low charges
- You can transfer shares, unit trusts or investment trusts you already own in a PEP – sometimes free of charge

The flexibility of PEPs
The PEP rules have been revised many times over the years. The maximum contributions have been increased, the range of investments has been widened and the choice of markets that PEPs can invest in has been extended. Last year, a decision to allow corporate bonds to be invested in PEPs unleashed a massive sure of activity and opened up the PEP market to a wider audience.

New wave Corporate Bond PEPs
"the inclusion of bonds in PEPs will provide the link between deposits and equity unit trusts. Many savers need high income now, and for them bond PEPs will be ideal" –

Philip Warland, Director General of The Association of Unit Trust and Investment Funds

The inclusion of corporate bonds in PEPs does seem to have provided a stepping stone for many investors who are looking for a high income but do not want their investment linked to equities. It has also been suggested that because short term interest rates are currency low, corporate bond PEPs provide a new and competitive option for building society and TESSA investors.

8 key rules for investing in a PEP
- Investors must be aged 18 or over and resident in the UK for tax purposes to hold a PEP
- The PEP must be managed by a PEP Plan Manager approved by the Inland Revenue
- All dividends and capital growth within a PEP are free of income and capital gains tax
- A maximum of £6,000 can be invested in a general PEP each tax year which can be invested in qualifying unit or investment trusts. Qualifying in trusts are those which have at least half their assets in the UK/European union. General PEPs can also now invest in corporate bonds and certain other fixed interest investments, or in unit trusts investing in corporate bonds
- You can cash in all or part of your PEP at any time, though they are best viewed as long tem investments
- Everyone is entitled to their own £6,000 annual PEP allowance
- You do not have to declare a PEP on your tax return
- On the death of a PEP investor the tax free status of the PEP ceases. Income and capital to the date of death are tax free, but future income and gains will be liable to taxation and the proceeds to inheritance tax.

Past performance is not necessarily a guide to future performance. The value of investments and the income from them can go down as well as up, you may not get back the amount you invested. The value to you of the tax benefits will depend upon your own circumstances. The tax regime of PEPs could change in the future. M&G does not offer any investment advice or recommendations regarding investments. We only market the packaged products and services of The M&G marketing group.

*Source: Inland Revenue

Personal Equity Plans

Charles Dickens, a quote from "David Copperfield"

"Annual Income Twenty pounds, Annual expenditure nineteen nineteen and six, result happiness"

For more information about how to save as little as £50 per month with M&G either call us now on (01245) 390000 or write to: The M&G Group, Bristol BS38 7ET, or e-mail on hb@MandG.reply.Co.UK

Issued by M&G Securities Ltd (regulated by IMRO and the Personal Investment Authority). M&G does not offer investment advice or make any recommendations about investments. We only market the packaged products and services of the M&G marketing group.

Managing your money for the longer term

Lump-Sum Investment

investment trusts, plus the standard initial and annual charges on any unit trusts included – though a few managers will rebate part of the initial charge or pass on any discounts they negotiate.

PEPs offered by unit trust groups generally have no plan charges other than those on the trusts themselves. Both these and plans run by investment trust companies normally allow the investor to choose which trusts are included, but, of course, the choice is generally restricted to their own range. Also, now that the investment allowance for trusts is the full £6000, few of these managers offer a facility to include shares, so if you want a plan with a mix of holdings you may find more choice with a stockbroker or independent adviser.

Advisory PEPs

Advisory PEPs are available from stockbrokers, investment managers and independent advisers. They generally offer a completely free choice of investments and the final decision is up to the plan holder, but the manager will offer advice on what to buy and sell and when. This type of plan is best suited to investors who already have a fair knowledge of the market but still prefer to have some guidance.

As with the managed share PEPs, there are likely to be initial and annual plan fees, as well as the charges arising on the investments themselves. If you plan to buy and sell actively, the dealing charge is the most important; this can vary from as little as 0.5 per cent to as much as 1.9 per cent. Several managers also have a minimum charge, which makes it expensive to deal in small amounts.

Obviously, the quality of advice is important, but so is the quantity. If you intend to invest actively, you need to be sure you can get advice when you need it, otherwise good opportunities could slip by. You also need to check who takes the initiative – whether it is up to you to request advice or whether the manager will contact you if he thinks the time is right to buy or sell.

Self-select PEPs

As mentioned, PEPs must always be operated by an authorised plan manager. The nearest you can get to a do-it-yourself PEP, under which the investor takes all the decisions, is a self-select plan. These plans are run mainly by stockbrokers and, while in principle any qualifying investment can be selected, the main emphasis tends to be on shares.

The minimum investment can be as little as £250. But because you are buying your own individual holdings, rather than a stake in a managed pool of money, these plans are better suited to larger investments, which will enable a reasonable spread of shares to be bought.

The prime advantage of self-select PEPs is, of course, that you are not restricted to any one range of unit or investment trusts, or a manager's selection of shares. However, not all self-select plans offer a completely free choice. A few have restrictions on the shares that may be bought, although the limits are generally quite broad – for instance, shares included in the FT-SE 100 Index or the FT-SE-A All-Share Index. More importantly, some exclude unit trusts or investment trusts or both, so you should check before you buy that the plan will meet your particular requirements.

Perhaps surprisingly, self-select PEPs can be more expensive than managed plans. Although you are not paying for any management expertise, there are still set-up and continuing administrative costs which will be met through initial and annual charges. More significantly, there will be dealing charges each time you buy and sell. In a managed plan these are kept to a minimum because the manager is dealing in very large sums on behalf of all the plan holders pooled together; with a self-select plan you have to meet all the costs yourself.

This is another reason why these plans are not suitable for small investments. A number of managers have a minimum dealing charge which can be as much as £50, so it is uneconomic for small sums. Aside from that, dealing charges can vary enormously, from as low as 0.25 per cent up to 1.95 per cent of the transaction value. The more actively you intend to run your plan, the more these dealing charges will mount up and eat into any profits you are making.

Since the investment performance is entirely down to your own efforts, charges are the major factor in choosing a plan, but you should also check the services offered and the quality of administration, in particular the speed of response when you give

Lump-Sum Investment

Picking a PEP?
Buying a Bond?

Garrison saves you more!

With over 25,000 clients, Garrison is the UK's largest Discount Broker. By cutting our commission AND organising extra allocations for our clients we can save you up to 4% on PEPs and simply loads on Distribution and With-Profits Bonds, Unit Trusts, Pensions and AVCs etc, etc.

- ★ We deal with all the leading companies
- ★ There are no registration or membership fees
- ★ FREE comprehensive Newsletter
- ★ No Salesman will call

We have been saving our clients money on the best investments for 10 years – savings you will not make if you go direct to the investment company.

ACT NOW – Before you put pen to cheque book contact us for full details and your copy of our latest comprehensive newsletter. It will cost you nothing and could save you an awful lot of money.

Ring the Discount Hotline on **01142-500720** now or write to:

Garrison Investment Analysis Ltd
FREEPOST, Kingfield Road, Sheffield S11 8TE
Offices also at Beverley, Gainsborough & York
Regulated by the Personal Investment Authority
The value of investments and the income from them can go down as well as up.

Garrison Investment Analysis Ltd, FREEPOST, Kingfield Road, Sheffield S11 8TE   DTIG
Please show me how to save money on PEPs, Bonds, Unit Trusts & Pensions – without obligation.

Name ....

Address ....

....

.... Postcode ....

I am interested in ....

Personal Equity Plans

Discount Brokers
The route to cost effective investment

When investing, many people assume that they can save money by going direct to the company they are investing with and cutting out the middleman - i.e. the broker. However, this **is certainly not the case with most products in the financial services sector.** Quite simply, your investment will cost you the same whether you go direct or invest via a broker - and here lies the secret of the Discount Broker.

If you invest in a unit trust, PEP or investment bond direct, they will deduct their initial charge (generally between 2% and 6%), say "thank you" and pass the commission they have saved on to their advertising department. If your application has the stamp of an authorised intermediary on it, the company will still deduct the same standard charge - but will pass a proportion of the money to the intermediary as a "thank you" to them.

What the Discount Broker does is to pass most of this commission back to the client - and the increased turnover this generates more than compensates for the reduced commission. The final result is that you have precisely the same investment as your neighbour who chose to go direct, but it has cost you less.

However, it's not simply a matter of sharing commission. Because of the volume of business they generate Discount Brokers have the financial clout of a Sainsburys or Tesco and can use this to improve the basic product. The typical commission on a PEP will be 3% - but Discount Brokers will frequently be able to negotiate discounts of 3% or 4% for their clients - and still retain 1% for themselves. Similarly, with a well known Distribution Bond, the insurance company offers direct investors a 1% bonus - but clients of Discount Brokers will receive a further 3% bonus.

So where do you go from here? These organisations are not "bucket shops". The largest have been established over 10 years and have over 25,000 clients. They will offer advice free of charge and without obligation. Alternatively, you can do your own research and simply contact them with a shopping list.

At the end of the day you must choose - Do you want to go direct to the investment company or do you want to use a Discount Broker. On a mixed Bond/PEP/Unit Trust portfolio of £50,000 the savings could add up to over £1,500 - the choice is yours!

the manager instructions to buy or sell your holdings. If you spot a good investment opportunity that needs immediate action, it will be no good if the manager takes a week to respond, so you need to be sure you can get ready access to give instructions and that they will be carried out without delay.

Because the onus is entirely on the investor, these plans are suitable only for the more experienced, with a fair slice of capital to invest and the time to keep track of market movements. If you are already investing in equities on your own account, then the charges become less important – you would face them anyway – and the plan can be used as a convenient trading service, with the manager taking care of all the paperwork.

Corporate bond PEPs

As mentioned above, corporate bond PEPs may invest in fixed-rate bonds issued in sterling by UK companies with terms of five years or more. Bonds in this context are debt certificates issued by a company which pay a fixed rate of interest and carry a guaranteed repayment value on a specified date. Government bonds – gilts – are not allowed, nor are bonds issued by financial institutions.

Other allowable investments are preference shares, which offer fixed dividends, and convertibles, which also carry a fixed dividend, plus the option to convert them to ordinary shares at a fixed price on some future date.

Although the concept was set out in the November 1994 Budget, the introduction of the new plans was delayed to July 1995 by debate over what was acceptable for inclusion. Despite a slow start, it has been estimated that they could attract some £6 billion a year by the end of the century.

The attraction is that they offer a high, fixed income – of the order of 8.5 per cent gross. Thanks to the PEP environment, this is tax-free and therefore compares very favourably with the much lower taxed rates offered by building societies, or even with a tax-free TESSA.

There is more risk involved than with a building society account, although generally less than with equities. The price of bonds will fluctuate from day to day, so you should not invest money you may need to get at in a hurry. The guaranteed repayment value is also only as good as the company giving the guarantee and this can vary considerably, from large, well-founded firms to small ventures issuing so-called 'junk' bonds. As a general rule, higher rates of income will indicate higher risk, the first being offered as compensation for the second.

Another potential problem is that high demand for the PEPs, and therefore for the underlying bonds, will push up prices, which will lower the yields. It may also force managers to seek issues from smaller companies, increasing the risk level.

There is also the consideration that high initial income tends to restrict the potential for capital growth. Hence the PEPs are likely to be more suitable for older investors, for whom capital is less important, while younger investors should consider equities for better potential total returns over the longer term.

Corporate PEPs

Corporate PEPs are set up by companies, through an authorised plan manager such as a bank, building society or stockbroker, to allow their shares to be held in the tax-free environment of a PEP. They are usually aimed chiefly at the company's own employees and existing shareholders but are available to anyone. A wide range of corporate PEPs is now available, generally based on large companies such as British Gas, BAA and ICI.

A few plans offer the investor a choice of company or specify a minimum holding in one company, after which the investor can choose any quoted shares for the rest of the portfolio. For the most part, though, shareholdings are confined to the one company, so these plans are pretty inflexible. Under PEP rules, corporate PEPs come under the 'general' category, which means you can invest up to £6000, but you cannot take out another general PEP in the same year, so it is very much a case of having all your eggs in one basket.

Of course, you are not committed for all time, only for the current tax year; thereafter you can take out a more balanced plan, or you may already have one from previous years. So if you hold a large chunk of shares in one company, and you have no other current PEPs, it may be worth putting your holdings into a corporate PEP for the tax advantages.

Shares that you already hold cannot be transferred directly into

Lump-Sum Investment

a PEP except within six weeks of buying a new issue. What you can do, however, is a 'bed and breakfast' operation, which means selling your shares and then buying them back again within the PEP.

Once the shares are inside the PEP the investment will be free of any income and capital gains tax, but beware that the tax gains are not eaten up in plan charges. Many plans have no, or only a small, initial charge, while the annual charge is usually 0.5 per cent, but can be up to twice that. For a basic rate taxpayer this could outweigh the savings.

Single company PEPs

Single company PEPs are similar to corporate PEPs in that they are based on the shares of a single company. This means that they are usually inflexible, but they have the advantage that they carry their own separate investment allowance, of £3000 a year, and can be held in addition to a general PEP.

There are three types of single company PEP: those that are based on one particular company, those where the choice of share is at the manager's discretion and those offering the investor a choice of share. The first type operate very much like corporate PEPs and are likely to have particular appeal to employees of the company who are participating in a share scheme.

Holding the shares within a PEP will bring the usual income and capital gains tax exemptions. But unlike general and corporate PEPs, shares that are already held can be transferred directly into a PEP providing that they have been acquired through an employee share scheme and that the transfer takes place within 90 days.

Non-employees can also invest in this type of PEP, either directly or, if they already hold shares in the company, by using a bed and breakfast transaction. One advantage is that the charges are generally low, with only a nominal or possibly no initial charge and annual fees of around 0.5 per cent.

'Managed' single company PEPs are almost a contradiction in terms, since there is little management involved in a portfolio that consists of a single company's shares. Of course, the manager may decide to switch from one company to another if it appears to give better prospects; there is also the argument that to pick a

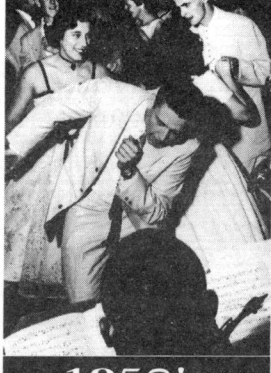

HELP US MAKE TODAY AND TOMORROW AS GOOD AS THE MEMORIES

Leave a legacy
for the future
of older people

MAKE A WILL

FOR FURTHER DETAILS TELEPHONE

01865 854000

ACHIEVING QUALITY RESPONSES BY FULFILLING THE WANTS
AND NEEDS OF OLDER PEOPLE THROUGH HOUSING AND CARE
Charity Registration Number 1052183. Company 3147851

single share that will perform well can be a harder task than managing a portfolio where a few wrong choices will be compensated by a few right ones. Even so, the charges on these plans can be quite high – as much as 5 per cent at the outset and up to 1.5 per cent as an annual management fee. In some cases, a discount is offered on the initial charge if you also take out a general PEP with the same manager. Otherwise, there may be better value in the corporate style plan, if there is one available for the share that interests you, or a self-select plan.

Some self-select plans offer a completely free choice of share, while others provide a list for investors to pick from. Again, it is important to check the charges. These tend to be fairly low – one or two plans have no charges other than the dealing costs on the share – but the initial charge can be as high as 4 per cent, which is a hefty sum when you are making your own share selection. Similarly, annual charges vary from none to as much as 1.5 per cent.

Corporate-style single company PEPs generally offer a monthly savings facility and the minimum for lump sums can be as low as £300. Managed and self-select plans are mainly geared to lump-sum investments, from £500 to the full £3000.

Single company PEPs have most appeal for those who have a large amount of money to invest and want to maximise their tax allowances, or for employees acquiring shares in their own company. For the average investor, putting £3000 into the shares of just one company carries a high level of risk, even with the tax advantages, and a general PEP should certainly be considered first.

Choosing a PEP

The first step in choosing a PEP is to decide on the type of plan that you want. Broadly speaking, advisory and self-select PEPs are for the more experienced investor, corporate and single company PEPs are for the specialist, while managed PEPs suit a range of types, from the more cautious seeking the safer spread offered by unit and investment trusts to the more adventurous seeking to invest in equities but preferring to leave the decisions to a professional. Once you have decided on the type that suits you

Personal Equity Plans

With ShareLink, one size fits all – we offer the most flexible self-select PEP in the country. That's because you can tailor our Premier PEP to fit your particular needs. For example, you can choose how and when to invest – with a lump sum every now and then, or through a regular savings scheme. We also make it easy for you to transfer shares you already own into your PEP. And, as market conditions change, you can adjust your portfolio to suit your circumstances. You even have the option of taking a tax-free income from your Premier PEP. One thing you won't have to adjust is your purse strings. From as little as £4 to a maximum of £30* per quarter, ShareLink's charges won't eat into your investments. We're open seven days a week, so call now and find out about the PEP that lets you breathe more easily.

Our PEP adjusts to fit your circumstances.

0121 233 9955

SHARELINK
Helping investors help themselves.

*Plus VAT

Issued by ShareLink Limited, a member firm of the London Stock Exchange, an Inland Revenue approved plan manager and regulated by SFA. The levels and bases of taxation may change.

DTG

Lump-Sum Investment

best, there are various other considerations which may help to narrow the field.

Growth versus income
This distinction applies chiefly to managed PEPs. With advisory and self-select plans, you can simply pick the investments that match your requirements, and corporate and single company plans can also encompass either strategy, depending on the particular share chosen. However, it is worth checking on the plan's procedure for dealing with dividends. If you are looking for a regular income, you may want to receive the dividends as they are paid, so check that this is possible, without an exorbitant charge being levied. Conversely, if you are looking primarily for growth, you are better off with a plan that will reinvest the dividends automatically without a new set of initial or dealing charges.

Managed PEPs may also offer a choice between income and growth objectives, but some are specifically set up for one or the other. It is sometimes said that smaller investors will get more benefit from an income PEP, primarily for tax reasons: few people pay capital gains tax anyway, and over the shorter term, the income tax benefits will be more visible and immediate.

However, the choice depends very much on your investment aims and any other holdings you have in addition to the PEP. For instance, if you require a measure of income, then it will usually make sense to hold income-producing investments within a PEP, to benefit from the tax shelter, particularly if your other investments are not large enough to make capital gains tax a concern. Beware, however, of simply choosing the PEP showing the highest current yield. Often this will be achieved only at the expense of opportunities for capital growth and increasing income in the future, which can prove much more valuable.

If you are not looking for income, but simply want to accumulate capital for future use, then a growth PEP may be more suitable. Even if capital gains tax is not a problem today, the regime could change in the future, and over the medium to long term you can build up a sizeable sum in a PEP which would then be protected against any such changes. Growth PEPs can also be useful to meet specific financial needs in the future, such as

>
> For more than 200 years the Royal School for the Blind, Liverpool, has been teaching the visually impaired and now claims the enviable reputation as one of the leading institutions of its kind in the world. Over the years the school has been involved in all facets of education of the blind but its present role is the education of blind and multi-sensory impaired children between the ages of 2 and 19 years, who have moderate to severe learning difficulties and additional disabilities. Our children can come from all over the country but are mainly from the North West and are either day pupils or weekly boarders.
>
> We are presently engaged in a large scheme of redevelopment and extension of our existing facilities to improve the degree of excellence and to enable us to accept more children.
>
> Please help us to give our children the best start in life that we are able to give them. We are greatly dependent on voluntary contributions. Pleae give what you can – a donation, legacy or deed of covenant.
>
> Remember "You can see what the children need – they can not."
>
> **The Royal School for the Blind, Liverpool**
> Church Road North, Wavertree, Liverpool L15 6TQ.
> Tel: 0151 733 1012   Fax: 0151 733 1703

paying for school or higher education fees, or boosting retirement income.

Charges and services

Charges on the plan are obviously an important factor as they will eat up a portion of the profits made. As mentioned, unit trust PEPs generally add nothing to the underlying charges on the trusts held, but with share PEPs in particular, there is a danger that the additional running costs of the plan could outweigh the tax gains.

In the past couple of years, a number of unit trust and investment trust plan managers have reduced or abolished the initial charge on their plans. In several cases, this has been combined with the introduction of an 'exit' fee if you take your money out, which applies on a reducing scale for the first three to five years.

If you keep up the plan beyond the exit fee period it can be very attractive, as the initial charge may be only 2 per cent or less,

Lump-Sum Investment

instead of the usual 5–6 per cent. But if you need to take your money out suddenly, you can face a penalty of up to 4.5 per cent. In almost all cases this is based on the current value of the plan, so if it has grown since the outset the total charge will be more than if you had paid a normal up-front fee.

The plan managers argue that PEPs should be viewed as a medium- to long-term investment. With a lower initial fee, more money is invested at the outset, which should lead to higher returns. But over longer periods, the recurring annual management fee can have a greater impact on returns, so you should check that this has not been bumped up to compensate for a lower initial charge.

On top of initial, annual and dealing fees, there are a number of others that can crop up. A few plans make a charge for collecting or paying out dividends. A more common extra is a charge for investors to attend shareholders' meetings, where they are entitled to do so. This can be as much as £100 a time, which is a substantial sum if you hold five or six shares and want to go to all the meetings.

Charges may also reflect the services provided. Commonly, statements and valuations of the plan holdings will be sent out half-yearly, but it may be more frequent and there may also be newsletters and reports. Most important is the quality of administration and this can only be tested by experience. It is now possible to transfer from one PEP manager to another, so you should not be afraid to vote with your feet if you are not satisfied with the service you are getting, but again there may be a charge made to transfer out, in or both.

Past performance
Corporate PEPs, and single company plans where the same holding is maintained, can be judged by the track record of the company concerned but managed PEPs, and particularly those investing in shares, are so diverse that comparisons would not be on a like-with-like basis.

With unit trusts and investment trusts, you can check the track records of individual trusts and of the management group generally. As the saying goes, past performance is not necessarily a guide to the future, and today's league leaders are not always the heroes of tomorrow, but a consistent past record is a reasonable indication of potential. Other points to consider are the overall investment philosophy of the plan manager; whether the attitude to risk broadly accords with your own; how actively the plan will be managed; and the degree of commitment to PEPs – whether they are viewed as an important part of a company's business or just a sideline.

PEP facilities

Share exchange
A number of PEP managers offer share exchange schemes through which you can convert existing holdings of shares into a PEP investment in different shares, unit trusts or investment trusts. This is particularly useful if you have small holdings, such as privatisation issues, that would be expensive to sell through normal channels, as the charges are usually low and in some cases the scheme is free.

PEP mortgages
A number of lenders will now accept a PEP as a repayment vehicle for a mortgage in place of the more standard endowment and pension contracts. They can offer greater flexibility, but, of course, there is no guarantee of the eventual proceeds, so lenders may be quite fussy over the plans they will approve. As a rule they will expect you to make regular savings into the PEP, rather than occasional lump sums.

Keeping track of your investment

Prices of unit trusts, investment trusts and shares are quoted in newspapers such as *The Daily Telegraph* and *The Financial Times*. This can give you a general idea of how your investments are performing, although the actual value of the PEP may be affected by additional charges. More accurate information will be given in the statements and valuations sent out by the plan manager, usually at half-yearly intervals, and they may also provide reports on the companies or trusts included in the plan, plus newsletters or commentaries on the investment strategy.

Lump-Sum Investment

Where to find out more

Chase de Vere publishes the *PEP Guide*, which currently lists 1190 plans from over 200 managers. Listings include the investment aim of the plan, the minimum investments accepted, the various charges and facilities such as share exchange. There is also a quarterly supplement which gives performance figures and annualised growth rates for qualifying and non-qualifying unit and investment trusts and companies that currently make up the FT-SE 100 Share Index. The *PEP Guide* costs £12.95 and can be obtained from Chase de Vere, 63 Lincoln's Inn Fields, London WC2A 3JX, telephone 0171 404 5766.

On the second Saturday of every month, *The Daily Telegraph* publishes a performance table covering all the major unit trust and investment trust PEPs, showing performance over one, three and five years. There are also regular articles on PEPs in the personal finance pages.

Phone ShareLink for a PEP talk on 0121 233 9955.

10

Life Assurance and Friendly Society Investments

Within the last generation, life assurance companies have become sizeable players in the savings market. This is not to say that they have abandoned their traditional role of supplying straightforward protection products such as term assurance, or the savings-plus-protection vehicles such as endowment plans. In fact, this range has been expanding, with the introduction of the likes of critical illness insurance and long-term care plans.

But the fact remains that insurance is generally sold rather than bought, so to maintain a healthy flow of new business, insurance companies have been broadening their horizons in the investment field. Many have associated unit trust companies, but they are also competing for lump-sum investments with their own products.

This chapter looks at the main types on offer. Single premium bonds are a version of collective investments, like unit and investment trusts, that provide smaller investors with a stake in a large portfolio of assets, thereby spreading risk. Annuities are income-producing vehicles and are also put to use in 'hybrid' plans, which aim to produce a fixed level of income plus the prospect of capital growth. They therefore offer greater opportunities than fixed capital investments such as building society accounts, but with a measure of capital risk.

Second-hand endowments are policies which have been sold by their original holders and provide a lump-sum route into what is traditionally a regular savings product. Fourthly, the chapter

Lump-Sum Investment

AS BRITAIN'S longest registered company, MGM Assurance has been helping policyholders with their financial problems since 1852. Originally founded to provide life assurance for Victorian mariners and ships' officers (hence its full name Marine & General Mutual Life Assurance Society), the company has since grown into a modern, innovative financial services organisation offering a wide range of other products including pensions and investment plans.

When it comes to investing money, MGM's City-based fund management team never lose sight of the fact that it is policyholders' money they are investing. Their investment philosophy is both disciplined and research-based, seeking to add long term value through modest short term out-performance. Out-performing the market indices on a year on year basis will, the team believe, translate into significant long term out-performance.

The success of this approach is evidenced by the performance of MGM's fund and the team picked up several prestigious investment awards during 1995.

Investors can take advantage of MGM's investment expertise through a range of quality products, such as the MGM Capital Investment Bond, the MGM With Profits Bond (Series 3) and the MGM Personal Equity Plan.

Recognising the fact that many investors, particularly those with capital held on deposit, welcome the prospect of the higher returns offered by as asset-backed investments (e.g. equities or property) but are reluctant to give up the security of a bank or building society, MGM recently launched the MGM Millennium Bond.

A with profits investment, the Millennium Bond gives individuals access to the potential returns of asset-backed investments, but also offers the degree of security offered by the with profits formula. In addition, the bond offers a cast iron guarantee that investors can withdraw all of their original capital (less any withdrawal) plus growth on the fourth policy anniversary, irrespective of market conditions. In other words, even if the stock markets were to crash the bond can be encashed and the capital is fully protected.

To find out more about the Millennium Bond, or for further information on how MGM Assurance can help you invest for your future, contact your financial adviser or call MGM direct on 01903 204631.

Please bear in mind the value of investments is not guaranteed and may fluctuate.

Life Assurance and Friendly Society Investments

MGM Assurance

We've managed to out-perform *again!*

FACT When it comes to performance, the MGM Managed Fund is in a class of its own, achieving growth in 1995 of 16.1% and beating the sector average by nearly 2.5%.

FACT This kind of out-performance is certainly no flash in the pan. Since it was launched in 1983 the same fund has achieved an impressive annual growth of 11.8% pa, and currently sits comfortably amongst the top ten funds in its sector.

Annualised growth since 1983

10.3%	Sector Average
11.8%	MGM Managed Fund

FACT Some people will miss out on this kind of top quality performance during 1996. Make sure you're not one of them, speak to your financial adviser or call 01903 204631 to find out more about MGM's award winning investment performance.

MGM
assurance Britain's longest registered company.

Source: Micropal, offer-offer basis, calculated 2/1/95 and 14/11/83 to 2/1/96.
Past performance is not necessarily a guide to the future.
MGM Assurance and MGM Unit Managers Ltd are regulated by PIA and IMRO.

Lump-Sum Investment

looks at friendly societies, which have similarities with life assurance companies but certain tax advantages.

Finally, there is a review of health insurance products. While these are obviously not investments as such, they can protect your ability to enjoy the fruits of your investments.

Single premium bonds

Single premium bonds – so-called because they are based on a one-off contribution – offer a broad investment choice and a spread of risk for sums starting at around £1000. Although technically they include an element of life assurance, it is relatively small – often it is simply the current bid value of the bond. This means that the investment potential is maximised rather than money being siphoned off to pay for life cover.

The bonds can be invested in a wide range of underlying funds operated by the company. These are similar to the various categories of unit trusts; for example, there are equity funds covering the UK, North America, Europe, Japan and the Far East, as well as broadly based international funds. There are also types that are not found among unit trusts, such as managed funds, with profits funds, currency funds and, to a large extent, property funds.

Managed funds invest in a mixture of equities, fixed interest securities and property, thus giving the widest possible spread of assets and risk. For this reason, they are the most popular, appealing both to very conservative investors and to those who prefer to leave all the investment decisions to a professional. There can, however, be considerable differences between one managed fund and the next, depending on the investment strategy adopted.

Essentially, there are two types: those which have a more or less set division between equities, fixed interest and property, which are sometimes called 'three-way' or balanced funds; and those where the manager takes a more active role in determining the proportions. A fairly recent trend is to offer more than one managed fund with differing degrees of risk; for example, Adventurous, Balanced and Cautious (or Conservative). The Adventurous fund will have a higher proportion in equities, which carry the highest risk/reward prospects, while the Cautious fund will lean more towards fixed interest securities.

In theory, a more actively managed fund should produce a better return by responding to changes in market conditions, but equally there is more scope for wrong decisions. The three-way fund, on the other hand, is likely to produce steadier, if unexciting, returns. Some examples of the past performance of managed funds are shown in Table 10.1.

In the late 1980s and early 1990s, property funds were in the doldrums, thanks to the sliding fortunes of the property market, and many shrank considerably in size. But from mid-1993 performance started to improve, as demand increased with the upturn in the economy. At the time of writing, expectations are for steady, if not spectacular, growth in both the commercial and residential sectors.

The drawback of property funds is that they are unwieldy – property cannot always be sold readily, so the portfolio cannot easily be adjusted to changing market conditions. Managers also reserve the right to delay making repayments to investors for up to six months, to avoid having to sell at a loss to raise cash quickly. In practice, this has only ever been imposed on funds invested in residential property, while the bulk focus on commercial property. Smaller funds are often invested instead in the shares of property companies, which are more tradable, although the returns are subject to different influences.

With profits funds, like managed funds, are invested in a mix of assets, but instead of the value of your holding depending on the value of investments in the underlying fund, with profits funds

Table 10.1 *Past performance of managed funds*

Percentage increase in fund value over different periods			
	1 year	3 years	5 years
Best	35.0	66.9	179.4
Average	19.2	31.8	65.3
Worst	4.0	10.3	23.8

Note: Figures to 29 February 1996, on an offer-to-offer price basis.

Source: HSW

work by adding bonuses. The bonus rate is declared annually and depends on the investment profits made by the fund, but a part of these is usually held in reserve to boost rates in bad years. So there should be a 'smoothing' effect on market fluctuations, which reduces the risk. Some companies set a minimum guaranteed bonus rate and there may also be a terminal bonus, although this is not guaranteed.

Companies also reserve the right to make a 'market value adjustment' when money is paid out or switched to another fund. This would arise if the actual investment performance has not matched up to the value that has been credited, and is designed to protect continuing investors in the fund. Although this is likely to apply only in the early years – and is not normally applied on death – it does detract from the apparent safety of these funds.

Taxation

The taxation of bonds is governed by the rules applying to life assurance companies. As regards the underlying fund, this will pay tax on investment income and is also subject to capital gains tax on profits from the disposal of assets, hence the fund will set aside a reserve against future liabilities. The tax paid by the fund cannot be reclaimed, which is a major drawback for non-taxpayers.

Basic rate taxpayers have no tax worries on their own score – their liabilities are covered by what the fund has already paid. For higher rate taxpayers, however, it is a different – and rather complex – story. To start with the good news, up to 5 per cent of the original investment can be withdrawn from the bond, free of tax, each year for 20 years – this counts as being a return of capital. If the allowance is not used every year, it can be carried over, so if, for instance, you take nothing out in the first year, you have 10 per cent to play with in the second, and so on. The bad news comes at the end, when you cash in the investment. Tax is then assessed by a procedure known as 'top-slicing'. First, the total profit made from the bond is calculated, taking into account any withdrawals that have already been made, and the resulting amount is divided by the number of years for which the bond has been held. This figure is then added to your income for the year

in which you cash in the bond to determine if you are liable to higher rate tax. If so, the higher rate will be applied to the whole of the profit made, and you will have to pay the difference between that and the basic rate tax which has already been paid.

There are two ways to mitigate the tax bill. If you can, you should put off cashing in the bond until a year when you are a basic rate taxpayer – after retirement, perhaps. Then you will have no further liability. You should also opt for the bond to be split into separate segments, each of which is effectively a policy in its own right; some companies do this automatically, others may do it on demand. The advantage is that, if you want to withdraw more than the 5 per cent allowance, you can cash in all of one segment, which gets more favourable tax treatment than making a partial withdrawal above the limit.

Bonds versus unit trusts

Bonds and unit trusts have certain similar characteristics – both offer low-cost access to pooled funds and charges are comparable. Hence there has long been debate about their respective merits for investors.

One drawback of bonds is that capital gains tax is paid by the life assurance company on profits within the bond. With unit trusts, the capital gains tax liability falls on the investor, which means it only arises when you cash in and then you can make use of the annual exempt allowance, currently £6000 for the 1995/96 tax year.

Against this, the returns from a bond are treated as having had basic rate tax already paid, whereas in practice the charge incurred by the insurance company may be well below 25 per cent. Hence the returns may be higher than could be achieved on unit trusts. There is also the annual 5 per cent tax-free withdrawal allowance, which is useful for higher rate taxpayers. If you can cash in at a time when you are subject only to basic rate, and if you are also already using your capital gains tax allowance on other investments, bonds can be tax-efficient.

However, unit trusts can be held within a personal equity plan, which offers complete exemption from both income and capital gains tax for investments of up to £6000 a year. If you have not

Life Assurance and Friendly Society Investments

For Worldwide Growth Potential ...

PERFORMANCE BOND

The offshore investment offering a unique approach to fund management

Irish Life International, Irish Life Centre, Lower Abbey Street, Dublin 1, Ireland
Telephone: +353 1 704 1500 Facsimile: +353 1 704 1922

Irish Life International is authorised to conduct business within the Dublin International Financial Services Centre.
This product is not available to residents of the Republic of Ireland.
Holders of policies issued by the company will not be protected by the Policy Holders Protection Act 1975 if the company should become unable to meet its liabilities to them. Some fund management activities are carried on by Irish Life Assurance plc, which does not act independently of Irish Life International Ltd.
Irish Life International Ltd. is incorporated in the Republic of Ireland No. 218391 (not maintaining a permanent place of business in the United Kingdom) and is a member of the Irish Life Marketing Group which is a life, pensions and investment organisation. Other members are: Irish Life Assurance plc (incorporated in the Republic of Ireland and registered in England and Wales as a branch No. BR001381) City of Westminster Assurance Company Ltd. registered in England and Wales No. 925554.
All members are regulated by the Personal Investment Authority.

already used this allowance, it should be a prime consideration.

The other main attraction of bonds is the facility to switch between different underlying funds at low cost and without any tax liability. If you move from one unit trust to another, there may be a capital gains tax liability and you will have to pay a new front-end charge; even with a discount offered for staying with the same management group, this is likely to be at least 2 per cent. Bonds generally offer one or more free switches per year, after which there is a small charge of perhaps 0.5 per cent. Of course, you are restricted by the range of funds offered by the company, and it is unlikely that any single company will top the investment tables across the board.

For different investors' needs and circumstances, one or other product is likely to have the edge, so it is a good idea to seek advice before you commit yourself.

Variations on the bond theme

Guaranteed equity bonds

Guaranteed equity investments are a fairly recent innovation, born out of the disillusion with the stock market of many smaller investors after the 1987 crash. At first sight, they seem to be the perfect investment: they guarantee to return a high percentage of any increase in a given stock market index over the investment period, or your original capital if the index should fall.

However, you need to check the small print to be quite sure what you are being promised, as there are a number of variations on the theme. The investment period is commonly five years; if you take your money out before then, you normally forfeit the guarantee and there may be early surrender penalties as well. So if the market starts falling just before the end of the period, you could lose all the gains made up to then. Some products have a periodic 'lock-in' facility, whereby gains to date are consolidated into the guarantee; while others average the index value over the last 6 or 12 months, to protect against a last-minute fall.

In several cases, the guarantee applies only to the capital growth in the index, which means the income from share dividends is sacrificed. Over longer periods, this can be quite a lot to give up.

The message is that guarantees only come at a price, but these

Life Assurance and Friendly Society Investments

FRIENDLY SOCIETIES
...tax-free savings from £10 a month

Friendly societies give you and your family a unique opportunity for tax-free savings.

And now the Government has raised the amount you can save. You can start a 10 year plan with Homeowners Friendly Society from just £10 a month – but if you want to maximise your tax-free savings, you can save up to £25 a month.

So if you wish to benefit from the investment expertise of one of the UK's top friendly societies and take advantage of your new tax-free savings allowance, call Homeowners now FREE on 0800 210 270 or return the coupon, no stamp needed. You'll receive a FREE Sheaffer Pen along with your Action pack.

FREE Sheaffer Pen
Yours just for finding out more!

PJ   **PHONE FREE OR POST THE COUPON TODAY. NO STAMP NEEDED**
PHONE FREE   0800 210 270   PHONE NOW

PLEASE QUOTE   **PDT361**

The Government limits the amount each individual can save tax-free with a friendly society. But everyone in your household, including your children, can have a friendly society tax-free savings plan. So we can send you details appropriate to your circumstances, please complete the following:

Title _____ Forename _____
Surname _____
Address _____
_____ Postcode _____
Daytime Tel. No.   Your Date
(inc STD code)* _____   of Birth ___ / ___ / ___
* So that we may call and offer further information.

No. of adults in your household ☐   No. of children under 10 years ☐
The Society will not make your name and address available to unconnected organisations. Naturally, we will tell you about other investments offered by ourselves and associated organisations. If you would prefer not to receive this information, please tick this box. ☐

HFS   HOMEOWNERS FRIENDLY SOCIETY LIMITED
REGULATED BY THE PERSONAL INVESTMENT AUTHORITY.
Post to: Homeowners Friendly Society Limited, FREEPOST, Moorfield Road, Yeadon, Leeds LS19 7YY
Registered and incorporated under the Friendly Societies Act 1992. Reg. No 964F
Please remember that the value of your investment can fall as well as rise and you may not get back all you invest.

National Deposit
Friendly Society Limited

Formed in 1868 as the Surrey County Deposit Benefit Club by a group of local worthies led by the Reverend Canon George Portal, the Society was not given its present name until 3 years later, when the expansion of the Membership into nearby counties made it obvious that it would become nationwide – as indeed it rapidly did.

In fact in 1912 a shortage of only 10 votes to achieve the necessary two-thirds majority required at a General Meeting prevented expansion into Canada and a further name change to the International Deposit Friendly Society!

However, the National Deposit continued to expand and played a large part in the administration of State Benefits introduced in the National Insurance Act of 1911 – attracting 450,000 new Members to the Society in the first six months.

Responsibilities in this area carried right through to the implementation of the National Insurance Act in 1948. This introduced what used to be completely free medical treatment – the National Health Service – and many of the Society's staff were transferred to the Ministry to run the service.

During all this time the Membership had been increased – as had the assets of the Society, which are today in excess of £100 million; not a huge sum compared with many commercial companies much younger than us, but one that is of sufficient size to ensure our survival whatever the future holds in store.

The Society has an enviable record of service and stability – over a century and a quarter – and a future that the Membership is determined will be as great as our past.

Let us examine the last sentence again – because it is the Members of the Society who have a say in determining the future direction of the Society. Through over 300 Districts and 30 Divisions, 30 Members are elected to represent the interests of the entire Membership on the Committee of Management. All unpaid and voluntary! Why? Because they care.

Anyone joining the Society, by taking out a plan, can play a part in the management of the Society should they so wish. It is not difficult to imagine the wealth of different skills and experience that are represented on the Management Committee – all of which are directed at improving the conditions for the rest of the Membership.

Few commercial companies could claim that their controlling management was unbiased, not affected by vested interests and only worked for the benefit of the customer! A very rare attitude in this rather materialistic age, but one that characterises the friendly society movement.

As a registered and incorporated Friendly Society we also gain from the advantage that we receive preferential tax treatment in respect of the investment we make on behalf of our Members that fall within the Tax-Exempt limits laid down by government legislation.

Needless to say we constantly update and revise our products to maintain our competitiveness in an ever increasing market place, thereby making sure that our Members continue to benefit from the knowledge that their health and their financial future can be left safely in our hands.

You're never too young and may not be too old

to benefit from tax exempt saving

Why not benefit from the preferential tax treatment received by Friendly Societies by investing a lump sum, or regular monthly or annual contributions, into a National Deposit Savings Plan?

A National Deposit 10 year With-Profits Savings Plan maturing in 1995 showed an annual return of just over 13 per cent per annum – equivalent to a gross investment return of over 17 per cent!* (Based on a male aged 29 at outset in 1985 contributing £35 a month over the 10 year period.)

WHO CAN HAVE ONE?
Anyone in good health – including children – up to the age of 70 next birthday.

The Society is run by a Committee of Management consisting of Members (policyholders) solely for the benefit of the Members. Although the Society is now incorporated, there are no shareholders, all surpluses being passed back to the Members by way of enhanced benefits.

For details, dial 100 and ask for FREEPHONE NATIONAL DEPOSIT or write to us at the address on the right.

*Past performance is not necessarily a guide to future performance.

National Deposit
Friendly Society Limited

A proud past – a secure future

National Deposit Friendly Society Limited
FREEPOST, 4-5 Worcester Road, Clifton,
Bristol BS8 3JL.
Telephone: (0117) 973 9003
Fax: (0117) 974 1367
Registered Friendly Society No. 369F
Regulated by the Personal Investment Authority

Any advice or recommendation which is given or offered by this advertisement relates only to the package of products of National Deposit Friendly Society Limited.

bonds can be attractive for short periods if you are nervous of stock market movements. For larger sums, though – say, £10,000 upwards – you could put together your own package to offset risk, so it is worth taking independent advice.

High income bonds

These are another fairly recent idea, stemming in this case from the plunge in interest rates during 1993 which was a severe blow to building society investors dependent on income.

The bonds generally run for five years, during which time they offer a guaranteed level of income – recently, this has tended to be between 8 and 10 per cent a year. They also offer a guarantee on the capital return at the end of the term; this varies a little from bond to bond, but is commonly such that the total return, including all the income received, will be not less than the original investment.

The bonds use quite sophisticated derivative instruments to provide the guarantees, but in essence what happens is this. Part of the original capital is siphoned off to provide the ongoing income, while the rest is invested with the hope that, over the five years, it will grow enough to replace the full original sum, in addition to the income paid, or perhaps even show a profit.

In other words, capital is being sacrificed up-front to provide income, but there is the potential for it to be replaced through investment growth and in the worst case, if the stock market falls, there is a guarantee that you will get back your original investment less the income you have already been paid.

The bonds have attracted a fair amount of criticism, focusing on the concepts of 'income' and 'guarantee'. First, it is argued that the payments made are not truly income, because they are made from capital. Second, the capital guarantee has been called misleading, as it provides for a return of your initial investment *including* the income already paid, not in addition to it. As a result, the regulatory authorities have laid down strict rules on how the bonds should be described in advertisements and product literature and the warnings that should be given.

Certainly you should make sure you know exactly what you are being promised. If the stock market falls, and you get back only the minimum amount guaranteed, you will effectively have lost out on the interest you could have earned meanwhile from a building society account, which would also have preserved your capital intact.

But if, say, you need a 10 per cent annual return to live on, and a building society account is paying only 5 per cent, you would need to draw on your capital anyway. The advantage of a bond in this case is that there is the opportunity for capital growth to replace what you spend, whereas with a building society your capital would simply dwindle.

What you should check is the required annual rate of return on the bond to get back your original capital in addition to the income paid. This will vary from bond to bond, depending on the exact structure and the economic conditions at the time the derivatives are bought, plus the level of income offered. The greater the income, the higher the rate of growth required to pay back all the capital, so there is a trade-off between the income you receive and the chance of getting back your full investment or showing a profit.

Another point to bear in mind is that the money is generally locked in for the full term: withdrawals may be banned completely or very restricted, possibly invalidating the guarantees.

Distribution bonds
These are bonds designed to pay out the dividends accumulated by the underlying fund, so that investors can receive an income without cashing in holdings. They tend to focus on UK equities and gilts, which offer higher dividends than overseas securities.

The income is free of tax for basic rate taxpayers, and also for higher rate payers as long as it is within the 5 per cent annual allowance. But they share with other bonds the drawback that the fund itself is liable to capital gains tax and income tax, which cannot be reclaimed by those not liable.

Personalised bonds
These are bonds which allow you to have your own choice of investments held within the medium of a bond. They are designed for sizeable investments – around £50,000 upwards – which would normally be managed by a stockbroker. Personalised bonds enjoyed some popularity when the top tax rate was 60 per

Lump-Sum Investment

You don't need to start an endowment policy to enjoy the benefits

With-profits endowment policies are one of the most popular forms of saving in the UK. They comprise a basic sum assured to which reversionary bonuses earned each year are added and these cannot be taken away. This makes them a very secure investment.

Unfortunately, circumstances such as being made redundant or needing to clear debts frequently force policyholders to cash them in early and the amount offered back by the Life Office is often significantly less than the policy's full value. This differential provides an opportunity – both for investors to acquire an investment in a mid-term policy with guaranteed bonuses which have accumulated over the years, and for policyholders to sell their policies for a higher cash sum.

When an investor buys a Traded Endowment Policy (TEP) they pay the purchase price and take over the payment of premiums. The policy is legally assigned to them which entitles them to all future benefits under the policy at maturity or the earlier death of the life assured (life cover is not transferred, but remains on the original policyholder).

TEPs provide an appealing way to save regularly and policies are available with levels of premium to suit all investors. They are increasingly being used for retirement planning either within a pension fund or in addition to existing pension arrangements. They are also ideal to provide for school/university fees or special gifts, for example for weddings or 18th/21st birthdays. In the past policies were selected by their maturity date so that a cash lump sum was available on a particular date. This is no longer necessary as policies can be re-traded at any time prior to maturity to suit the investor.

It is the combination of the qualities of TEPs which make them an attractive and unique investment. Particularly important to investors who are averse to risk is that they have a Guaranteed Minimum Value at maturity (the sum assured and attaching bonuses which cannot be taken away). But low risk does not have to mean low returns. TEPs have the potential to provide an excellent investment return because they are invested primarily in stocks and shares which gives them the strongest opportunity for asset growth. Unlike direct investment in the stock market, however, their value does not constantly fluctuate. This is because returns are "actuarially smoothed" by the Life Offices which means that a small portion of the profits of the stock market's growth from good years is kept in reserve to pay out in years when returns may not be so good. In this way peaks and troughs are avoided and the policy's value grows steadily. Another extremely attractive benefit is that in many cases, the payout can be entirely free of tax.

Beale Dobie is the most experienced market maker in TEPs and is part of the Hambro Group of Companies. It is committed to the highest standards of investment work and, uniquely in the TEP market, employs two qualified Actuaries to ensure that the valuation of policies is carried out meticulously.

Policies have been bought and sold by assignment for over 150 years but until 1989 buyers and sellers had to attend an auction. Now policies can be traded very easily through market makers like Beale Dobie, the leading company in this field.

Every fortnight Beale Dobie issues a list of around 150 TEPs for sale. Policies issued by the majority of the well established UK Life Offices are on offer with prices from £2,000 to £200,000.

If you would like to find out more about investing in TEPs, Beale Dobie publishes a guide which is free on request on 01621 851133.

Life Assurance and Friendly Society Investments

TEPs:
a unique investment.

A Traded Endowment Policy (TEP) is a with profits policy part-way through its term with attaching bonuses and a Guaranteed Minimum Value. They are suitable investments either to hold to maturity or re-trade at any time in the future prior to maturity.

Potential for excellent returns – often tax free
As TEPs are primarily invested in stocks and shares they participate in the long term growth of the stockmarket. And in many cases the payout can be entirely free of tax.*

Low risk
Their Guaranteed Minimum Value which often equates to, and sometimes exceeds, their purchase price makes them very secure investments.

Equity invested by the UK's most experienced fund managers
The investment expertise of the Life Office fund managers provides the strongest opportunity for asset growth.

For a free guide to investment in TEPs and our latest list of policies for sale, write to us or call us.

This investment is not suitable for everyone. If you have any doubt about whether it is suitable for you, you should seek expert advice. Levels and bases of, and reliefs from, taxation are subject to change.*

Telephone 01621 851133 Fax 01621 850724

Beale Dobie & Company Limited, Dept. KP41BF, Fullbridge Mill, Maldon, Essex, CM9 5FN.

Beale **Dobie**
& Company Limited

A Member of the
Hambro Insurance Services Group PLC

AP
MM
Regulated by the Personal
Investment Authority

Lump-Sum Investment

cent, as the bond environment offers tax protection for investment income. Now that tax rates have fallen, this market has gone quiet, but there are still a few offers available.

Broker bonds

Broker bonds are offered by a number of independent financial advisers, not necessarily insurance brokers as the name suggests. They had their origin in the early 1980s, when advisers who managed bond funds on behalf of clients used the power of proxy to make block switches instead of making the same move individually for each client.

Broker bonds have moved on a long way since then. The concept is that clients' money is pooled into one fund, which the adviser will manage, moving it between underlying funds to make the most of current market conditions. These funds can be 'fettered', meaning they are invested with just one life company, or 'unfettered', which means they can be invested across a number of companies, depending on where the adviser sees the best prospects. The latter are more common and offer greater scope for the adviser to give added value, compared with an individual bond.

The advantages of a broker bond are that you have your investment professionally managed, without being required to approve every move, but still have access to the person doing the managing, which would not be the case if, say, you simply put your money into a life company's managed fund. In return, you will be faced with an extra layer of charges levied by the adviser.

So will performance justify the extra cost? Anyone offering a broker bond must be authorised to do so, and life companies are responsible both for vetting the advisers in the first place and for monitoring their performance. There are, however, no rules on what action should be taken if an adviser fails to achieve performance bench-marks, so you should always satisfy yourself as to the adviser's track record.

Annuities

Annuities are a means of transforming capital into income. The basic concept is simple: you pay a lump sum to a life assurance company and in return you get an income, at a predetermined level, for the rest of your life. A basic annuity is irrevocable; once you have given up your capital, you cannot have it back.

Annuities operate rather like a mirror image of life assurance. Instead of paying out a lump sum when you die, they pay an income until you die. So the older you are, the fewer payments are anticipated and the higher the rate will be. For this reason, annuities are not normally suitable for anyone under about 65; the income offered would be too low to justify giving up the capital for good.

The income from an annuity is taxable, but only in part. A portion of it is treated as being a return of your original capital, and is therefore tax-free, while the rest will be taxed as income at your normal rate. The capital element is determined by scales laid down by the Inland Revenue, based on your age; the older you are, the shorter the likely payment period, so a higher proportion of the return will be treated as capital. However, new scales were brought in at the beginning of 1992 – previously they were based on mortality tables that were around 40 years old, when life expectancy was lower than it is today. The new scales reduced the capital element for any given age, making the after-tax return rather less attractive than before. Examples of current rates are shown in Table 10.2. One exception to this tax rule is an annuity bought with money from a pension fund. This is known as a 'compulsory purchase annuity', because you are obliged to buy it (though you may still have a choice of companies to buy it from), and it is wholly taxable as income. Ordinary annuities that you buy voluntarily are called 'purchased life annuities'.

Variations of annuities

The main failing of a basic annuity is that it dies with you. To take an extreme example, if you handed over £100,000 and died the very next day, your estate would be £100,000 the poorer and the insurance company equally the richer. For insurance companies, premature deaths make up for clients who live unexpectedly long, but for your heirs it could be a serious blow.

There are several ways of overcoming this problem. First, the annuity can be guaranteed for a certain period, such as five or ten years. Payments will then be continued for that time, regardless

Lump-Sum Investment

———— Advertisement Feature ————

Savers still missing out

Amazingly, the majority of taxpayers in the UK are still unaware of the considerable tax-saving opportunities provided by friendly society savings plans – even though they have been around for years.

Even fewer savers seem to know they can invest a lump sum in a highly tax-efficient way by taking out such a plan. In fact, the Government allows up to £270 a year to be put into a 10 year friendly society scheme, with all capital growth and cash returns accorded tax-free status.

Everyone can take advantage, regardless of their age or any other tax-free investments held. So a friendly society plan perfectly complements a PEP or TESSA.

Friendly society brings you tax-free benefits

Family Assurance, the UK's largest tax-exempt friendly society with over 660,000 members, offers a choice of plans for savers seeking the ideal way to provide for future family needs. Both the Family and Junior Bond aim for a balance of growth and security, with flexibility in the level of lump sum you can invest. And both plans pay out tax-free cash after 10 years – or the term of the Junior Bond can be extended to pay out on a child's 18th, 21st or 25th birthday. Please remember that investment values can fall as well as rise.

You get extra reassurance knowing that Family Assurance is committed to achieving good fund performance combined with low charges. And when you join the UK leader, you're a member for life.

Don't miss out any longer. To find out more about providing for your family or giving a special child a great start in life, call Family Assurance free on 0800 616695.

Family Assurance Friendly Society Limited is regulated by the Personal Investment Authority and incorporated under the Friendly Societies Act 1992 (Reg. No. 939F).

Life Assurance and Friendly Society Investments

Invest a lump sum in your family's future – TAX-FREE

- Save with the UK's leading tax-exempt friendly society
- Go for tax-free growth in a 10 year Family Assurance Bond
- Available even if you have a PEP or TESSA
- Tax-free cash payable at end of term
- The ideal way to provide for your family's future.

Please remember that investment values can fall as well as rise.

Post the coupon to: Family Assurance Friendly Society Limited, FREEPOST 2206, 16-17 West Street, Brighton BN1 2BR.

Call FREE on 0800 616695

LEADING THE WAY IN FAMILY FINANCE

Please send me details of your ☐ Family Bond ☐ Junior Bond. *Please tick.*

Mr/Mrs/Miss/Ms First Name _____

Surname _____

Address _____

Postcode _____ Tel No _____

Date of Birth __ / __ / __

Post the coupon to: Family Assurance Friendly Society Limited, FREEPOST 2206, 16-17 West Street, Brighton BN1 2BR.

We may send information to you about other products offered by the Society. If you do not wish to receive this information, please tick here. ☐

We may telephone you as part of our customer service programme. If you do not wish to be contacted in this way, please tick here. ☐

Family Assurance Friendly Society Limited is regulated by the Personal Investment Authority and incorporated under the Friendly Societies Act 1992 (Reg. No. 939F).

REQUEST CODE 13924

Lump-Sum Investment

of whether you die sooner. In practice, if the annuity-holder dies, the insurance company may offer his heirs the option of commuting remaining payments to a lump sum.

Second, if you are married but have no other dependants, you could opt for a joint life, second death annuity. As the name implies, this will continue paying income until the death of the second partner.

Third, you can ensure that you (or your estate) at least get back the original outlay through a capital protected annuity. If at your death the income payments so far are less than the purchase price, the insurance company will pay over the difference. All of these options cost money, in that the rate will be reduced, as can be seen in Table 10.2. Rates for women will be lower again, as they have a longer life expectancy.

Annuity rates are also affected by how often the income is paid, whether it is paid in advance or in arrears, and with or without proportion. The latter refers to the position if you die between payment dates – whether or not a proportion of the next payment is made. Obviously, it hardly matters if payments are monthly,

Table 10.2 *Annuity rates*

Purchase price £10,000	Level no guarantee	Level guaranteed 5 years	Escalating 5 per cent, per annum, no guarantee
Male 65, single life	£1138.80	£1111.20	£798.00
Female 65, single life	£1003.44	£985.20	£658.80
Male 75, single life	£1579.20	£1455.60	£1243.20
Female 75, single life	£1330.80	£1275.60	£1000.80
Male 65, female 60, joint life	£899.52	£866.16	£531.00
Male 75, female 70, joint life	£1041.01	£1118.16	£727.20

Note: The table shows gross annual rates assuming payment is monthly in arrears, without proportion.

Source: MoneyFacts, June 1996

but for annual income it could be useful. If you have no heirs and are in no immediate hurry for money, an annuity payable yearly in arrears, without proportion and with no guarantees, would give the best possible rate.

Another drawback of the basic annuity is that the income is fixed for life and therefore vulnerable to inflation. It is possible instead to have an increasing annuity, under which payments rise each year, either by a fixed percentage or in line with, say, the Retail Price Index. Two further, much less common, options are with profits and unit-linked annuities, where the income is linked to an investment fund. This means it is dependent on the fortunes of the stock market, so while the long-term trend should be upwards, it can fluctuate year to year. Both this and the increasing annuity will give a lower income at the outset than the plain level type.

Hybrid plans

One variety not mentioned above is the temporary annuity, which pays out for a fixed period of time rather than for life. These have little application by themselves, but are often used in packaged schemes offered by life companies. Sometimes called 'hybrid' or 'back to back' plans, these combine different products with the aim of providing a reasonable level of income plus the prospect of capital growth.

Plans fall into two types. With one, the lump-sum investment is used to buy a ten-year annuity; payments from this are used to fund the premiums for a ten-year endowment policy, while the surplus provides a running income. At the end of the ten years, the maturing endowment should provide a return of the original capital. With the second type, part of the original lump sum buys a temporary annuity to provide income, while the rest is put into an investment such as a bond, unit trust or personal equity plan, again designed to return at least the original capital at the end of the term.

Some of the packages around now are quite sophisticated. With the second type, for example, you may be able to choose the level of income you want, either by adjusting the amount put into the annuity or by taking additional income from the second investment. But there are two important questions to ask. First, what return would there be if you die during the term? The annuity will normally die with you, so the return may be less than you invested. Second, what rate of growth is needed from the investment to return the original sum, and how realistic is this? Remember that the higher the income you take, the less money will be left to build up capital.

One other point is that the package will usually combine products from the same company, which may not be good for both annuities and investments. You might get a better deal by putting together your own combination from different companies.

Second-hand endowments

These are with profits endowment policies which have been sold by their original holder before maturity owing to a change of circumstances. They can be bought either through auctions or through 'market-makers' – firms which buy up policies to sell on to investors. When you buy a policy the details stay the same – it is still based on the life of the original owner – but you take over responsibility for paying the remaining premiums due. These can usually be commuted to a lump-sum payment, but this is not always beneficial; the discount offered may be negligible and the policy will become non-qualifying in status, which means there may be a tax liability on the maturity proceeds.

While policy auctions have been around for decades, market-makers are a fairly new phenomenon. The market, however, is expanding fast, as selling a policy can give a much better return than the surrender value. For the investor, a second-hand policy can be attractive if you need a lump sum at a specific time in the future; for example, to meet school fees or for retirement.

Policies will normally have run for around two-thirds or more of their total term, so in addition to the basic sum assured they will have built up bonuses which, once they have been allocated, are guaranteed to be paid at maturity. In some cases, the value of the sum assured plus bonuses can be as much as the purchase price, so your profit then depends on the level of bonuses

Life Assurance and Friendly Society Investments

SAILORS' FAMILIES' SOCIETY
NEWLAND, COTTINGHAM ROAD
HULL, HU6 7RJ
TEL: 01482 342331

SAILORS FAMILIES
SOCIETY 1821-1996

The Sailors' Families' Society supports the families of deceased, disabled and distressed seafarers throughout the United Kingdom. Continually, we are taking onto our Support Schemes children who have lost a parent at sea. We provide assistance for their welfare, education and upbringing.

YOU CAN MAKE A WORLD OF DIFFERENCE – Donations and legacies ensure that we can continue to provide for children, widows, disabled and elderly mariners in the years ahead. Tragedies at sea are all too common and we are always there to "Throw out a lifeline". — *Thank you for your support*   Reg. Charity No. 224505

---

allocated during the remainder of the term and the amount of the remaining premiums.

The price is determined by the current value of the policy, its original term and the period remaining, the future premiums and the seller's mark-up. Sellers usually quote an anticipated rate of return at maturity, but whether this will be achieved or not depends on the future pattern of bonus rates. The recent trend has been downward, and since most policies bought have fairly short terms to run – between three and ten years – it is not likely that they will pick up again significantly.

Unless you already have some experience in this area, you would be wise not to buy at auction. Like car auctions, they can offer bargains, but you could equally end up paying over the odds if you lack the specialised knowledge. Similarly, policies issued by 'top name' insurance companies offer the safest prospects though they may not be the cheapest. It is usually worth taking some professional advice.

Lump-Sum Investment

Friendly societies

Friendly societies have been around for a couple of centuries. In some respects their operations resemble those of insurance companies, but on a smaller scale, as they have been subject to tight restrictions on their activities. However, the Friendly Societies Act 1992 has opened the way for expansion and most societies incorporated in 1993. This means that they may own assets directly instead of through trustees and may set up subsidiary companies that can manage unit trust schemes and personal equity plans or do insurance broking. They are also due to be brought under the Policyholders' Protection Act, which has not previously applied to friendly societies.

The societies' chief advantage over insurance companies is that they can issue tax-exempt policies, which invest in funds that are free of income and capital gains tax and pay the proceeds tax-free to the investor. These are ten-year plans designed for regular savings, but many offer a lump-sum version, using an annuity from which payments are drip-fed into the plan over its term.

The bad news is that there is a limit on the premiums that may be paid into these plans and this in turn has meant that charges have tended to be relatively high. However, the 1994 Budget raised the limit to £25 a month or £270 a year, which may allow some leeway on charging. The Budget also proposed to abolish the existing restriction on surrender values, under which, if a plan was surrendered before it had run for three-quarters of its term, the return could be no more than the premiums paid in.

Investors may take out only one plan each, but children are also entitled to have plans, so a family of four will now be able to invest up to £1200 a year through monthly savings. Plans do not always have to cease at the end of ten years: some offer the choice to continue paying premiums or to take an 'income' by making regular withdrawals.

Private health care

What would be the use of the highest return on a lump sum investment if you were not healthy enough to enjoy it – or worse, not around at all?

According to research commissioned by PPP healthcare group, 51 per cent of those polled rated health as their most important priority, ahead of personal relationships and financial security. There is a strong argument for using some of your spare funds to pay for private health care in one form or another to insure a reasonable quality of life. However, as there are several different types of health insurance, it is important to sort out which one is relevant to your needs.

Private Medical Insurance (PMI)

Currently 11 per cent of the population has some form of PMI, a figure which is expected to rise to 50 per cent in the next 35 years. The number of PMI providers is increasing as mainstream insurance companies and foreign firms have joined the traditional private health insurers. There are now 25 providers and between them they offer more than 400 different products.

Products fall into three broad ranges: low cost, middle range and up-market policies. The more you pay, the more coverage you buy. At the top end of the spectrum are plans which include fully comprehensive dental treatment, childbirth, full refund for specialist's fees and out patient treatment. Their annual costs vary from about £600 per year to more than £5000, depending on how old the insured is, where he lives and the scope of the hospitalisation benefits which he chooses.

Lower levels of cover vary with the amount of hospitalisation charges which would be met, whether or not there is an excess which the insured bears in the event of a claim and several other factors. The lowest cost plan included in *Which?* magazine's most recent survey of the market costs £165 per year for a single person aged 29. There is a compulsory excess (undefined), all out-patient and specialist refunds and no maximum hospital costs. But this is only an indicative specification because products, exact prices and terms need to be clarified at the time the policy is taken out.

The choice can be somewhat baffling at first glance as the industry players seek to differentiate themselves and establish competitive advantage. There are also derivative products which have a minimal level of cover or may be intended only to meet the cost of major surgery, dental care, hospital costs or accidental

Lump-Sum Investment

Health Care matters

SOME six million people are currently covered by private medical insurance. Industry experts have forecast that by the millennium this could increase to more than eight million. The majority currently have their premiums paid as part of their employment package. However, the greatest growth is among those paying their own premiums out of taxed income.

There is, of course, no investment element in medical insurance. This means that its sale is not subject to the stringent regulations governing financial services. Currently it is classified as General Insurance and so falls within the Association of British Insurers' code of practice, in the same way as motor and household cover. The Office of Fair Trading has been looking into the selling of health insurance and its report should have appeared by the time this is published.

Until a few years ago the market was shared by the Provident Associations and there was little apparent competition. One Insurer had some sixty five per cent of all policies written but this is now down to about forty five per cent. These figures illustrate the growth in competition in the recent past. There are now more than twenty Insurers offering a bewildering array of policies. The new entrants have been innovators, offering expanded benefits and keen prices, and some of the established Insurers have been slow to react. Competition has helped to temper inevitable premium increases and encouraged new products. However, the private sector cannot replace the NHS. Although many more operations, such as open heart surgery, are now routinely available long term or incurable conditions are not covered by most policies. Private medicine helps to relieve the NHS and should be looked on as a complement rather than a complete replacement. Increasing numbers of people are opting for the convenience of being able to choose when, where, and by whom treatment is received.

The entry of the new Providers makes it even more difficult for the lay person to make an informed choice from the ever expanding choice available. Calls to Insurers will produce a large pile of glossy brochures, many of which are full of colour photographs but give little detail on what a policy offers and its cost. The benefits offered by apparently similar products can vary tremendously. Purchasers may think that they are fully covered but this is not always so. Poor benefits can lead to the policyholder having to meet the gap between what the policy will meet and the actual treatment cost, known as a shortfall.

It may also be that your policy will meet only certain costs. The normal concept of medical insurance is that, within any limits, it picks up the bills from the moment your GP refers you to a Specialist. This is certainly true of standard or comprehensive policies. It is, though, unreasonable to expect that a low cost policy will offer all this. In an attempt to widen the market there are now many policies which eliminate outpatient costs, paying costs only while you are admitted to hospital. It must be remembered that out-patient costs are not merely the cost of one appointment with a Specialist. There may well be tests, scans, investigations and aftercare such as physiotherapy. The cost of these can run into many hundreds of pounds. If your policy does not cover them you must either fall back on the NHS or meet the costs out of your own pocket.

It is becoming increasingly common for people to check that their medical insurance remains good value, just as most do with motor and household cover. However, your claims record may make it difficult to change. Conditions for which your current Insurer has met costs may well be excluded by a replacement policy. Many policies are sold direct to the public by insurers. This can be via mailshots, newspaper adverts or through the efforts of their tied sales force. Currently most individual policies are sold in this way. However there is a growing realisation that there really is a wide choice available and consumers are becoming less likely to buy purely because they know the name.

Remember that with the bewildering variety of policies now on offer it is essential to take the utmost care when making your choice. You are free to buy from whomsoever you choose but remember that a tied salesman can normally sell you only the products of the company he represents. Your usual broker may also be able to help and there are now Specialist intermediaries who deal only in health insurance; either should be able to give you proper advice and a choice of Insurers and policies. They will also be able to ensure that you continue to receive good value and advise you of developments which may be of interest to you.

Advertisement feature

Life Assurance and Friendly Society Investments

Private Medical Insurance

CONFUSED?

THINKING OF TAKING PRIVATE MEDICAL INSURANCE?

You need make only one call
for professional and unbiased advice
to

HEALTH CARE *Matters*

CALL *FREE* ON
0500 136 442

Lump-Sum Investment

Income Protection – A Healthy Investment

Whilst most people think that they will not suffer a serious accident or illness, the sad reality is that all too many people do, and with it financial hardship when their main source of income dries up. The statistics are quite disturbing.

- There is a 1 in 6 risk that you will be incapacitated for longer than 6 months at some time in your life.
- You are 14 times more likely to suffer an illness lasting longer than 6 months than you are to die before age 65.
- Few employers guarantee sick pay beyond 6 months.

It is therefore obvious that some form of Income Protection is a key requirement for just about everybody, to help pay the mortgage, meet the bills and cover everyday expenses.

The government has signalled its clear intention that individuals must learn to take more care of themselves in the event of a prolonged illness or injury. The choice is stark – protect yourself or find yourself receiving state benefits that thrust you straight on to the breadline.

April 1995 witnessed substantial changes to state benefits for the long term sick and disabled. In many cases, those who are unable to work due to ill health will find that their state benefits have either been radically cut or are now much harder to come by.

Invalidity and Sickness Benefit has been replaced by the new Incapacity Benefit. Not only are benefit payments now taxable but the criteria for receiving benefit has been tightened up so much so, that it is estimated 75,000 fewer people will now be able to claim benefit as a result. GP's will continue to assess a person's ability to resume their normal occupation for the first 28 weeks but thereafter, all individuals will be independently assessed by the Benefits Agency Doctors with benefit only paid to those deemed incapable of work. This means any work, not just the work they were doing before becoming incapacitated.

Income Protection or Permanent Health Insurance as it is often known, is the ideal financial solution. Whilst many people make adequate provisions for pensions and life assurance, Income Protection lags way behind in the list of priorities. But just consider what would happen if your income dried up because you were unable to work, how would you continue to pay for other insurance or investment products? Clearly protecting the source from which all else derives is a fundamental requirement.

Prime Health, a wholly owned subsidiary of the Standard Life Assurance Company, has recently launched a new Income Protection plan designed specifically to combat the recent government changes. Unlike many of its counterparts it is extremely simple to understand and operates a straight forward formula for calculating benefit which is related to gross income. Benefit payment consists of one third of the first £10,000 of a persons salary and two thirds of the balance. This is paid in addition to any state benefits received and is tax free for the first year.

Unlike other plans, it also has a unique basis for underwriting whereby provided you can answer no to a few simple health questions on your application form, you will be accepted for an annual benefit of up to £20,000 without the need for any further evidence of health, subject to our standard exclusion for pre-existing conditions.

Prime's Income Protection plan is available to individuals up to the age of 54 who reside in the UK and have an annual income of over £10,000. You can choose to start receiving your cash income after 8, 13 or 26 weeks and there is an automatic benefit increase of 5% annually to keep pace with inflation.

Premiums are extremely competitive, for instance, an employed male in his forties wanting a policy payable to age 60, and with a waiting period of 13 weeks, can get up to £1,000 of cover per month at a premium of just £21.30, the equivalent to most people's car insurance but for protection that is potentially far greater!

For more information on Prime Health's Income Protection plan telephone 0800 252369.

Life Assurance and Friendly Society Investments

Prime Health
A member of the Standard Life Group

A Healthy Investment for the Future

At Prime Health we are specialists in health insurance. We offer some of the most innovative and comprehensive products available today, at highly competitive rates:

- *Private Medical Insurance*
  Prompt access to private hospitals in your area.

- *Income Protection*
  A regular income to cover prolonged illness or disability.

- *Critical Illness*
  A lump sum payment giving you financial help when you need it most.

- *Long Term Care*
  Covering the cost of professional nursing care in the home.

- *Optional Add-on Benefits*
  Valuable cash benefits for Personal Accident, Hospital Cash and Major Dental Expenses.

In fact, with a portfolio of over 10 health insurance plans it may come as no surprise that we are now the fifth largest private medical expenses insurer in the UK today.

To discuss your healthcare needs or receive a free quotation, simply contact us on the number below.

Prime Health Limited is a wholly owned subsidiary of The Standard Life Assurance Company, which is the largest mutual life assurance company in Europe.

Prime Health Limited,
Wey House, Farnham Road, Guildford, Surrey GU1 4XS Tel 01483 440550

For further details on any of our plans please call

0800 252369

cover. As with all insurance there is the question of whether certain types of cover are really necessary, to which the counter argument is: 'You won't know whether you need the cover until it's too late.'

One of the problems in picking out just how much cover you need to take out in money terms is knowing the cost of the care itself. As examples, a consultation with a doctor could cost £90, an X-ray £100, having your tonsils out could come to £1000 to £1500 and major heart surgery might run to well in excess of £5000.

How to choose
It is important to research the market. At the end of this section (page 254) is a list of the major players and their telephone numbers. They will all be pleased to send details of the plans they offer and premium rates.

Which? magazine can help in doing a good deal of the donkey work for you in its periodic market surveys. It also allocates best buy ratings to various plans, although in the latest September 1995 survey all 14 of the 'standard policies' category were, apparently, best buys.

A useful reference book is *Laing's Review of Private Health Care*, for which details are given below. This lists a range of useful information about the PMI market and also the names of specialist brokers.

Brokers who really understand the market and the differences between the products and who keep up to date with what is going on can be a real help in cutting through the information undergrowth to find the most appropriate policy.

Permanent Health Insurance (PHI)
If you are employed, your employer may have taken out cover such as a sick pay scheme for the possibility that you fall prey to a long-term illness and are unable to work. It is worth checking. If you are self-employed or working in an industry where such benefits are not common it is worth considering taking out PHI.

As with a mortgage protection policy, you can usually rely upon receiving an agreed benefit after a 'waiting period' which can be as short as four weeks or as long as several months. Whereas with a mortgage-related product the pay-out would be the amount of your monthly mortgage payments, in the case of PHI it is usually three-quarters of your gross earnings. Obviously the longer it is until the PHI policy pays out, the cheaper the premium, because there is a higher chance of your getting well again in the meantime.

The cost depends on variables such as age, occupation, whether or not you are a non-smoker and how much your regular earnings are. Payments usually continue until you recover from the illness or until you would have retired from your job or occupation.

Critical Illness Insurance (CII) and Long-term Care (LTC)

Whereas life assurance is geared to paying out a lump sum when you die, CII pays out if you are struck down by a long-term disabling illness. Current research suggests that only 2 per cent of the population has taken out this sort of cover and yet complete disablement would lead to the worst of both worlds, a life of lingering suffering and poverty. It is surprising that it is not more popular than life assurance itself.

LTC enables you to pay now for the benefits of having long-term care paid for in later life. Recent press coverage of the rate at which the population is ageing and the lack of state provision for care of the aged has brought LTC to greater public attention. Furthermore, if your savings and assets, including property, exceed £16,000, you will be disqualified from receiving local authority support for residential care.

Mixing and matching

Because all the above types of insurance contribute to healthcare in one form or another, it may be possible to pick a selection of them as part of a planned healthcare programme available from one of the providers. Once again, this will depend on the services which individual providers are able to offer. The larger insurers are likely to be able to provide the widest range of complementary services.

Private Medical Insurance Check-up

- Does your policy pay for all your pre-hospitalisation outpatient costs?
  Even if you are not eventually admitted?
- Does your policy pay all your in-patient costs without limit?
  Including anaesthetists' and surgeons' fees in full?
- Do you have total freedom of access to any consultant or hospital that might be appropriate for your complaint?
- If you have to be admitted to a hospital outside of your chosen band, do you know how much it will cost you?
- If you are treated in hospital as an NHS patient, what benefit, if any, do you get?
- And after you are discharged from hospital, will your Policy continue to pay for necessary care – say at home?
- Do you know how many times you will be faced with age related increases in premium up to say 75?

  And the amounts involved?

  And at today's costs, what that is in percentage terms?
- Does your policy allow you the choice of contributing a known amount toward your medical costs in any one year – with the appropriate reduction in premium?

  Or do you have an excess which applies to every claim and for which you get a small flat discount?
- If you have a No Claims Bonus, do you know, how much your premium will increase if you claim once in a year?

  Twice ?
- Do you have access to Complementary or Alternative medical treatment?

  If so, is this direct or do you have to get your GP's consent?

  And does any excess apply to the costs?

If you do not know or are simply unsure of the answers to these questions, you should seek professional advise from your Insurance Broker, or Insurance or Financial Adviser. You may be surprised at how different Private Medical Insurance policies are – and how much you may be able to save in cost both now and in the future.

If you or your family have acquired medical problems since you effected your current medical insurance, you should not change your policy until you have received independent professional advise. Changing may prejudice your cover.

To find out more about OHRA's Private Medical Insurance simply phone OHRA on 01703 620620 or fax 01703 620200.

PRIVATE MEDICAL INSURANCE
What you see is not always what you get

Private Medical Insurance increasingly features in the personal financial columns of the National Press. The ongoing debate about the efficiency – or lack of it – in the National Health Service is prompting more people to look for an alternative way of obtaining necessary though perhaps not life-threatening medical treatment and for most the only affordable way to do this is through insurance.

Medical Insurance is not regulated – at least at the moment. It is not subject to the stringent rules applicable to financial products and those selling it do not have the same onerous obligations to explain to a potential purchaser the value of the product nor do they have to disclose the income they will derive from a sale. The pressure from competition within the Private Medical Insurance industry has resulted in the introduction of a number of products which range from what are termed Budget Plans to Comprehensive Insurance. The pricing of these products, however, does not necessarily relate to the value of cover given.

It is important, therefore, to look very carefully at the cover provided under whatever policy is being offered and to relate that cover to the cost of other insurances where, perhaps, the cover may appear to be precisely the same but in fact isn't and, when a claim is made, the cost may be radically different either immediately or in the long term. The simplest way to do this is to apply the following questions:

1. Consultants Fees
Once the General Practitioner has referred the case to a Specialist (Consultant) are all the Consultants fees, which may include expensive tests, scans etc, covered in full? Does the policy contain a limit on the amount which the insurer will pay the Consultant Surgeon and Anaesthetist if an operation is necessary? Will the policy continue to pay Consultants costs after the patient is discharged from hospital?

2. Hospitalisation
Are all the hospital's charges paid in full? If the patient is admitted to a hospital outside of the chosen hospital Band what are the financial penalties? (Some policies provide only a limited amount which is applied to the TOTAL hospital costs including nursing. £220 per night only will be a small contribution if the patient is receiving intensive care which could cost as much as £1,000 per night. Other insurers apply the Out of Band costs ONLY to the "hotel or accommodation" costs of the hospital where the difference will be relatively small and it may be possible even to negotiate those charges down to the Out of Band benefit). What happens after the patient is discharged? Is there any provision for the cost of care in a nursing home or at home? And for how long? (These are very important factors if both adult members of a family work and the family income will be seriously affected if one member is forced to stay at home to look after the other)?

3. Choice
Does the policy offer a real choice of hospital within your location? There are policies which limit choice of hospital. This could create difficulties if the best Specialist for the surgical procedure required does not operate in the hospital listed. Also, consider the future. You may not always live in the location where the limited list of hospitals will be adequate. What will happen if you move to another area where the nearest listed hospital is many miles away and to which none of your local medical specialists has access? An illness acquired since you took out your current policy may prevent you from moving to insurers who can provide the care you need.

4. Time
Do you have a choice of time? Do you realise that the so called 6 weeks deferred contract means that cover is there if the operation cannot be carried out by a National Health Service hospital within 6 WEEKS OF THE CONSULTANT DECIDING YOU NEED THE OPERATION, not when you first feel ill? Some, but not all, policies will pay for immediate access to a Consultant, others pay the Consultant's fees if you are subsequently admitted to hospital as a

Lump-Sum Investment

private patient (you may not be paid if the NHS carry out the operation).

5. Premium
It is advisable to check the rate at which premiums increase for age. After 60, when your Private Medical Insurance is likely to be most useful in maintaining your quality of life, you may find that premiums rise very rapidly. Some companies increase their premiums annually, others every five years and some every ten. Always insist on seeing a rate chart with these details. There are insurers offering cover where the premium increases for age are limited - Exeter offer a contract with no increase for age after inception. A simple comparative graph will demonstrate how your premiums will affect your income in later years when it may be relatively fixed.

6. Discounts
Are the INITIAL discounts offered just that – INITIAL? Such an initial discount of 15% will mean an automatic increase in premium at next renewal date before any inflation or age related increases of 17.6%. Some insurers offer an initial no claims bonus discount. Do you know what happens if you claim? Do you realise that a claim under a PMI policy will affect the no claims bonus on the policy as a whole even if only one out of, say, five people claim? No claims bonus on PMI policies does not operate in the same way as it does on multi vehicle motor insurance policies. A family paying £750 in the first year where an introductory no claims bonus of 25% has been allowed will find their premium increasing to £900 at next renewal date before any age related or inflation increases have been applied, even if only one person claims during the first year.

An excess can be a useful way of reducing premium. Does an excess apply to every claim or only to expenses incurred during the insurance year? The combination of an excess with no claims bonus can prove to be very expensive. If a claim is made you will be faced with paying both the excess and losing no claims bonus unless the balance of any claim is paid to preserve the bonus. Where no claims bonus isn't a feature, you merely pay the excess and can claim the remainder of the costs without fear of further financial penalty.

What is the discount offered for the excess? Is it realistic? (A 10% discount offered on a premium of £1,000 for a £100 excess is a much better deal than the same discount offered on a premium of £250).

7. Fringe Benefits
These may include travel insurance, dental or optical treatment, General Practitioner surgery and maternity cash benefits. Will claims under these sections affect any no claims bonus? Will they be subject to any excess?

8. Complementary and Alternative Medicine
There is growing interest in complementary medicine as a genuine alternative to conventional medicine especially where this relates to non-life threatening illnesses. If the policy offered includes complementary or alternative medicine what are the limits? Again, if a claim is made, will it prejudice any no claims bonus? Will an excess be applied? Do you have direct access to treatment or does it have to be through your General Practitioner? Not all GPs will be happy to refer a patient to non-conventional medical practitioners.

9. National Health Service
Some insurers have adopted the view that admission to hospital in an emergency situation where the treatment is not part of a planned and agreed treatment provided for under the PMI policy will not be paid for. Does the policy you wish to purchase allow you to transfer either way between the NHS and private treatment? If you are treated in an NHS hospital as an NHS patient do you receive any cash compensation? If so, what amount?

As will be seen, the subject is quite complex. It is recommended that professional insurance advisers are consulted before purchasing Private Medical Insurance and that when that happens the adviser is requested to put forward alternatives with reasons for his recommendations. That will at least test whether he is really qualified in giving advice on this subject and whether he is really independent or simply a "tied" agent.

Private Medical Insurance is supposed to give you choice. Make sure that your choice is not being eroded by what may appear to be attractive ways of reducing cost. At the same time, remember that the most expensive contracts available at not necessarily giving the best value for money.

Life Assurance and Friendly Society Investments

LET OLD MUTUAL MAKE YOUR MONEY WORK HARDER FOR YOU

Want to make the most of what you've got?

Worried about going through the financial minefield alone?

Not with an Old Mutual Professional by your side.

Let a professional take the strain and make your money work harder for you. An Old Mutual financial adviser has the experience and professional qualifications to discuss your needs, understand your problems, your worries, your desires and long term goals. Like everything in life, no one person's needs are the same. An Old Mutual financial adviser is there to ensure you make the financial decisions in life that are best for you.

To arrange your personal and confidential financial review

Call us now on Freephone 0800 525221

Information and advice will only be provided on Old Mutual products relevant to individual needs.

Life Assurance Company Limited, Providence House, 2 Bartley Way, Hook, Hampshire RG27 9XA
Telepnone: 01256 768888 Telex: 858049 Fax: 01256 768804
Registered No 943621 England Regulated by the Personal Investment Authority

Lump-Sum Investment

Politics and Taxation

Since 1990 tax relief (currently at 24 per cent) has been allowed against contributions to PMI policies for policy holders who are over 60. For the time being this presents an opportunity for those who are both the right age and can afford the premiums.

The Labour Party has, however, already vowed to do away with this benefit should it form the next government. There is also the prospect of VAT being levied on insurance premiums which would increase the cost of cover for everyone, in addition to the 2.5 per cent of gross premium charged for insurance premium tax which was introduced by the current Conservative government.

The extent of political risk to the private health care market is not clear. Nevertheless, changes in demographics, population statistics and long-term lack of provision by successive governments mean that social benefits look set to become increasingly inadequate unless there is considerable taxation and investment in the benefits system.

For the time being the prospect is for a greater number of providers to enter the market with even more choice of private healthcare products to offer the public. The consumer is likely to be required to make provision for his own well-being in the future to a greater extent than ever before. This points to the need for us all to understand the market and the products and make our own choices as to benefits and the future lifestyle we require.

Contacts for the main providers

Abbey Life 01202 292373	BCWA 0117 929 3742	BUPA 0800 289 577	Clinicare 01438 747733	Cornhill 01483 552975
Halifax 0800 142142	MFIA 01162 362 420	Norwich Union 0800 142142	Provincial 01539 723 415	Exeter Friendly Society 01392 75361
Healthcare Agencies 01753 532 092	Nationwide 0800 335555	Permanent Health 01923 770000	Saga 01483 553 553	Guardian Direct 0800 282820
Johnson Fry Healthsave 0171 451 1000	NPS 01536 713 713	PPP healthcare 0800 335555	Staffordshire 01902 317 407	Guardian Health 01303 853 400
Lloyds 0800 750750	Northern Bank 01232 333361	Prime Health 01483 553553	Sun Alliance 0800 374 351	WPA 0500 414243

Further reading

- *Which?* magazine. Last surveys August and September 1995.
- *Laing's Review of Private Healthcare*, 1995, Laing & Buisson (London).

11

Retirement Planning

Pension planning can be as complex as any other investment described in this book, and twice as important. Once you retire, your income will very largely depend on the investments you have built up during your working life and a pension can be the core element. It may seem out of place in a book devoted to lump-sum investment, as pension planning is (or should be) chiefly a matter of regular saving. But there are three good reasons why it should have a prominent place in any investment strategy.

1. Very few people have the maximum possible pension provision. In fact, it is estimated that fewer than 2 per cent of members of company-run pension schemes will retire on the maximum two-thirds of final salary that is allowed by the Inland Revenue. This can arise because the company scheme is not geared to producing maximum benefits, or because the employee does not put in a sufficient number of years of service. Most people, indeed, are likely to end up with a far lower pension than they expect or imagine.

2. Pensions are extremely tax-efficient as an investment. All contributions, to whatever type of plan, qualify for tax relief at the highest rate of income tax you pay and the funds in which they are invested are themselves free of all income and capital gains tax. In addition, when you retire, you can take part of the proceeds as a cash lump sum, tax-free; the exact proportion depends on the type of pension you have and when it dates from.

3. There has been a host of developments in pensions legislation in recent years, aimed at improving private provision and, alongside that, reducing the burden on the State. As a result there are now greater opportunities to make your own pension arrangements, through lump-sum investments as well as regular savings.

Personal pensions

Personal pensions, which came on the scene in July 1988, are arguably the most important development of recent times. They are open to anyone who has earnings that are not already covered by a company pension scheme. That includes not only the self-employed, but also those who have freelance earnings in addition to a main job – or, indeed, in addition to a current pension. Moreover, employees have the choice of opting out of a company scheme and taking a personal pension instead.

On the face of it, this is not an attractive choice. For a start, if you take a personal pension, all the costs fall on you – both the charges of the plan and the payments into it. Your employer may make a contribution to it, but there is no obligation for him to do so.

Then there are the benefits to consider. Most large company schemes operate on a 'final salary' basis; this means that the pension is equivalent to a proportion of your salary at the time of leaving the company, typically one-sixtieth per year of service. Should runaway inflation suddenly double your salary, or investment performance not measure up to expectations, that is the company's problem. With a personal pension, all the risk is on your head: you will only get what you put in and the investment growth it achieves.

On top of this, a company scheme will normally offer additional benefits: life assurance, should you die before retirement, which can be up to four times your annual salary; a widow's or widower's pension, of up to two-thirds of your own prospective pension; and guaranteed or discretionary increases in your pension once it is being paid. In fact, from April 1977, it will be compulsory for final salary schemes to provide increases in line with the Retail Price Index up to 5 per cent.

Lump-Sum Investment

Secure your future in the most tax-efficient way

Brian Barker, Pensions Manager at Sun Alliance explains how a lump sum can be used to boost your pension.

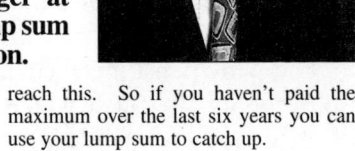

Making adequate pension provision has become a priority for people concerned about their standard of living in retirement. With diminishing State support, changing working patterns and the long term effects of inflation, investing in a pension makes good financial sense. A pension is one of *the* most tax-efficient way of saving. You enjoy full income tax relief on your contributions, investment gains are tax-free and a proportion of your final pension fund can also be taken tax-free.

With a lump sum to invest, you're in an ideal position to start a pension or top up existing arrangements. Let's take a look at the options.

Personal pension plan (PPP)

Providing you are working, you can take out a PPP if you do not already belong to a company pension scheme.

You can start a Sun Alliance PPP with a lump sum of £5,000.

If you already have a PPP, you can use a lump sum to make additional single contributions. With a Sun Alliance PPP you can pay in any amount from £500 at any time.

Take it to the limit

The Inland Revenue limit what you can put into a PPP, but most people never reach this. So if you haven't paid the maximum over the last six years you can use your lump sum to catch up.

Topping up a company pension scheme

Few people today belong to a company scheme for long enough to maximise their pension. If you are already a member, it will almost certainly be to your advantage to remain so - especially if you are a long-serving employee. You should, however, consider 'topping up'. You can pay up to 15% of your earnings a year.

If your scheme rules allow, you can top up by paying a lump sum into your company pension. Alternatively, you can pay additional voluntary contributions into your company AVC scheme or your own portable free standing plan (FSAVC).

You can start a Sun Alliance plan to top up your pension with as little as £25 a month. And you can pay additional contributions from £500 at any time.

It's never too late

Whatever age you are today, you can still improve your retirement prospects. For further information about Sun Alliance Pension Plans, call **0345 700 950** or speak to your financial adviser.

Past performance is not necessarily a guide to the future. The value of investments can go down as well as up. In the case of plans invested in the unitised with profits fund the nominal value of units may be adjusted up or down to take account of investment market conditions. Full terms and conditions are available on request.

Information on product and taxation is correct at time of publication but is subject to change.

Sun Alliance and London Assurance Co. Ltd. No. 894616, Sun Alliance Linked Life Insurance Ltd. No. 889209, Sun Alliance Pensions Ltd. No. 50603, regulated by the Personal Investment Authority. These companies form part of the Sun Alliance Life Marketing Group and are registered in England. The Registered Office of each is 1 Bartholomew Lane, London EC2N 2AB.

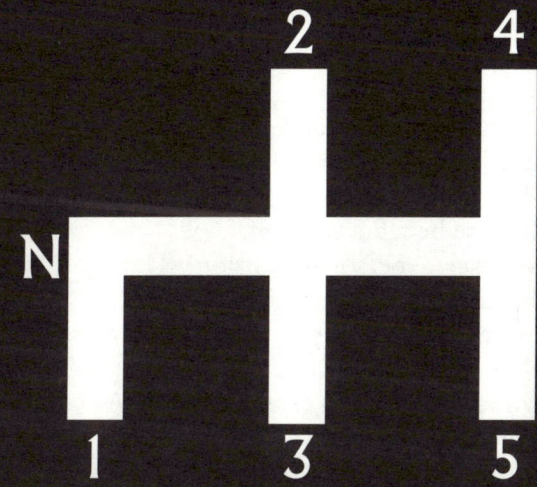

A SUN ALLIANCE PENSION PUTS YOU IN CONTROL.

Sun Alliance has designed a pension that adapts to the changes in your life. For instance, should you have a lump sum to invest and wish to move your pension benefits up a gear, you can. Or if you need to shift down to a lower level of contribution for a while, your pension will continue to thrive. You can even stop and start your contributions without penalty.

For more information, including terms and conditions, ring Sun Alliance on 0345 700 950 any weekday between 8.30 am and 5.30 pm quoting reference DT or speak to your financial adviser. The flexible pension plans from Sun Alliance make the difficult decision of choosing a pension easier.

SunAlliance

TOGETHER WE MAKE SOME ALLIANCE

Past performance is not necessarily a guide to the future. The value of investments can go down as well as up. In the case of plans invested in the unitised with profits fund the nominal value of units may be adjusted up or down to take account of investment market conditions. Sun Alliance and London Assurance Co. Ltd. No.894616, Sun Alliance Linked Life Insurance Ltd. No.889209, Sun Alliance Pensions Ltd. No.50603 are regulated by the Personal Investment Authority. These companies are members of the Sun Alliance Life Marketing Group and are registered in England. The Registered Office is 1 Bartholomew Lane, London EC2N 2AB. 512211

Under the rules, employees who opt for a personal pension are still eligible to have life assurance through a company scheme, but again, there is no obligation on the employer to provide this. If you decide to go it alone, you will have to think in terms of paying for all these benefits yourself.

So why consider a personal pension? The most important reason is job mobility. If you leave a company, your pension entitlement is based on your years of service to that point and your final salary at the time of leaving. Since the beginning of 1985, companies have had to revalue these preserved rights by the lesser of the inflation rate and 5 per cent, which means so-called 'frozen' pensions have been somewhat thawed. But higher rates of inflation, or promotional salary increases, can still make this entitlement look pretty feeble.

Alternatively, you can take a transfer value out of the scheme to put into a new company scheme or a private arrangement. However, transfer values are usually conservatively assessed, so each time you move you are likely to lose out. In contrast, a personal pension can be continued intact across any number of job changes, so, for younger people in particular, it can be a much more stable means of building up benefits.

Smaller companies are also turning increasingly from final salary to 'money purchase' schemes, which are less of a financial commitment. Instead of promising a pension based on salary, these schemes build up a fund of money for each employee which is then used to buy a pension at retirement. This is similar to the way a personal pension operates so, if your employer is prepared to contribute to a personal pension in place of the company scheme, you could be no worse off.

There are limits on the contributions you are allowed to make to a personal pension, which start at 17.5 per cent of annual earnings for those under 35 and increase with age to a maximum of 40 per cent. There is also an overall earnings cap on the calculation, which for the 1996/97 tax year stands at £82,200. However, if you do not use the full contribution allowance in one year, the rest can be carried forward for up to six years. So if you find yourself with windfall cash, you may be able to tuck away a sizeable lump sum by picking up unused allowance from past years.

Retirement Planning

Special Olympics United Kingdom

**The Otis Building,
43-59 Clapham Road, London SW9 0JZ
Tel: 0171 735 9131   Fax: 0171 735 4639**

Special Olympics is an international movement which gives people with a mental handicap (learning disability) the challenge, the incentive and the opportunity to develop their true potential through physical effort and sporting competition. Special Olympics commenced in the UK in 1978 as part of the worldwide growth of the movement, and is a registered charity in the UK. With well over 100 voluntary groups across the country we train and coach over 30,000 athletes to participate in Special Olympics events at local, regional, national and international levels. The athletes take part enthusiastically in many sports programmes including athletics, gymnastics, swimming, tennis, equestrian, sailing, powerlifting, table tennis, netball, basketball, football and skiing. Their joy is the true Olympic spirit – their achievement is to take part – and their courage makes every competitor a winner.

"Let me win, but if I cannot win, let me be brave in the attempt" – *Special Olympics Oath.*

Types of plan

Personal pensions are available from insurance companies, banks, investment trust groups and unit trust groups and offer a variety of investment choices: with profits, unit-linked, deposit-style and investment and unit trusts. Deposit-type plans offer maximum security with the lowest growth prospects, and are suitable mainly for those very close to retirement who need to know their capital is safe. With profits plans invest in a mix of assets and aim to smooth out fluctuations, thereby offering a balance between risk and reward. Unit-linked, investment trust and unit trust plans provide direct exposure to the equity market through a range of funds, which themselves offer different levels of risk and growth prospects. Broadly speaking, the further you are from retirement, the more risk you can afford to take, in return for the likelihood of higher growth.

One other type of plan, which first appeared in 1990, is the self-invested personal pension. This is a 'do-it-yourself' option that gives you a free choice of all allowable investments, which include

Lump-Sum Investment

equities, unit trusts and investment trusts, insurance company funds, deposit accounts and commercial property. These plans are geared towards larger investors, and would not normally be cost-effective for lump sums of less than about £20,000. The attractions are that you are not tied to the investment fortunes of one company and there is generally a fixed fee structure which is economical for very sizeable sums.

Contracting out of SERPS

If you are a member of a company pension arrangement, you cannot normally have a personal pension as well. The one exception to this rule is that you can have a 'rebate-only' plan for the purpose of contracting out of the State Earnings Related Pension Scheme (SERPS). In return for giving up your rights under SERPS, you receive a rebate of part of your, and your employer's, National Insurance contributions and this money can be invested in a special personal pension.

From April 1997, this rebate will be based on your age, varying from 3.4 per cent up to 9 per cent. Currently, the rebate is a flat rate, except that an extra 1 per cent is given to those over 30 contracting out through a personal pension. With a flat rate, contracting out ceases to be worthwhile after a certain age, around 40 to 45 for men and 35 to 40 for women. If everyone were to opt back into Serps at these ages, the State would not be able to afford the scheme, hence age-related rebates are being introduced in the hope of encouraging people to stay contracted-out.

Under the new system, contracting out should be attractive for men up to their mid-fifties and women up to their mid-forties or so. At younger ages, however, it will have less appeal, as the age-related rebate will be lower than the current flat rate. Income is also an important factor: for those earning less than about £11,000, the charges on a personal pension may outweigh the gains on the rebate. It is also important to remember that a plan based only on the National Insurance rebates is not going to produce an adequate pension. So if you are not also in a company pension scheme, you should be making further contributions of your own.

Retirement Planning

Could you reap greater rewards from your investments?

With current low interest rates you may find that the High Street isn't the most rewarding home for your investments, particularly if you're looking for higher returns.

Now is the ideal time to reap the benefits of investing in the financial expertise of Ecclesiastical, the country's leading church insurer.

We have a range of attractive investment schemes to meet your needs, from the long term growth and security of our Centenary and Capital Bonds to the Amity Fund, which invests only in companies committed to ethical practices.

And whichever plan you choose you can rely on our commitment to courteous service and efficient administration. Call now on **01452 419221** or return the coupon for written details or to arrange a visit from one of our consultants.

ECCLESIASTICAL
INSURANCE YOU CAN BELIEVE IN

Beaufort House, Brunswick Road, Gloucester GL1 1JZ. Telephone: 01452 419221

Regulated by the Personal Investment Authority. The value of unit prices may fall as well as rise.

To Ecclesiastical, Customer Services Department, Freepost, Beaufort House, Brunswick Road, Gloucester GL1 1BR (no stamp necessary)

Please send me more details on investing with Ecclesiastical ☐
Please contact me to arrange a visit from an Ecclesiastical Financial Consultant ☐

Name Mr/Mrs/Miss/Ms _____
                                                                              DT/96
Address _____
_____ Postcode _____
Tel _____ Date of Birth _____

If a representative of the Company calls at your request, any advice you may receive will only relate to the investment products of Ecclesiastical.

Lump-Sum Investment

CHOOSING THE WRONG PENSION CAN BE VERY COSTLY

The state pension which everyone is entitled to for 1995/6 is £58.85 a week for a single person and £94.10 for a married couple. There is also a state earnings related pension scheme (SERPS) entitlement based on national insurance contributions available to anyone not "contracted out". The value of the state pension has been falling for years. In comparison with average salaries it is now around 17% and by 2020 could be under 10% assuming the universal pension available to everyone still exists in the future.

If you are in an occupational pension scheme then you are going some way to provide an adequate pension for your retirement, particularly if you stay with the same employer for a considerable number of years.

Personal pension plans were first introduced in 1988. They are designed to provide a retirement income for the self-employed, or those whose job doesn't provide a pension. You have considerable flexibility over when you start your pension and whether you wish to provide a pension for a spouse or dependent. Personal pensions may also be used to contract out of SERPS.

Even if you are currently a member of an employer's occupational pension scheme, particularly if you have frequently changed employer, your final pension may not be as high as you expect and therefore you may want to consider increasing your future retirement income by free standing additional voluntary contributions (FSAVC).

Tax Advantages

A personal pension is an extremely tax efficient form of savings for your retirement. There are four major benefits:

- Income tax relief is given on contributions at your higher marginal rate. This means that for a basic rate tax payer for every £100 invested in a pension the actual cost will be £75 and for a higher rate tax payer the cost falls to £60.

- Contributions are invested in a fund free of all UK tax on investment income and capital gains.

- You can take part of the accumulated fund on retirement as a tax-free lump sum.

- Death benefits are usually written in trust to avoid exposure to inheritance tax.

But personal pensions are not all the same. To choose a personal pension provider you should consider four factors:

i) *Charges*

The cost of taking out a personal pension varies enormously from one insurance company to another, but until this year it was difficult to see by just how much. New disclosure requirements since 1 January 1995 mean that companies now have to show what their charges are and the commission they pay. The cost of choosing the wrong company can be huge leading to a difference of as much as £20,000 over twenty five years on contributions of £100 per month. It is often household names who are amongst the most expensive.

A whole series of surveys analysing companies' charges has appeared in the press recently and the Bristol based company Merchant Investors Assurance has featured prominently. As quoted in the magazine Planned Savings in a review of personal pensions in February "the most consistently good projections for unit linked lump sum and recurring single premium investments came from Merchant Investors Assurance and Provident Life . . .".

ii) *Flexibility*

It isn't just the initial cost of buying your pension which can prove expensive. Times change and peoples circumstances change with them. In the future you may need to vary what you pay into your pension or even stop contributing for a while. Many people are locked into a poor inflexible long term investment by penalties which companies often build into their products. But now certain pension providers are offering flexible products with no penalties. This means that you can start a pension secure in the knowledge that you will be able to adapt your pension to changes in your life. It is also comforting to know that if you wish to transfer to another provider in the future you can do so without penalty.

iii) *Investment Performance*

The performance of the pension providers' investment team will also make a huge difference to the value of your pension. This can be extremely difficult to predict, however, a look at past performance can be useful. The trouble is that most companies can claim some investment success at some time. A good investment performance over the last twenty five years may appear impressive but what if this was due to the excellent investment team of years ago? A look at the last five or ten years performance and an awareness of the investment strategy of the fund managers is probably a reasonable approach though it must be remembered that past performance is not necessarily a guide to the future.

iv) *Security*

Finally, the financial strength of the company that will provide your pension is of utmost importance. You must be as sure as you can that the company is likely to have long term stability and security.

Harry Kerr
Merchant Investors Assurance Company Limited
Telephone: 0117 926 6366

THE PENSION YOU'RE LOOKING FOR

With a Merchant Investors pension you always know exactly what's going on...

LOW, LOW CHARGES: Crystal clear and explicit; amongst the lowest available.

IMPRESSIVE TRACK RECORD: Since 1991 we've won 21 major investment awards and over the last decade many of our funds have ranked in the top 25% of their sector. *Past performance is not a guide to the future.*

MORE INVESTMENT CHOICES: We offer you a large and unique range of unit-linked investment options including funds which invest in investment trusts. In this area we're considered to be... *'one of the best investment trust specialists in the UK'* *

TOTAL FLEXIBILITY: You decide when and how much to contribute and when to retire – there are no penalties if you vary contributions or retire early. You're in control.

YOUR MONEY'S IN SAFE HANDS: We're a part of Allianz, Europe's largest insurance group.

* Julian Gibbs, Money Marketing, November 1994

Merchant Investors
Assurance
Regulated by the Personal Investment Authority

PLEASE CALL 0800 374857 FOR DETAILS

OR WRITE TO PORTFOLIO ADMINISTRATION
MERCHANT INVESTORS ASSURANCE COMPANY LIMITED,
ST BARTHOLOMEW'S HOUSE, LEWINS MEAD, BRISTOL BS1 2NH

Additional contributions

As mentioned, you cannot make contributions to a personal pension if you are a member of a company scheme. You can, however, make extra payments through an Additional Voluntary Contributions (AVC) scheme. This can be an in-house scheme provided by your employer, or a free-standing plan operated by an insurance company.

Why should you do this? The answer is that a company scheme can fall short of the ideal for a number of reasons: it may offer less than the standard one-sixtieth per year of service; the final salary assessment may not include extras such as bonuses and overtime payments; it may not provide the maximum possible death benefits or spouse's pension. Most of all, if you change jobs, you will not clock up the necessary number of years of service, and benefits from previous employment may be partly or wholly frozen.

The choice between in-house and free-standing schemes depends on your circumstances. Briefly, an in-house scheme is convenient, as payments are usually deducted directly from salary and the employer will bear the plan charges; but a free-standing scheme can offer a wider investment choice and is yours to take from job to job.

Members of company pension schemes can put in up to 15 per cent of earnings a year, tax-free. Compulsory contributions are normally around 5 to 6 per cent, so there is plenty of scope for making AVCs. However, while it is possible to have a single premium plan – to which you can make one-off payments as and when you can afford it – the allowance cannot be carried forward from year to year, so there is less scope for large lump-sum payments than there is with a personal pension.

An alternative route to building up savings for retirement is a personal equity plan. Unlike a pension, there is no tax relief on the money going in, but there is greater flexibility: the investment limits are generally higher; you can get the money out whenever you like; and all the proceeds can be taken as cash, whereas an AVC can only be used to provide income. The two are not mutually exclusive: to maximise savings, you can have a PEP in addition to an AVC.

Retirement Planning

START Skin Treatment & Research Trust
Understanding Skin, Enhancing Life

The reason – the millions of reasons – why START was established are all around you. Psoriasis, eczema and other common chronic skin disease blight the social and working lives of millions of men, women and children in the UK. Please support START's research by making a donation – whatever the amount it will help. For more information contact:

START – Skin Treatment and Research Trust
Chelsea and Westminster Hospital,
Fulham Road, London SW10 9NH
Tel: 0181 748 8174. Fax: 0181-746 8887
Registered charity no. 298474

How much to save

The chief drawback of pensions is that you cannot draw on the money until you reach a minimum age – 50 for personal pensions and normally 60 for company schemes. Other investments may be difficult to convert into cash, but a pension is by nature non-negotiable. Hence most of us contribute only grudgingly – on average, around 4–5 per cent of earnings.

A glance at Table 11.1 shows how inadequate this can be. Even contributing at 10 per cent a year, starting at age 30, will not produce the maximum allowance of two-thirds final salary at 65. This is based on a fairly conservative assumption for investment growth, but the truth is that the danger of over-funding is pretty remote, while under-provision is extremely common.

On top of that, you may not want to soldier on to the age of 65. If you retire early, not only will you have accumulated fewer rights from a company scheme, say $^{35}/_{60}$ths instead of $^{40}/_{60}$ths, but

Lump-Sum Investment

Table 11.1 *How much should you put into a pension plan?*

The columns show what level of pension (expressed as a percentage of final salary) can be expected, assuming that contributions of 10 per cent of salary are made each year

Age now	Pension[a] at age 65	
	Male	Female[b]
	%	%
30	58.9	53.4
35	47.6	43.2
40	39.5	35.8
45	28.7	26.0
50	20.6	18.7
55	14.7	13.3

[a] These figures assume a 2 per cent 'real' growth rate on the pension fund, and that pension contributions keep pace with salary increases, i.e. they are always 10 per cent of salary. They also assume that all the fund is taken as a pension, rather than a proportion as a lump sum.
[b] The figures for women are lower at all ages because pension rates are lower for women (they live longer).

Source: Allied Dunbar

most schemes also levy a penalty, often up to 6 per cent a year. Hence there is all the more reason to plan now for your future leisure.

The good news is that pension plans are becoming much more flexible. Many insurance company products will allow you to switch without penalty from, say, a free-standing AVC to a personal pension, if your employment circumstances change, and contributions can be made in the form of occasional lump sums instead of, or in addition to, regular savings. So there is no excuse for not acting!

Where to find out more

The financial pages of newspapers run frequent articles on pension issues, as do specialist magazines. For specific suggestions on your own circumstances, you should think of consulting a financial adviser.

Retirement Planning

There are also a number of bodies which can offer certain types of information and help. The Occupational Pensions Advisory Service can advise on the rights of members of company schemes and can be contacted on 0171 233 8080. To track down pension entitlements you may have from past employment, contact the Pensions Register, on 0191 225 6237. If you have any disputes that you cannot resolve with your pension provider, there is the Pensions Ombudsman's Bureau on 0171 834 9144, or, for aspects of personal pensions, the Insurance Ombudsman's Bureau, on 0171 928 7600.

12

Tangibles and Other Investments

This chapter looks at alternative investments which do not fit into any of the categories covered so far. Chief among these are 'tangibles' which, as the name implies, are physical objects rather than financial instruments. They can be highly specialised – rarity is often a key factor in their value – and may therefore require a high degree of expertise. Hence investors should be prepared either to do considerable research on their own part, or to put their trust in an expert. Tangibles also tend to be less liquid than financial investments, partly because there is not always a ready market, and partly because of indivisibility – you can sell a small parcel of shares, but you cannot sell one arm of an antique chair.

Tangibles

Tangibles are extremely wide-ranging and can be categorised in a number of ways, but a broad breakdown can be made as follows.

Objects of intrinsic value
This would include items such as precious metals and gemstones whose value is determined more or less by objective criteria rather than any artistic or cultural merit. For this reason, they can be easier to get to grips with, though an understanding of the market is still useful.

Arts and crafts
This group covers items such as paintings and antiques, ranging from furniture to silver or porcelain. Specialist knowledge is

Tangibles and Other Investments

Think about your funeral now. Then forget about it for the rest of your life.

When people don't plan ahead for their own funerals it is their loved ones who have to make the decisions and meet the financial burden. That's why it is sensible and practical to plan for your funeral now.

With a Co-operative Funeral Bond you can tailor-make funeral arrangements at today's prices. No further costs will be incurred regardless of when the funeral takes place. There are no hidden extras. So when your loved ones need us, we'll be there to carry out your wishes and they won't have to meet the cost.

For peace of mind cut out the coupon below or call us on 0500 112 121.

The Co-operative FUNERAL BOND

W*hen* you need us, *we'll* be there

Name...
Address...
....
Postcode.................... Telephone..................

co-op FUNERALS

Please send to: Co-operative Funeral Bond, FREEPOST, 12 Lower Bridge St, Chester CH1 1YZ.

DTC 96

more or less essential and some objects may need particular storage conditions. Security and insurance are also important considerations; it is worth checking out specialist art insurers, who can offer better rates with fewer specifications on security measures than the big general companies.

Collections
Collectable items range from those with recognised markets and dealers, such as stamps and coins, to the more esoteric, such as matchboxes and beer mats. The latter, of course, are usually collected for pleasure rather than financial gain, but even in the former case, enthusiasm for the subject is often the key to financial success; the essence of a good collection is that the items have been hand-picked, rather than simply thrown together, so that the sum is greater than the parts.

Other items
Tangibles that do not come into the above categories include, for example, jewellery, exotic rugs and classic cars. Like collectables, these are often bought for pleasure rather than investment gain; for the latter purpose, specialist knowledge or advice is desirable, as the most aesthetic objects are not necessarily the most financially rewarding.

Although there is such a wide variation in types, tangibles do have some common characteristics, which should be borne in mind if you are buying primarily for investment purposes.

1. They produce no income, which can be an advantage to higher rate taxpayers, but meanwhile they involve running costs for storage and insurance. Hence the prospects for capital gain should be enough to finance this ongoing 'deficit' as well as producing a profit.
2. While some tangibles such as gold and precious stones have intrinsic worth, in many cases the price depends on current supply and demand rather than 'face' value. This in turn may be influenced by fashion as much as market trends, as well as economic factors such as inflation which detract from financial alternatives.

3. Some items, especially collectables, may not be freely marketable, so money invested should be truly 'spare' capital that you will not need access to in an emergency.

4. Because the markets are often limited, with little competition, dealing costs or mark-ups may be high, so you need to invest over a longer term before there is an appreciable profit.

Precious metals

As alternative investments go, precious metals have a certain glamour, but investors should not get too carried away with the glitter. Investment value and beauty are two very different characteristics; jewellery, for example, may have increasing value but should not be considered purely for investment purposes, because the retail mark-ups are high and the cost of the workmanship involved can outweigh the intrinsic value of the metal.

Both gold and platinum can be bought in the form of bars and coins. Gold is the more popular choice with investors; while platinum is much rarer, and is underpinned to some extent by industrial demand, it does not have the same history as gold of being seen as the ultimate store of value and haven in troubled times.

In the UK, the one-ounce gold Britannia coin is minted for investment purposes. Other options are the South African Krugerrand and the Canadian Maple Leaf; there are also sovereigns, which are smaller, but these are not always available singly – a minimum purchase might be 20 coins.

An important point to bear in mind is that if you buy coins in this country they will be subject to VAT at (currently) 17.5 per cent. This can be avoided by buying offshore, usually in the Channel Islands, and this can be arranged through a high street bank. On top of the price of the coin, you will also have to pay a dealing charge and transportation costs, including insurance while the coins are in transit.

To continue to avoid VAT, the coins will need to be held offshore, which the bank will do for you. This is also convenient in terms of security, but it does of course mean further charges, for both storage and insurance. Together these would currently come to around £80 a year upwards, depending on the number of coins and their value. Furthermore, any urge to see your treasure should be resisted, as this can incur yet another charge, on top of your own travelling costs.

Given that there are these various running costs, and no income being generated, gold is only attractive if there are good prospects of capital growth. The increasing sophistication of 'hedging' instruments such as futures and options has meant that gold is no longer the prime refuge from inflation that it once was, and after the 'gold rush' of 1980 the metal spent many years in the doldrums. However, there has recently been an upsurge in the price, as demand has outstripped supply.

An alternative way of investing in gold is to buy shares in gold mining companies, either directly or through a unit trust. These tend to move ahead of the price of the gold itself and are even more volatile: over 1995, the gold price went up 7 per cent, while share prices rose by a massive 44 per cent. Offshore funds are another possibility; these may invest in shares, physical gold or gold futures, so will respond to different market factors.

There are also both onshore and offshore commodity funds, the former investing only in shares of associated companies, while the latter can include direct investment; these may include some exposure to gold, but within a spread of holdings which can reduce the risk. Finally, you can buy gold options, but these are not currently traded in London, so the dealing cost is relatively high.

Diamonds

Diamonds share some of the characteristics of gold: a hard-headed approach is needed, and jewellery should be ruled out for purely investment purposes, because too much of the cost relates to the settings and there is also the fashion element which can affect the value. Again, it is best to buy and store the stones offshore, which a dealer can arrange for you, but there will be storage and insurance costs.

Diamonds offer rather more scope than gold to pick and choose what you want, because there are a wide range of grades. Stones are categorised by the 'four Cs': cut, colour, clarity and

Tangibles and Other Investments

Launch Release of Huge Quantity Extremely High Value Stockpiled Persian Carpet Barter Merchandise

Finest Export & Contract Qualities Fully Guaranteed Genuine Authentic
HANDKNOTTED PERSIAN & EASTERN RUGS & CARPETS
redirected for immediate disposal as final phase of unique one-off Exchange Trade project at the new London riverside storage & liquidation depository

EAST WEST PERSIAN CARPET INTERTRADES MARKET
Albion Wharf, Hester Road, Battersea Bridge, London SW11
(first turning on left going south over Battersea Bridge) **Tel: 0171-978 4288**

This vast and exceptionally valuable merchandise was stockpiled by Middle East/Central Asian exchange trade specialists East West Intermediaries in a series of targeted barter transactions with Iranian counterparts following identification of a uniquely advantageous opportunity for sourcing huge quantities of fine quality Persian carpets under conditions of unprecedented potentiality which arose from a remarkable convergence of circumstances in the years 1992-1995

- **Crash** of the Iranian currency from 70 Iranian Rials to the US$ (1982-1992) to IR 1,600/US$ (1993), IR 1,800/US$ (1994), finally IR 7,000/US$ in April/May 1995 - i.e. a 1000% devaluation inunder 3 years*
- **Abolition** of notorious Iranian Customs valuation system for Persian carpet exports in 1989, which had reduced Iranian exports of Persian carpets to lowest-ever recorded level, simultaneously artificially creating most expensive global Persian carpet wholesale/retail prices known, thereby undermining traditionally unassailable Persian domination of the handmade Oriental carpet market. Abolition permitted immediate source price reductions to reinvigorate the export market, motivating a new vitality and search for excellence among all Persian city workshops, village looms and tribal weavers. Notwithstanding such benefits, system was reintroduced in May 1995, resulting in 90% fall in Iranian Carpet Exports since, with price increases/reduced availability consequently imminent.
- **Chaos** in the International Oriental Carpet Trade, devastated by bankruptcies, foreclosures and legal disputes occasioned by change from the low availability-artificially high source, wholesale & retail prices-easy credit conditions of the 1980s carpet market to the high availability-high quality-low price climate of the early 1990s created by Iranian export deregulation, this coming on top of the massively debased value of average trade stockholdings made up of lower quality Persian carpets bought at hyperinflated prices with interest-laden bank loans in the Eighties' boom, rendered virtually worthless by the spectacular crash of the Iranian Rial - the sheer scale of the problem became apparent through advertisements of Persian Carpet of Banruptcy Auctions and Closing Down Sales filling the pages of the world's leading newspapers throughout the 1992-95 period.

The misfortunes of others provided an extra benefit for the East West Persian Carpet project, allowing tailored exchange trade packages to be selected from the wealth of top quality Persian carpets log-jammed in Iran without even token competition from the major trade buyers, inevitably sidelined during the dark days of the carpet trade's nemesis, as the strongest buyers' market in history passed them by.

In May 1995, the bubble burst - legislation by Iranian Government, on brink of bankruptcy itself, pegged the Rial to fixed rate which holds today, + reinstated Persian carpet payman export system. East West Intermediaries, having foreseen the window had to close eventually, moved into the final phase of their Project, a regulated release of the massive number of items amassed in the unique barter period.

The East West Persian Carpet Exchanges Market provides the central focus of this operation, showcasing a new, consumer-centred approach evolved from client-satisfaction studies of Persian carpet and other 'excellence-motivated' buyer-collectors, aimed at making the East West Persian Carpet Exchanges Market at Battersea Bridge the unique London source for the lowest prices, the widest choice in size, category, style, colouring and price range relating to the highest export calibre authentic handmade Persian carpets ever available, supported by the ideal browsing environment, expert advice and tailored services which Persian carpets and their admirers both need and deserve

✪Open Every Saturday & Sunday, 10 am - 5 pm each day✪30-Day Full Exchange Guarantee✪All prices incl. VAT✪Free Parking✪Payments: Cash, cheque, major credit cards✪Stock includes other Oriental rug groups included in the Persian barter packages as found, also old/antique examples, kelims, soumacs, saddlebags - in fact, any handmade knotted/woven artefact in transit or available in Iran during project period✪Certificates of Authenticity with all purchases✪Deliveries inside M25 by arrangement✪East West Persian Carpet Exchanges Market managed by Specialised Intermediaries Ltd, UK Affiliates of East West Intermediaries

Lump-Sum Investment

TAX FREE RETURNS
INDIVIDUALLY TAILORED & MANAGED FINE WINE INVESTMENT PORTFOLIOS

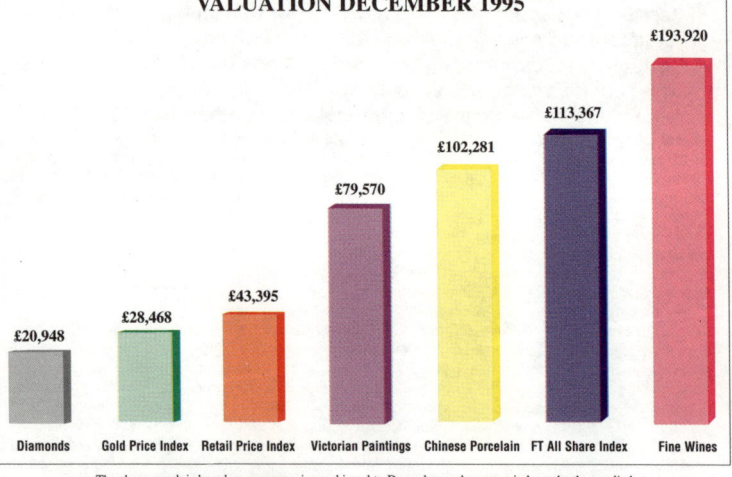

£10,000 INVESTED JANUARY 1975
VALUATION DECEMBER 1995

	Diamonds	Gold Price Index	Retail Price Index	Victorian Paintings	Chinese Porcelain	FT All Share Index	Fine Wines
	£20,948	£28,468	£43,395	£79,570	£102,281	£113,367	£193,920

The above graph is based on average prices achieved to December each year, as independently supplied

£10,000 Invested in January 1975 would now be worth

	1992	1993	1994	1995
Fine Wines	**£107,000**	**£112,400**	**£150,600**	**£193,920**
FT All Share Index	£79,840	£95,020	£102,630	£113,367
Chinese Porcelain	£89,000	£82,990	£89,630	£102,281
Victorian Paintings	£55,180	£85,970	£72,760	£79,570
Retail Price Index	£37,500	£38,000	£39,450	£43,395
Gold Price Index	£21,000	£24,500	£25,880	£28,468
Diamonds	£17,600	£17,500	£19,030	£20,948

Tel: 0181 905 4495 Fax: 0181 905 4496

Registered Office: Croffield House, Queen Street, Tring, Herts HP23 6BQ. Company Registered in England and Wales 3141325

Send to: **Premier Crû Fine Wine Investm,ents Ltd. Premier Crû House, 34 Orchard Drive, Edware, Middlesex HA8 7SD.**

☐ *I/We would like to meet with a Fine Wine Investment Consultant* ☐ *Please Prepare a Portfolio for my/our approval without obligation.*

Name _____ Single Investment _____ £2,500 minimum
Address _____ Annual Investment _____ £1,500 minimum
_____ Monthly Investment _____ £150 minimum plus £2,500 single
_____ Term of Investment _____ 3 years minimum
Tel Home _____ Investment amount to be *inclusive or *exclusive of management fee
Tel Work _____ at 2.5% of original investment subject to inflation (delete accordingly)

FINE WINES – TAX FREE INVESTMENTS

Fine Wines have proved to be one of the most successful and consistent, low risk, high yielding, Tax Free investments in the world, showing an average return of 16% per annum for the past 20 years.

Experts have been exploiting this market for hundreds of years. However before now, like Fine Art and Antiques you would need considerable knowledge to enter the market purely for monetary gain. Premier Crû Fine Wine Investments Ltd was formed with the specific intention of offering structured and managed investments to people with little or no knowledge of Fine Wines.

STRUCTURE INVESTMENTS

Fine Wine as an investment has many advantages over e.g. unit trusts and equities. These include freedom from all taxes on growth, stability and ease of realisation without penalties. Wine experts Premier Crû are the first company, to bring Fine Wine investments to the forefront with structured lump sum and monthly Portfolios.

Records that go back over 250 years show that Fine Wine has remained the steadiest form of investment in the world, generally unaffected by interest rate changes, general elections and stock market fluctuations. The foundations for the present Fine Wine market have been in place since 1855 when Napoleon III ordered the classification of the best Bordeaux wines. Those decisions took into account the quality and prices realised over the previous 100 years.

COMPLETELY TAX FREE

All gains realised on Fine Wine by private investors are free of UK taxes. Under current UK taxation rules table wines are classed as a "wasting asset" (life expectancy under fifty years). And so are not subject to Capital Gains Tax. There is no charge to Income Tax, as wines are a pure capital growth investment.

Financial advisers say in order to avoid easy mistakes it is essential to deal through a specialist wine investment firm who will advise which wines should and shouldn't be bought, depending on when you wish to realise your investment. A wines value will rise and fall according to its age.

STORAGE

Correct storage of your wines is of great importance. The atmosphere, temperature and light will

Lump-Sum Investment

all affect the eventual quality of your wine, which in turn will affect its value. It is recommended wines bought for investment are kept in a Bonded Warehouse which has been specifically designed to store quality wines. If you invest with Premier Crû they arrange all the necessary documentation for you. You can buy and sell your wines under Bond; and so avoid paying VAT and Duty.

A RARE COMMODITY

In the creation of this rare commodity variable weather conditions play their part, and over the past 60 years there have only been 4-5 vintages out of every decade which are of a high enough quality for the wine to be used for investment. In addition, the Appellation Controlee Authorities, backed by both French Law and EEC directives exercise a tight control over the industry, which extends from the methods of cultivation and varieties of vine grown to the amount of wine produced from a particular property.

The top 25 Chateaux, have an average size vineyard of just 108 acres, and the limited production means only 200 cases of fine wine per acre can be made. This means supplies of top quality wines will always be in demand in the face of the increasing world-wide market.

RECORD BREAKING

More and more investors are becoming aware of the value of Fine Wines. On November 11th 1995 Sotheby's New York held their scheduled auction which broke all records in American history, producing total sales of $2,092,534 in a record eight hour sale. On November 15th 1995 at Sotherbys in London a Far Eastern buyer bought two cases of Chateau Cheval Blanc 1947 (still drinkable) for £50,600. This years Auctions have continued to be buoyant with the Bordeaux wines reaching higher than expected prices. May's sale produced some fantastic results for Mouton Rothschild 1982 which was sold for £3,960 per case and Chateau Latour of the same vintage which realised a high price of £2,440 a case.

On a more realistic scale (for most of us) figures provided by Premier Crû show that a portfolio of six cases of established high quality Fine Wine bought for £2,500 in July 1994 was valued in March 1996 for £4,010. That's an impressive increase of 60.40% in just 20 months.

Investors are rapidly becoming aware of the benefits in the Fine Wine market, which has been reflected in continuously rising prices. For a comparison of how Fine Wines have performed against mainstream investments see Premier Crû's advert on the next page.

Premier Crû – 0181 905 4495

carat (in other words, weight). Each of these may be good, bad or somewhere in between, so there are various possible permutations which will influence the current price and the future prospects.

The conventional rule is that investment stones should be at the upper end of the scale in each category, as quality stones are more likely to hold their value, but you need to take expert advice in the light of how much you want to invest and how long for. It may be, for instance, that several lesser stones will suit you better than a single one of very high quality, as it would give you greater flexibility in selling; but depending on supply and demand in the market, lower quality stones may be less readily marketable.

Tastes can also change. For example, colourless stones used to be preferred to coloured ones, but it is now the latter that fetch the highest prices. In all cases, it is essential to have a certificate from an independent assessor on the quality of the stone.

Like gold, diamonds used to prosper in times of high inflation, but have been less talked of in recent years. As well as market influences, they are subject to investment fads, so can experience sudden booms when prices reach unrealistic levels, as happened in the late 1970s, but can equally undergo long periods of disinterest.

Wine

Wine drinking has enjoyed increasing popularity in this country in recent years, leading to a growing interest in fine wines and corresponding opportunities for investment. Getting it right, though, can be tricky, as there are fashions in types, as well as acknowledged good and bad vintages.

The most popular wines among investors are claret and port. As these take some years to mature, prices and prospects will depend on the time-scale on which you are prepared to invest. If you are willing to tie up your capital for ten years, say, you can go for a fairly young wine and wait for it to reach its prime; if you are taking only a five-year view, you may need to look at something older, which will be more expensive. You can even make your investment before the wine is bottled, through the wine futures market, in the hope that it will mature successfully to command a high price in years to come.

Lump-Sum Investment

The minimum investment could be as low as £200, depending on what you choose. Remember, though, that you need proper storage conditions, which may require a certain outlay. An alternative is a wine investment fund, launched in 1995. Specialising in Bordeaux, this gives you the opportunity to invest in 25 wines picked by the fund manager, for a minimum investment of £2500. There is a charge of 1.5 per cent to 2 per cent to cover insurance and storage costs plus an exit charge of up to 2.5 per cent. Profits are not taxable, as wine is considered to be a depreciating asset, but the scheme is also not covered by the Financial Services Act, so you do not have the protection of the Investors Compensation Scheme should things go wrong.

There are numerous books available on wine, as well as occasional press articles, and Christie's and Sotheby's both hold regular auctions.

Forestry

One of the main attractions of an investment in forestry is that it attracts substantial tax concessions. For a start, commercial timber that is growing is free from both income and capital gains tax. The 1992 Budget also doubled the business property relief from inheritance tax, from 50 per cent to a full 100 per cent, on commercial woodland. This applies after the first two years of ownership and means that, on the investor's subsequent death, there will be no liability to inheritance tax. With the tax rate currently at 40 per cent for assets outside the nil rate band of £200,000 (except property inherited by a spouse, which is exempt from tax), this represents a considerable saving.

The condition is that the woodland must be run as a commercial enterprise, which may mean you have to employ a qualified manager. The other drawback is that you can no longer claim tax relief on plantation expenses under Schedule D, as this has been phased out. This has removed the attraction of the traditional route into forestry, which was to buy bare land and plant it, offsetting the costs against other income for tax purposes, and then passing on the forest to your heirs as a long-term investment.

During the first 25 years of its life, a plantation incurs a good deal of expense in management and tending, while producing no return, as the trees are too young to be felled. Although the tax relief has been replaced by the Woodland Grant Scheme, this does not offer the same degree of financial support during the maturing phase, hence investors are turning away from new or young plantations towards those that are already mature enough to offer some felling opportunities and thus produce an income from the start. As a result, good quality woodlands of an appropriate age are moving into short supply.

The current outlook for forestry as an investment is good, with timber prices on the increase. But while it is possible to buy part shares through a management company, it has to be remembered that this is essentially a large-scale, long-term investment rather than one of quick returns and in many cases, the tax advantages are a significant part of the appeal.

An alternative route is an investment fund. Again, this is a long-term commitment – a fund launched recently requires money to be tied in for up to 14 years, with a minimum investment of £10,000. But the return on offer is a basic 6.9 per cent a year, worth 11.5 per cent to a higher rate taxpayer, plus a proportion of any rise in timber prices over 1 per cent a year.

Theatre productions

You do not have to be rich to become an 'angel' – a sponsor of a theatre production – but you do have to be sanguine about losing money. There have been some notable successes, but for many productions, even commercial viability is a stiff target. By the time the initial cost and the running expenses have been met, ticket sales have to be very good for you to make a return – many shows fail to make enough even to recoup the original investment.

As well as being philosophical about losses, you need to be hard-headed in your choice of show or producer. Worthy causes are generally not the money-spinners; what matters is not what the critics say, but what the audiences think. The recommended approach is to back a successful producer, rather than choosing an individual production.

The Society of London Theatre operates a scheme on behalf of

Lump-Sum Investment

its members to put investors in touch with producers looking for backers. The minimum investment required is usually £500 or £1000.

Information can be obtained from:

The Society of London Theatre
Telephone 0171 836 0971

Enterprise Investment Scheme

Just as there are theatre angels, so there are 'business angels' – private investors who provide finance for entrepreneurs. They help to fill a gap at the bottom end of the market, backing very small companies for which bank financing may be unsuitable or even impossible to arrange. In many cases, they will also contribute management expertise as well as cash.

However, this is a highly risky area, because the companies are small and are likely to have no track record and no security for the funding. Two alternative routes into the venture capital arena are offered by recent government initiatives, which also carry tax advantages: venture capital trusts (VCTs), which are described in Chapter 8, and the Enterprise Investment Scheme (EIS).

The Enterprise Investment Scheme (EIS) was announced in the 1993 Autumn Budget as the successor to the Business Expansion Scheme, which was phased out at the end of 1993. Dubbed 'Son of BES', it has the same aim of encouraging investment in small, unquoted companies.

The scheme differs from its predecessor in certain respects. The maximum you can invest each year is £100,000, as against £40,000 for the BES, but income tax relief on the investment is limited to 20 per cent. This makes the scheme less attractive for higher rate taxpayers, who could get a full 40 per cent relief from BES investments.

In fact, the scheme as originally announced found few takers; during 1994, the total raised was only about £5 million and no scheme reached its maximum subscription level. This was addressed in the 1994 Budget, which improved the scheme with further tax concessions.

Investors may get 'rollover' relief on capital gains made from the sale of other assets if they reinvest the proceeds into an EIS.

Tangibles and Other Investments

Although this only defers the tax – it will have to be paid eventually when the EIS shares are sold – it does mean that the upfront relief on the EIS investment can be equivalent to 60 per cent – 20 per cent income tax and 40 per cent capital gains tax relief.

Moreover, there is no capital gains tax liability on the EIS shares themselves. You must, however, hold them for at least five years to qualify for the tax benefits.

The scope of the EIS has also been extended, to include property-backed businesses such as hotels, leisure clubs and housebuilding. In addition, schemes may offer a 'contracted exit', meaning that there is a guaranteed return to investors.

This can cut the risk considerably, although any guarantee is only as good as the underlying security – the company could fail and so might its guarantor. You should also remember that investments are locked in for at least five years, even if you are guaranteed an exit thereafter. But if you are a higher rate taxpayer and have money you will not need to access, this is an area worth considering.

Further information is available from:

Local Investment Networking Company (Linc)
0171 236 3000
British Venture Capital Association
0171 240 3846

Enterprise zone trusts

Enterprise zone trusts are based on enterprise zones, which are government-designated development areas around the country that attract special tax reliefs for construction. The trusts offer investors a stake in a portfolio of commercial properties, which should generate an annual income from rents.

Investments can be made during a trust's subscription period, with a normal minimum of £5000 and no maximum. Tax relief is available at your highest rate, but applies only to the portion of money used to buy or build properties, not to acquire the land. The Inland Revenue decides for each trust what proportion relates to land and is therefore disallowed for tax relief; on average, this is about 10 per cent, although it could be up to 30 per cent.

Lump-Sum Investment

Besides the tax relief, a further attraction is that investments can be funded by borrowing that is itself tax efficient. You can borrow up to 70 per cent of your gross investment and interest on this loan will be set against the income earned for tax purposes. Hence you will need to provide very little, if any, money up front, while the income tax bill on your returns will be substantially reduced.

The income comes from rent on the properties, which is distributed to investors, less an amount to cover the scheme's costs. Several trusts offer a guarantee for an initial period, which will provide a set return if no tenants are found or if the rent drops below a certain level.

But these guarantees should be treated with caution. For one thing, the payments are fully taxable and no tax relief is given against them for interest on money you borrow to invest. Second, the value of the guarantee depends on the financial strength of the guarantor; there have been cases where schemes have collapsed. Third, the guarantee period is generally no more than five years and income thereafter will depend entirely on the rent received, which in turn will depend on the quality and location of the properties.

Enterprise zone investments also represent a long-term commitment, as tax relief is normally clawed back if investors pull out within 25 years. The exception is that, after seven years, the trust may sell a lesser interest in its properties, thereby raising capital which can be distributed to investors.

While returns can look attractive, enterprise zone trusts should be viewed as high risk. The administrative costs can be high and the potential for capital appreciation is becoming more limited, as many zones are nearing the end of their 10-year life and the shortage of new investment opportunities is driving up prices. Hence it is well worth seeking advice from a specialist.

Lloyd's of London

Becoming a member of the Lloyd's insurance market has never been for the faint-hearted. The losses of recent years have only served to emphasise this: in 1989 they amounted to a record £2.06 billion. 'Names', as they are known, have had more than their fingers burned and the market has suffered considerable turmoil.

The primary feature of the market has always been that members have unlimited liability. To become a member, you must have minimum assets of £250,000 and this excludes the value of property which is your main residence. But in the event of losses, all your assets can be at stake, including your home and furniture. Underwriting profits and losses for any given year are not finally assessed for three years so, in the event of a disaster, there can be a long wait to discover the total extent of the damage.

There are currently around 12,800 Names, operating in 167 syndicates. The standard procedure for joining has been that, in addition to showing you had sufficient assets, you had to be supported by two existing members and satisfy the committee that you were suitable.

But the recent upheavals brought a radical rethink, as the market needed to put aside its difficulties and attract new money. In October 1993, Lloyd's members voted to allow limited companies to invest, to provide a back-up for underwriting syndicates. This has spawned a number of investment trusts, which provide a means for private investors to participate for as little as £1000. These are explained in Chapter 8.

A free guide to investing in the Lloyd's market is available from Sharelink (telephone 0121 200 4610). More information can also be obtained from:

Lloyd's of London
Lime Street
London EC3M 7HA
Telephone 0171 623 7100.

Charitable giving

Giving to charity may not rank as an investment in the ordinary sense, but it can be regarded as an investment in the future of society. Moreover, with a little organisation – as opposed to simply giving to street collectors – it can be tax-efficient.

The simplest arrangement is a payroll scheme, operated by an employer. This allows employees to make gifts directly from their salary, of up to £75 a month. The money is deducted before tax and paid to an approved Agency Charity with which the employer has an agreement. The employees, however, have a free choice of which charities their money goes to and the Agency Charity simply passes it on, although it may make a small charge for administration.

If your employer does not offer a payroll scheme, or you would like to make larger, one-off gifts, you can use Gift Aid. This carries a minimum for each gift of £250, net of basic rate tax, but there is no maximum. You give the charity a certificate which allows it to claim back basic rate tax from the Inland Revenue and, if you are a higher rate taxpayer, you may claim the extra 15 per cent.

The Charities Aid Foundation offers 'Personal Charity Accounts' for those giving through Gift Aid or covenants. The Foundation can reclaim tax on the gifts and also provides a 'cheque-book' of vouchers which you can make out to your chosen charities.

Further information on Gift Aid is given in the Inland Revenue leaflet IR113 and from the Gift Aid helpline on 0151 472 6038. The Charities Aid Foundation can be contacted on 01732 771333.

Ethical investment

Ethical investment is about knowing and approving of what your money goes into.

Although it may sound like a minority pursuit it is worth remembering that more than £1 billion of funds under management is now directed according to ethical criteria. If you add church-related pension and other funds whose investment is ethically guided the figure may be four or five times that. Furthermore, the concept is nothing new. Having copied the idea from post-Vietnam America, British ethical investment vehicles have been around since 1983.

How to invest

Ethical investment options include unit trusts, pension funds, endowment policies and PEPs. In its *Money & Ethics* reference work – which, incidentally, is a must for anyone wishing to investigate the subject in greater depth – the Ethical Investment Research Service (EIRIS) lists 28 funds which are run according to ethical criteria, as at October 1995. EIRIS lists each of the funds, appraising them according to no fewer than 24 'corporate criteria'. It is worth listing them just to get a feel for the subject and whether they would be on your ethical do's and don'ts list:

- sale and production of alcohol;
- testing of products on animals;
- gambling;
- production of greenhouse gases;
- health and safety breaches;
- operations in countries with poor human rights records;
- intensive farming;
- Ministry of Defence contracts;
- production or sale of military goods;
- nuclear power;
- ozone depletion;
- pesticides;
- pornography and adult films;
- road building;
- poor workplace conditions in South Africa;
- exploitation of the Third World;
- tobacco production or sale;
- extraction, sale or use of tropical hardwood;
- water pollution.

EIRIS also lists five activities which investors may wish to support:

- production and sale of basic necessities;
- corporate giving;
- disclosure of information;
- good record on environmental issues;
- good record on equal opportunities.

These two groups of issues place ethical investment securely in the twin camps of all that is morally 'right' and 'good' in the fullest, holistic sense and what is best practice in corporate governance. Shareholder power, participation and protest are certainly becoming red hot issues and some may argue that they are the natural counterweight to the concept of limited liability and corporate short-termism.

Freedom to invest

But how far do you take this in deciding where to invest? Do you avoid all privatised utility stocks, for example, on the basis that you disapprove of the government selling off the family infrastructure silver? Do you avoid a raft of otherwise appealing emerging market investment destinations and the companies which are active in those emerging markets because of alleged or perceived human rights abuses? Would there be any companies or countries left to invest in if you did?

The point about ethical investment is that you are free to exercise your right to invest in those things you approve of and avoid those which you do not. There is an implicit recognition that, beyond financial return, there are other values which should be taken into account when making an investment decision. Which they are is up to you. Of course, each time you set a criterion you narrow the range of investment options open to you.

Screened funds and returns

To take two funds as examples, the largest ethical fund in the UK excludes all but 15 of the UK's 100 biggest companies while another can select from only 400 companies worldwide because of the standards it sets itself. The technical term for this type of selective investment is 'screened funds'. Independent financial advisers and ethical fund investment managers can produce figures to show that this screening does not necessarily impair returns. For example, performance figures for unit and investment trusts show that the average ethical fund has outperformed the average across all types of unit trust by 10 per cent over the last 5 years.

Risk

Depending on a fund's ethical selection criteria it may, however, have a higher risk profile. The argument runs that stringent

Tangibles and Other Investments

AS *time goes by* YOU'LL BE GLAD *you chose* NPI

NPI started providing pensions in 1835. Since then over 150 years have gone by. ½ million people now invest with us. So who better to look after your pension? To find out more, ask your Independent Financial Adviser. You'll be glad you did.

PROVIDING PENSIONS SINCE 1835

National Provident House, 55 Calverley Road, Tunbridge Wells, Kent TN1 2UE.
Telephone: (01892) 705667 Fax: (01892) 705611.

Regulated by the Personal Investment Authority

Ethical Investment

The first ethical fund was started by the Friends Provident in 1984. Today there are over thirty similar funds, mainly unit trust and pension funds, with a total of £800 million invested. But despite growing interest, less than 1% of the public are offered ethical investment advice by their financial advisers.

Cancer charities want to avoid tobacco companies: other investors avoid weapons manufacturers, the fur trade and pornography. Many people care about the environment; they take care to avoid companies involved in making ozone-depleting chemicals and presticides, destroying rainforests, polluting air and water and producing greenhouse gases. It takes a lot of research to score different companies on ethical criteria. Mostly this research is done by the ethical research company, EIRIS, and by the managers of the ethical unit trusts or pension funds. Each private investor will have different concerns and a good adviser can point a client towards the most suitable investment fund.

Sometimes experts disagree on whether a company should be classed as "ethical" or not. Recently the Friends of the Earth objected when the TSB Environmental Fund, advised by David Bellamy, bought shares in Welsh Water, which has had more than thirty convictions for pollution offences. Professor Bellamy argued that as a shareholder he could put pressure on the company to mend their ways, and said that Welsh Water's record was improving. With the growth of the ethical sector, the pressure that can be put on companies to mend their ways will increase. This has already happened in the States.

Performance

The performance of an ethical fund depends on the companies it invests in. An ethical portfolio will include some of the very largest companies, such as Sainsbury's, British Gas and Severn Trent Water.

But according to a leading investment house, only 17 of the top 100 companies are ethically acceptable, so a substantial part of an ethical portfolio will consist of smaller companies.

Smaller company shares rise faster in times of economic growth, and fall faster in a recession, but overall they do better. The difficult economic environment of the early nineties has not favoured smaller company investment, and because of their smaller company holdings, most ethical funds have been average or below average performers over the past five years. But in the years ahead, research indicates that the longer trend will re-establish itself, which would move ethical funds to the top of the performance tables.

Offending companies are increasingly made to pay for their offences, so it makes good sense to invest in carefully selected ethical companies, which have fewer potential liabilities. For example, after a recent judgement in America, smokers now have the right to sue tobacco companies for causing their addiction. The cost of potential damages has been estimated in billions of dollars, which must affect the tobacco companies profits and the price of their shares. This problem is unlikely to affect investors in ethical funds, which do not invest in tobacco companies.

It is not possible to do justice to the subject of ethical investment in so short an article. We would be happy to hear from any reader who would like further information or advice on any aspect.

Tony Yarrow, Wise Investment.

Wise Investment
Cross Leys, Chipping Norton, Oxon. OX7 5HG
Tel: 01608 642233. Fax: 01608 642200

Tangibles and Other Investments

Wise Investment

INVESTMENT CONSULTANTS AND FINANCIAL ADVISERS

Managing money isn't easy. You have so many different things to cope with ~ conflicting advice, all the jargon, unknown risks, hidden charges ~ that it can be hard to know you are doing the right thing.

We have spent the last eleven years helping people to find investments they will be comfortable with and we are still looking after most of the people who took our advice eleven years ago.

Wise Investment specialises in investment for income, growth or a combination; setting up new portfolios and looking after existing ones.

We arrange and advise on all types of personal and company pensions.

As Independent Financial Advisors we are able to offer the best of what is available from Building Societies*, insurance companies, National Savings*, Unit Trust providers and others. Please phone Tony Yarrow on **01608 642233**.

An initial consultation is always free.

Wise Investment, Cross Leys, Chipping Norton, Oxon. OX7 5HG
Telephone: (01608) 642233 Facsimile: (01608) 642200

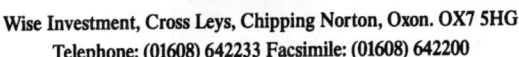

Regulated by the Personal Investment Authority
*Building Society accounts and National Savings are not regulated by the P.I.A.

Lump-Sum Investment

Ethical Investments

"An opportunity to invest for a profit that won't be made
at the expense of society or the environment"

"Ethical" and "Green" Funds – How they differ
Ethical Funds are based on self-determined criteria, typically they encourage good working practice and worker/management relations, but exclude interests in for example: oppressive regimes, nuclear power, armaments, tobacco and alcohol.
Green Funds are generally geared to companies that show a positive sensitivity to environmentally sound practice; recycling, energy conservation, pure air practice and water treatment.
"Ethical" or "Green" there are inevitably areas where they overlap.
Either fund type takes decisive steps in assuring their guidelines are followed by researching these investments and checking them against their criteria statements.
Considerable screening is often undertaken by an outside agency such as the Ethical Investment Research Service (EIRIS).

The Ethical track record
In investment terms, performance and principles are often viewed as incompatible partners. Sceptics hold the view that ethical standards have to be compromised if satisfactory returns are to be achieved. However, with the largest Ethical Fund now showing over ten years performance and a dozen others showing five year figures, it is clear that these funds are in no way under performers when compared to the overall market.
Indeed, there are a number of star performers. Since its launch over ten years ago, the oldest UK Ethical Pension Fund has achieved an average growth of 18.3% per annum. Over five years, figures show that the average UK Equity Ethical Pension Fund has returned 9.2% per year in comparison with the overall average UK Equity Pension Fund return of 8.0%. (Sources: Friends Provident January 1995, Pension Management January 1995).

The swing to Ethical Investments
Ethical and environmental issues are big issues in the media, in schools and in businesses – and are very much on the political agendas. Today, many investors welcome the opportunity to invest in and support those companies that make a positive contribution to the future welfare of our planet, while other investors avoid investing in those companies whose practices are considered harmful to people, animals and the environment.

What are the risks?
Ethical funds are carefully managed equity funds with the managers limited by the particular funds' set of investment criteria. Since smaller companies tend to fit ethical fund criteria more often than large conglomerates or blue chip companies, there is obviously some volatility in this field of investment.
Many people believe that Ethical investment is a sound defensive measure for investment, based on the premis that Companies already fulfilling rigorous trading standards will not be penalised in the future and therefore offer better potential profit margins.

Conclusion
Ethical Investment is well established and flourishing. It will go from strength to strength. As demand rises financial institutions will move further into this area. New funds and products covering a wider spectrum of risk options and further areas of application will be developed.
Those with principles they wish to adhere to in their investments will need specialist advice. Southernhays Ethical Investments are able to offer that advice objectively and independently.

Tangibles and Other Investments

SOUTHERNHAYS
Independent Investment Managers & Pension Consultants

Ethical Investments

22 Southernhay West • Exeter • Devon • EX1 1PR
Tel: 01392 410080   Fax: 01392 413638

If you care for the "environment" why invest in Companies that don't?

There are ethical/environmental investment opportunities in most areas of Lump Sum Investment.

For more information please contact:
Nicholas R. McKnight
MLIA (DIP)
Partner

The Balance Between Profit And Responsibility

(Please remember that the value of units can go down as well as up).

Lump-Sum Investment

criteria such as those listed above tend to exclude most, if not all, of larger, FT-SE 100 companies. Investments tend to be in smaller and therefore higher risk stocks which can be vulnerable to price fluctuations and public relations accidents, especially if other funds themselves become disenchanted and start to sell their holdings in a significant way, so affecting share prices. This points to the importance of risk spreading within the fund, which, as we have seen, is restricted anyway due to selection criteria: a kind of ethical-financial Catch-22.

There is still a deeply-rooted folk-belief that if you invest with conscience and responsibility you have to accept higher risk and lower returns. However, the spread of shareholder pressure and higher degrees of corporate governance should eventually increase the range of companies which fit ethical criteria and at the same time investors are likely to get more demanding in their performance expectations.

Ethical banking

While choosing the right ethical fund requires study of the funds available, leaving your money with an ethical bank is a more straightforward investment route.

The Co-Operative Bank set the pace in this field in 1990 by nailing its ethical policy securely and visibly to the mast. It says, for example, that it 'will not invest in or supply financial services to any regime or organisation which oppresses the human spirit, takes away the rights of individuals or manufactures any instrument of torture'. Its policy goes on to cover sales of weapons, money laundering, animal experiments, factory farming and blood sports among other things. The bank supplies a range of standard clearing bank services.

In the end, ethical investment comes down to a question of just how ethical you want to be. A good way to start deciding on what suits your conscience and your pocket is to contact with the Ethical Investment Research Service. They can cut short the process of research and help you to sift through the ever growing body of information which now serves the widening consumer interest in ethical investment in the increasingly caring 1990s.

Useful reading

- *The Ethical Investor*, Russel Sparkes, HarperCollins Publishers, 1995, £9.99.
- *Money & Ethics: A guide to pensions, PEPs, endowment mortgages and other ethical investment plans*, Ethical Investment Research Service, 1996, £12.50.

The Ethical Investment Research Service can be reached on 0171 735 1351. It can carry out an appraisal of your portfolio and tell you which of your holdings may be ethically challenged.

Investing in property

All sectors of the property market are putting a brave face on it at present. After the overheating in the 1980s and the recession of the early 1990s, any sign of increased activity is hailed by banks, building societies, estate agents and property companies as evidence of recovery. But with a lump sum to invest you are a buyer in a buyers' market, well-placed to get the best out of the property sector.

Domestic property

We all need somewhere to live. It still makes sense to avoid paying rent to someone else and, according to a recent survey, 92 per cent of home owners believe it is better to buy than to rent. Nationwide statistics show that 67 per cent of the housing stock is owner occupied. A lump sum investor does not need to borrow so, apart from maintenance costs, council tax, insurance and the other usual bills, he can have a roof over his head for free.

The benefit of this should not be overlooked. The purchase price of a four bedroom semi-detached house in good condition and in a reasonably sought-after area in suburban London could be £200,000. To rent a similar property might cost £300 a week. That saving represents a benefit of £15,600 per year or 7.8 per cent of the original purchase price. And there is still the asset of the house which can be sold in due course.

Which, of course, leads to the two snags which are besetting the domestic property sector in 1996. First, how much would the house be worth when the time came to sell; would it sell for more than it cost? And second, how long would it take to sell? The only reasonable answer to both questions in the current market is 'don't know' and that represents the investor's capital risk.

The lump sum investor can at least buy at the best price as a cash buyer and should press home that advantage as far as possible. But with the housing market across the country still in the doldrums it is prudent not to expect instant, 1980s-style short-term profits. A report earlier this year from a major bank noted that: 'The major mortgage lenders are currently forecasting that there will be no 'real' increase in house prices in England before 1998 (ie the nominal rate of increase in house prices will be no greater than that of the Retail Price Index).'

There are still tax advantages in investing in a domestic property although they have slowly been whittled away in successive budgets. Provided it is a main residence, any gain realised when selling the property is free of capital gains tax. Second, for those who are supplementing their lump sum investment with borrowing, there is still tax relief at 15 per cent on mortgage interest on the first £30,000 of a loan.

Second homes and timeshares

The advantage of not having to pay rent extends, of course, to second homes and timeshares. In the case of second or holiday homes, use of the property is likely to be entirely in the hands of the purchaser throughout the year. The property can be rented out to produce income. Furthermore, it can be nominated as the main residence and exempted from CGT. The switch in nomination between homes is up to the owner in agreement with the Inland Revenue; careful consideration of the best option with a tax specialist is advisable.

Timeshares entitle the owner to the use of a property such as a villa, chalet or holiday apartment for a given number of days or weeks. But most can be exchanged with owners of the same or other timeshares so that you are not locked into taking the same weeks of holiday at the same place for the term of the timeshare. Ultimately, it is possible to sell on the timeshare although the price is unlikely to be predictable. All told, it is worth totting up what you would have paid if you had had to rent other holiday accommodation during the term of the timeshare ownership and any profit can be a bonus. It must be said that, as with any other property investment, prices can go down as well as up and there is no telling which way they will go. Lastly, you should not forget to take into account annual maintenance charges and any other fees which may be payable. These can prove rather costly over the long term.

Commercial property
Although house purchase is the most obvious form of property investment, most of us also invest indirectly in commercial property through pension and life insurance arrangements. The main sectors of the market in which they invest are office buildings, retail outlets and industrial property.

The factors which are taken into account when fund managers invest can be useful in understanding their investment strategies and in making one's own property investment decision*:

- the position of the property;
- the description of the property;
- the tenure of tenants;
- the lease terms;
- the identity of tenants;
- the amount and timing of rental income;
- the initial purchase price of the property;
- the total yield on the property.

These considerations will be taken into account when the fund manager invests in a piece of property, perhaps as a group of institutions buying an office block or trading estate. At the same time he or she may invest in property companies whose portfolios are made up of a spread of such investments or they may invest in property funds which in turn invest in a variety of different types of property in selected locations.

UK property, along with UK equities, has traditionally been a mainstay of insurance company investment. It has been considered long term and sufficiently reliable. However, confidence

---

* Reproduced courtesy of *Commercial Property Investment, a Practical Guide*, published by Property for Investors, 43 Compayne Gardens, London NW6 3DD. Telephone 0171 372 3800.

Lump-Sum Investment

BEST VALUE FOR MONEY

The Chesham Building Society plays a maior part in the history of the UK mortgage market. Established in 1845, it is the oldest building society in existence and it has carried on the original building society tradition of putting its members first.

During the late 18th and early 19th centuries, the rapid growth of industry resulted in huge numbers of people leaving their life on the land in order to work in the new industrialised cities. These cities couldn't cope with the influx and living conditions were poor. In the nineteenth century building societies were very small organisations formed by skilled workers looking to improve their housing conditions during this Industrial Revolution.

Members of a building society would make regular contributions to the society until sufficient funds had been saved in order to buy the land and materials necessary to build a house. When the house was built, the society would then hold a ballot among its 20 or 30 members to determine which of them would be given the right to live in the house. The winner of the ballot would move into the property, while continuing to make contributions into the society. Eventually sufficient sums would be saved to build a second home and so it went on. After maybe 15 or 20 years, all of the members of the society were housed and the society was terminated. It wasn't until 1845 that the first-known permanent society was formed which accepted investments from people who didn't necessarily wish to build or buy a home. At the same time, their operations were extended, enabling them to lend money to people wanting to buy existing houses rather than organising and building new homes.

"People used to have to subscribe for shares in the society," says Keith Starkey, chief executive of the Chesham Building Society. "When shares became available, they were offered and people had to bid for them, usually at a premium. But it is very interesting to see who the original members of the Chesham were, for instance Arthur Liberty of Liberty fame was our eleventh member. In fact we still have some of the family names on our books now that we had in the nineteenth century, for instance one of our members is a seventh generation Chesham member."

Being such a close part of the local history of Chesham has stood the society in good stead, and it intends to stay close to its roots. Chesham Building Society has four branches: two in Chesham, one in Little Chalfont, and one in Aylesbury. It also accepts business from a limited number of financial advisers which are well established in the local market. Known to cover its local area, this extends as far as Bedfordshire, Berkshire, Buckinghamshire, Hertfordshire, Oxfordshire, and Surrey. Occasionally it does lend outside its area but this is usually for existing customers who move out of the catchment area, or for broker contacts who operate locally but have clients outside the region.

Most lenders try to win and retain customers with promises of personal service. But, however hard they try, there is a limit to how much personal service a major building society can offer. This is where small societies come into their own, offering easier access to senior staff including the person who decides whether or not to give you your mortgage - and tailoring their products to their market.

"We see a very good future for the smaller society operating in a local market that it knows and understands," says Keith Starkey. "We make it clear where we lend and therefore where we don't lend. We don't try to mimic a centralised lender or a national bank or building society. We just concentrate on the area we know and the people in that area. Because of this we can offer greater personal attention to the borrower and the mortgage."

The lender offers the usual mix of mortgages, from discounted rates to fixed rates. But, unlike most other lenders, the Chesham tries to compete on its standard variable rates as well. It tends to follow its competitors' leads when making rate changes, trying to alter the rates as soon as possible for its customers' benefit. But it also has a policy of undercutting the standard variable rate of the major lenders, taking the Halifax as its benchmark. It has been doing this for about 15 years and the maximum differential has been 0.5 per cent; it is currently 0.2 per cent lower than the Halifax. It is this strategy that has led to the Chesham Building Society winning a number of awards for offering the best value to its customers. In fact the society has recently won the What Mortgage Best Lender of the Year award for the fourth year in succession. The awards recognise those lenders who offer best value to their mortgage customers over the long term. Borrowers are only first-time buyers once, and we have all seen the special offers and incentives lenders are using to try and entice first-time buyers through their doors. But how do these same lenders treat their existing customers over time?

The award was made after research was carried out, calculating the actual interest rates charged by mortgage lenders on an interest only £50,000 mortgage, up to the end of 1995. Chesham Building Society came out as offering best value, beating every other lender. A £50,000 mortgage with the society over 10 years would have been more than £4,219.74 cheaper than one from the most expensive lender over the period. If this performance is extended over the normal 25-year mortgage term, the average homebuyer would save £10,549.35 by going to the Chesham for a mortgage – quite a saving for the same product over the same period.

Many people mistakenly believe that the smaller the society, the less secure it must be – and it is true that the industry is going through a period of long-term rationalisation. But again the Chesham dispels this myth. The society has celebrating its 150th birthday and, as Mr Starkey says, "We've survived since 1845 and we've weathered many downturns in the market. There is currently intense competition amongst lenders for market share, but we intend to compete aggressively with larger lenders, making the most of our local roots. And this can only be good news for our borrowers."

Tangibles and Other Investments

WHAT COMES AFTER A HAT-TRICK?

For the FOURTH year running Chesham Building Society has won the "What Mortgage Magazine" **Best Overall Lender Award!**

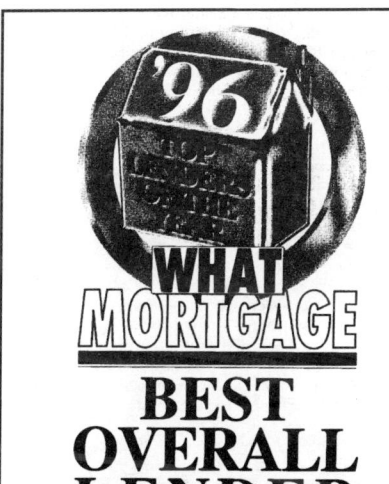

To find out why, call us on:
FREEPHONE CHESHAM BUILDING SOCIETY

Head Office:
12 Market Square, Chesham, Bucks. HP5 1ER
Telephone: Chesham (01494) 782575

CHESHAM BUILDING SOCIETY
(Established 1845) *Now celebrating its 150th year*

299

Lump-Sum Investment

Direct mortgages

Ronnie Macaulay, Senior Manager, Mortgages Direct examines the benefits of arranging your mortgage over the phone

WHEN Alexander Graham Bell invented the telephone back in 1876 little did he know that he would be providing the springboard for a telecommunications revolution over 100 years later. With more and more sophisticated telecommunications available, distance proves to be no problem in arranging anything from your weekly shopping to a multitude of financial services.

In the advent of these new services, the mortgage market has recently undergone a dramatic change as an increasing number of banks and building societies are now selling loans over the telephone.

Both Bank of Scotland Mortgages Direct and Direct Line, the motor and household insurer, launched their mortgage telephone service in autumn 1994. Other major telephone providers include the Woolwich Building Society and Abbey National. Many other lenders have plans in the pipeline.

This new generation of mortgages by telephone is based on speed, simplicity and price. It offers borrowers the convenience of arranging the finance for a new home – or switching an existing mortgage to a new lender – from the comfort of their own home, eliminating the hassle of parking in busy town centres to visit the local bank or building society branch.

Many people are also attracted by the fact that they can "dial a mortgage", at a time that suits them, rather than having to fit it in with traditional banking hours. Most telephone mortgage providers are open for business 7 days a week from early in the morning through to late at night, typically from 8am to 10pm. An added benefit to the customer is that the majority of lenders offer a freephone service too.

Some lenders do allow customers to carry out their entire mortgage application over the phone but post out partly filled forms for completion. Others do the whole interview on the spot and give provisional loan approval at the same time. Callers to Bank of Scotland Mortgages Direct are able to have provisional approval of a mortgage within 5 minutes.

Taking out a mortgage over the telephone is likely to be cheaper as well as faster than going to a High Street branch. The providers are able to offer savings because they have no branch network to support so their overheads are lower.

Another cost saving offered by the big telephone lenders is the abandonment of the Domestic Mortgage Indemnity (DMI) on loans right up to 85% of the valuation figure. This indemnity fee is normally charged by lenders for what are known as "high risk" loans and traditionally has been charged on loans of more than 75% of the property value. Now customers who are able to place a deposit of just 15% will qualify for a DMI free loan.

Some direct lenders have been accused of cherry picking as applicants require to have at least a 15% or 25% deposit. Bank of Scotland Mortgages Direct on the other hand offer 100% mortgages over the phone with the added advantage that you can include fees such as solicitors and valuation costs which frees up more cash for customers to purchase carpets and furniture without taking out personal loans.

Bank of Scotland Mortgages Direct has set the trend in innovation for direct lenders with the introduction of its Personal Choice mortgage which allows customers to implement a repayment schedule to suit changes in their personal and financial circumstances. The options allow customers to underpay, overpay, take a payment holiday for up to 6 months, pay the equivalent of 1 year's repayments in ten instalments, with the additional benefit of having an automatic further advance for up to 5% of the valuation.

Sceptics maintain that, while people may be happy to insure their car over the phone, they will balk at committing themselves to a 25 year mortgage for a considerable sum of money without going through a face to face interview. It is certainly true that customers need a lot of reassurance when they are taking out a mortgage – getting it wrong could lose them their home.

It is for this reason that the telephone providers typically employ experienced mortgage experts to man the lines. Applicants are guided through the mortgage maze in detail from the beginning and are contacted at each stage of the process to keep them appraised of what is happening. It is clear that an increasing number of people are turning to the telephone for a mortgage both for new purchases and transferring their existing mortgage.

The service is suited, in particular, to busy executives or house-bound mothers with young children who may not be able to get out to visit High Street branches but, as more big names continue to widen the choice for customers, mortgages by telephone stand to become a product for the mass market as the telephone insurance industry mushroomed from a standing start in 1985.

Tangibles and Other Investments

One option with a **personal choice** mortgage is **not to pay it.**

Personal Choice is the most flexible mortgage ever. You can pay more or less. You can take holidays from paying, or stop paying altogether. You can even sign cheques for further advances. Call between 8am and 10pm seven days a week for the full story (quoting reference DT.CG). We can give approval in principle in just 5 minutes.

BANK OF SCOTLAND MORTGAGES DIRECT

Call now on **0800 810 810**

All lending is subject to appraisal by the Bank of the applicant's financial status and valuation of the property. Full details and a written consumer credit quotation are available from Bank of Scotland, Mortgages Direct, PO Box 12304, Edinburgh EH12 9DX. The Bank requires security over the property, the assignation of an acceptable life assurance policy and house building insurance for reinstatement value. To apply for a loan or mortgage you must be aged 18 or over. Bank of Scotland is a Representative only of STANDARD LIFE, which is regulated by the Personal Investment Authority, for life assurance, pensions and unit trust business. Typical example: based on 90% loan to value: Repayment Mortgage: Monthly repayments of capital and interest for mortgage of £40,000 over 25 years. Assuming the rate at Mortgages Direct Personal Choice Rate (Variable) of 7.49% **(7.90% APR)** 300 net payments of £275.16 total net amount payable £82,548.

YOUR HOME IS AT RISK IF YOU DO NOT KEEP UP REPAYMENTS ON A MORTGAGE OR OTHER LOAN SECURED ON IT.

Traded Endowment Policies

> **We have a good selection of polices available for discerning investors**
>
> **GOOD SELECTION**

> **We create and manage tailored portfolios of policies (including a discretionary service).**
>
> **PORTFOLIO SERVICE**

> **We provide technical advice on all aspects of endowment policies (including taxation)**
>
> **TECHNICAL ADVICE**

> **We are always in the market to buy good endowment policies**
>
> **OUTRIGHT PURCHASE**

Neville James Limited

Tel: 0173 023 3000   Fax: 0173 023 3333

Page's Court, Petersfield, Hants., GU32 5HX
Member of the Association of Policy Market-Makers
Regulated by FIMBRA

Why invest in Mid-Term Endowment Policies?

Telephone, Fax or Write to Obtain our Guide to Investing in Policies.

Detailed Sensitivity Analyses (showing the effect of Bonus Rate Changes) are provided free of charge on policies purchased.
(Follow-up Analyses cost only £5.00p per policy per annum)

All policies acquired for re-sale are carefully evaluated using sophisticated actuarilly approved software developed and maintained in-house.

How much are your policies worth today?

Will they re-pay the mortgage on maturity or sooner?

Neville James can provide an Endowment Mortgage Policy Assessment Certificate for only £8.00p (per policy).
(Subsequent valuations of the same policy cost only £5.00p)

The Neville James Group is managed by Morris Bisdee, a Chartered Accountant, and Peter Gartside, a Solicitor and business school graduate.

AS *time goes by* YOU'LL BE GLAD *you chose* NPI

NPI started providing pensions in 1835. Since then over 150 years have gone by. ½ million people now invest with us. So who better to look after your pension? To find out more, ask your Independent Financial Adviser. You'll be glad you did.

PROVIDING PENSIONS SINCE 1835

National Provident House, 55 Calverley Road, Tunbridge Wells, Kent TN1 2UE.
Telephone: (01892) 705667 Fax: (01892) 705611.

Regulated by the Personal Investment Authority
National Provident Institution. Incorporated by Act of Parliament in England with limited liability No. ZC65.
Principal office: National Provident House, 55 Calverley Road, Tunbridge Wells, Kent TN1 2UE. Telephone: 01892 515151.

was quite severely dented by the aftermath of the property building boom of the 1980s, with projects such as London Docklands' Canary Wharf where boom was followed by bust within a short space of time. In mid-1996 we have seen investors returning and buying in at lower prices. Some of this new activity has been funded by bank borrowings and rights issues. But despite a blizzard of statistics from commercial estate agents and property analysts supporting the idea that recovery is on the way, many investors have yet to be convinced.

Where pension plans allow for individual policy holders to pick which funds they wish to invest in, UK property may appear among the available options. Bearing in mind the above criteria, it is important for investors thinking of looking at the property sector to delve into details of the composition of the fund on offer and what properties their money would be funding, as well as to receive regular updates about broad market trends and reports about the sites themselves.

Unit trusts

Both lump sum investors and regular savers can invest in property unit trusts. Lump sums can be as little as £1000 and even smaller amounts where they are additional investments to those already made. It is worth looking to see how funds are structured.

Its report as at 31 March 1996 shows that it splits its portfolio into seven separate sections: offices, retail sites, retail warehouses, industrial property, and three classes of property-related equities: ordinary shares, convertibles and convertible preference shares. This aims to achieve the widest reasonable spread within the sector. This is then split geographically with the largest area, London and the south east, representing 40.6 per cent of the direct property portfolio. The largest sectoral proportion is 33 per cent in office property.

Units can, of course, go up or down in price and Norwich Property Trust is no exception. The important thing is to be able to sell holdings as and when you want. Prices are quoted daily in *The Daily Telegraph* and the *Financial Times* and dealings in units also take place daily.

Tangibles and Other Investments

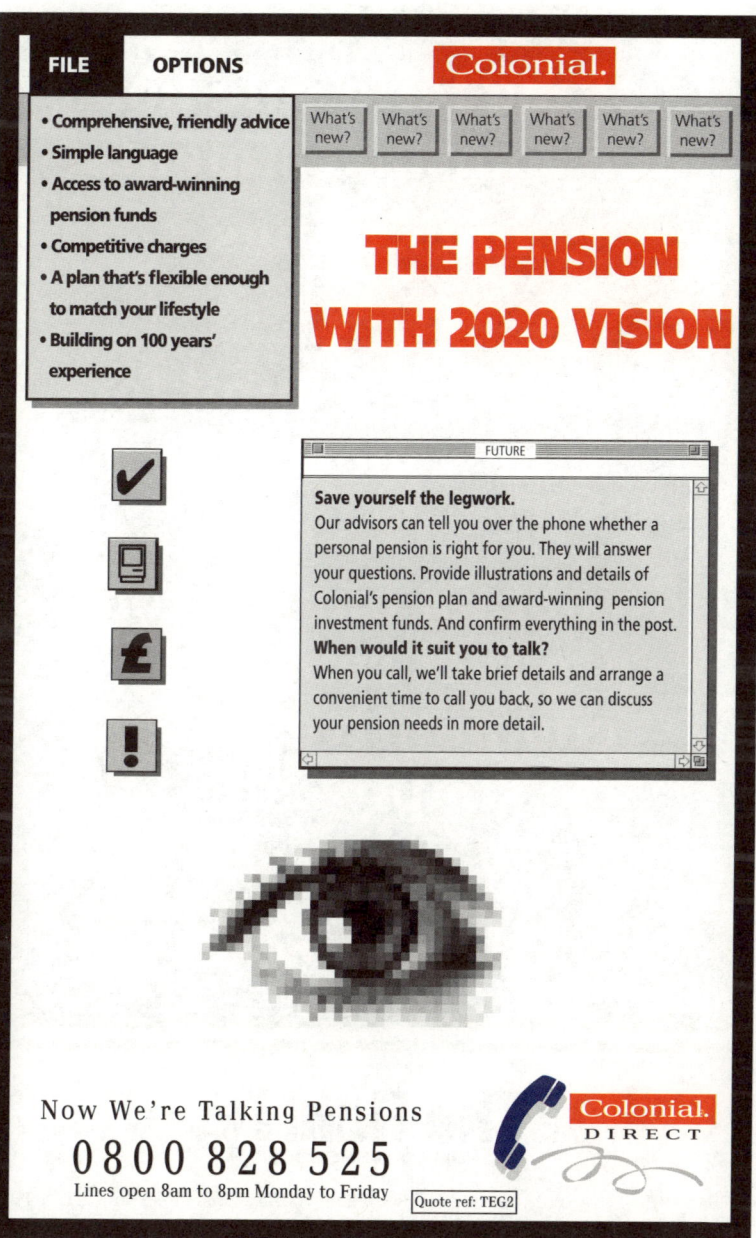

Lump-Sum Investment

Looking for a safe home for your investments and savings ?

Shopping around for a new mortgage ?

To obtain our current product range and competitive rates simply call

0800 838811

Head Office: Granville House, Festival Park, Hanley, Stoke on Trent, ST1 5TB
Telephone 01782 208733

YOUR HOME IS AT RISK IF YOU DO NOT KEEP UP REPAYMENTS ON A MORTGAGE OR OTHER LOAN SECURED ON IT. MINIMUM AGE 18. SUBJECT TO STATUS. WRITTEN QUOTATIONS AVAILABLE ON REQUEST. The Hanley Economic Building Society is a Member of The Ombudsman Scheme and subscribes to the Code of Banking Practice

MAKING AN INVESTMENT IN A WORTHY CAUSE

Vicki Pulman
Charities Aid Foundation

Giving to charity may not rank as an investment in the ordinary sense, but it can be regarded as an investment in the future of society. Moreover, with a little organisation it can be tax-efficient.

Around 80 per cent of people in the UK make donations to charity. Few, however, are even aware of the full benefits available through the tax system, not just to the charities they choose to support, but to themselves. Overall, government has introduced three schemes for tax-effective giving, enabling both private individuals and corporate donors to make their charitable giving more effective.

Donations made from taxed funds through any one of these schemes enables the Inland Revenue to repay the basic rate tax of around 25 per cent to the charity. If you are a higher rate taxpayer, you may reclaim the marginal rate of 15 per cent.

The schemes offer three very different methods of payment. These are by deed of covenant, payroll giving and Gift Aid. The *deed of covenant* is the oldest of the three and involves a contractual obligation to make regular donations over a period of four or more years. These payments can be made annually, monthly or in a lump sum, allowing the charity to subtract regular payments on its own behalf. Whichever method is used, tax is reclaimed and added to the total donation, increasing it by roughly one-third, at no extra cost to either you or the charity. There is no maximum amount payable under this scheme, although in order to cover the cost of administration, some charities may require a minimum donation.

Payroll giving was introduced by the government to encourage ongoing and regular gifts to charity. Since 1987, this scheme has enabled donors paying PAYE to make monthly contributions direct from their pay or pension at source, before tax is levied. The donor then pays tax at the usual rate but only on its remaining income. A donation, for example, of £50 per month, made from pre-taxed income, would cost you £37.50 in real terms and only £30 if you are a higher rate taxpayer. The maximum payable through this scheme is now £900 per annum or £75 per month and the real benefit, particularly to the charity, is in providing it with a regular source of income with which to budget and plan ahead.

Gift Aid is the most recent scheme and was introduced in 1991. It is the only scheme allowing single, one-off donations to be made tax effectively. In order to qualify, the gift has to amount to at least £250 but there is no obligation to repeat the donation. As with the covenant, however, tax is reclaimed by the charity at basic rate. This increases the minimum gift of £250 to £333.33 and allows higher rate donors to reclaim the marginal rate of around £50 for themselves.

There is one condition when making donations through any tax-effective scheme: the money has to go to a charity either registered with the Charity Commission or recognised by the Inland Revenue as being charitable. Organisations such as scout groups, places of worship, schools and hospitals, while not being registered charities, are all considered to be 'charitable'. Despite the obvious benefits of these schemes, for many they lack the flexibility and the spontaneity essential when giving to charity. There is a way, however, in which you can respond to a radio or television appeal, send off a few pounds in response to an advertisement or even give to a local street collector – tax effectively.

A personal charity account scheme, operated by an agency such as the Charities Aid Foundation (CAF), enables you to pay your tax-efficient donation into an account rather than direct to a single charity. As a registered charity itself, CAF reclaims the basic rate tax on the donor's behalf and adds it to the amount already in the account, deducting a small administrative contribution. So, on an initial payment of, say £120, a revised balance of £152 is created at no extra cost to you. Higher rate taxpayers would be able to reclaim a further £24 for themselves.

Once the money is in the account you are issued with a voucher book, similar to a cheque book, and a CAF Charity Card, a debit card designed specifically for charitable giving. This helps you to support any charity or cause of your choice and in whatever

Tangibles and Other Investments

We can't give Jamie his sight....... but with the help of legacy covenant or donation we can make sure he becomes confident, independent and secure in his daily life

Henshaw's Soceity for the Blind exists today thanks to the Thomas Henshaw's Legacy, in the year 1810, of £20,000 for the care of the Blind. Legacies are vital to the continuation of our work, allowing us to teach, house, advise, encourage and care for thousands of blind people of all ages. We need £6m each year to provide these services

If you would like to help please contact Janet Croker

HENSHAW'S
SOCIETY FOR THE BLIND

**Head Office
John Derby House**
88-92 Talbot Rd, Old Trafford,
Manchester. M16 0GS.
Tel: **0161-872 1234**   Fax: **0161-848 9889**
Registered National Charity No. 221888
Registered Housing Assoc. No L1737

Founded in 1837, Henshaw's Society for the Blind is to celebrate 160 years of service very soon. Please help them to continue for a further 160 years by investing in their future.
Henshaw's Society for the Blind
John Derby House, 88-92 Talbot Road, Old Trafford, Manchester M16 0GS
Tel: 0161-872 1234   Fax: 0161-848 9889

amounts, either by writing out a voucher in the charity's name or by giving the charity your card details.

Where would your donation go? Take, for example, the balance of £152 used above (which has cost the higher rate taxpayer only £96): £10 could be used to support a local community group, £50 could go to a place of worship; another £50 could go to an international aid agency and the balance perhaps to a local hospice. It is entirely your choice.

An added advantage to using an account is that CAF will honour only those donations made to registered or recognised charities, thereby protecting the money from going to an organisation which is not bona fide.

If you have slightly larger amounts to distribute – a bequest under a will or investments that you wish to give to a charity free of capital gains tax – setting up a charitable trust may be an ideal solution. It can provide enduring support for charities and causes even beyond your lifetime and can help to develop close links with those supported on a regular basis.

Before pursuing this option, however, it needs to be given careful consideration. First, there are legal and accountancy fees to be considered. Trustees need to be taken on, decisions taken over trust fund investment and accounting, separate bank accounts need to be opened and annual reports, returns and accounts all need to be submitted to the Charity Commission. It can take anything from 6 to 12 months simply to get the trust up and running.

By using an agency such as the Charities Aid Foundation, a trust can be established almost immediately and, coming under the guardianship of CAF's own trustees, there is no need to appoint them independently. Another advantage is that there are usually no initial fees or legal charges and CAF will take care of all administration requirements on behalf of the trust holder. Initially, all that is required of the donor is a sum of at least £10,000 – £7,600 plus tax reclaimed (or the commitment to reach that level within two or three years) – a name for the trust which, within reason, is up to the donor and a decision on the duration of the trust.

Once the trust has been established it operates rather like a bank account. The capital is invested by CAF although the

Tangibles and Other Investments

ANY LAST REQUESTS?

LEAVING A LEGACY

AMNESTY INTERNATIONAL UK SECTION CHARITABLE TRUST

Make your last request count. Leave a legacy to Amnesty International UK Section Charitable Trust and help end political killings and "disappearance"

CONTACT: HOWARD LAKE, TRUST FUNDRAISER, ROOM AG96,
AMNESTY INTERNATIONAL UK SECTION CHARITABLE TRUST,
99-119 ROSEBERY AVENUE, LONDON EC1R 4RE.
TELEPHONE 0171 814 6200 E-MAIL: trust@ai-uk.gn.apc.org
REGISTERED CHARITY NO. 1051681 REGISTERED COMPANY NO. 3139939

emphasis, such as high income or capital growth, is chosen by the trust holder.

The three investment funds operated by CAF are the Balanced Growth Fund, providing sustained capital growth and increasing growth of income, the Income Fund, which maximises income return with an element of capital protection, and the CAF Cash Deposit Fund, which pools investments to create a high rate of interest. The three schemes are designed exclusively for charities and trusts in a tax-effective way and are used by thousands of such organisations.

As with tax-effective giving, when it comes to distributing funds from the trust, donations may only be made to registered or recognised charities either by using a voucher book or standing order. Capital can be added to the trust at any time, and tax effectively, and all rights and responsibilities of the trust can be passed on at any time to a successor of the trust holder's choosing.

Under the current schemes, it has never been easier to support

Lump-Sum Investment

MAKE A WILL
It's Important

Church Army Officers work in a variety of different situations with those who are in need, and who are often at the edge of society.

The elderly, homeless, unemployed and those working with HM Forces and their families in Germany rely on us for practical help and spiritual support. A legacy to Church Army might make all the difference to someone in need. Thank you for your support; please send for our legacy booklet for more information.

Let your memorial be a helping hand to those in need.

ChurchArmy

Kevin Hawkes, Dept. KNL,
Church Army,
Independents Road,
Blackheath,
London SE3 9LG.
Tel: 0181 318 1226
Registered Charity No: 226226

HEARING DOGS FOR THE DEAF

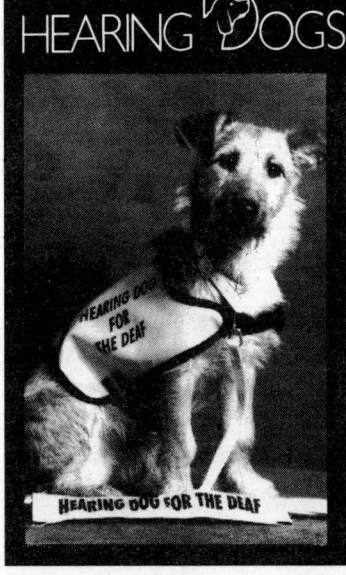

Rescued for a meaningful life

Den was just another unwanted pet in a rescue centre. Now as a fully trained Hearing Dog we have channelled his enthusiasm and energy into a useful and meaningful life. He is now assisting his deaf recipient, by hearing the sounds that most people take for granted.

Your donation or bequest would help us train many more dogs like Den. Please help in any way you can.

HEARING DOGS FOR THE DEAF TRAINING CENTRE
LONDON ROAD (A40), LEWKNOR, OXON OX9 5RY
TEL: 01844 353898
Patron: HRH The Princess Royal   Charity No. 293358

children's hospice SOUTH WEST

The South West has over 500 children with terminal illnesses. We provide love and care to sick and dying children and support to their families at the region's very own children's hospice, Little Bridge House.

We make no charge to families, but the cost of our specialised services is in the region of £800,000 per annum. Children's Hospices have little access to public funds, we are almost entirely dependent on public generosity. Your donation, convenanted gift or legacy will help us to continue our vital work.

Little Bridge House, Redlands Road, Fremington, Barnstaple, North Devon EX31 2PZ. Tel: 01271 25270. Fax: 01271 328640
Registered Charity Number: 1003314

BREAKTHROUGH
Deaf/Hearing Integration

Deafness is the most isolating of disabilities because it is a speechless invisible blank which deaf people cannot describe and hearing people cannot understand.

For 25 years, we have been working towards the integration of deaf and hearing people through training, education and interaction. Any help you can give will be music to our ears.
Registered charity No. 261951

BREAKTHROUGH TRUST
Charles W. Gillett Centre,
Selly Oak Colleges,
998 Bristol Road,
Selly Oak,
Birmingham B29 6LE
0121 472 6447 (voice)
0121 471 1001 (text)
0121 471 4368 (fax)

the charities of your choice tax effectively, whether you give in a sustained and regular way, make your donations spontaneously and with flexibility, or whether you simply want to ensure that both you and the charities you support gain the maximum benefit from your donations.

Further information on Gift Aid is given in the Inland Revenue leaflet IR113 and on the Gift Aid helpline on 0151 472 6038.

Lump-Sum Investment

Leave the gift of life
Include Blue Cross in your will

This 2-week-old kitten was thrown over a wall into a building site and left to die. We called him 'Everest' because he climbed so many mountains in his battle for life. He was just one of the thousands of animals saved by Blue Cross last year – animals that were rescued, adopted, nursed back to health and rehomed.

We couldn't save even one without our supporters. Especially those who care enough to include Blue Cross in their will. *You* can help us save lives. If we are to keep our pledge never to turn away an animal in need, we desperately need to find new supporters. Find out how you can help by filling in the coupon. It could mean 'the gift of life' to another defenceless animal like 'Everest'.

BLUE✚CROSS
We save lives

For further information, please write to, Tina Kew, Legacy Officer, Blue Cross, Freepost, Room 649c, Shilton Road, Burford, Oxon OX18 4BR. Reg Charity No. 224392.

Blue Cross has been helping animals in need for nearly one hundred years, and today is one of Britain's larger animal charities.

The Blue Cross veterinary service is provided for animals' owners who cannot afford private veterinary fees. We have three Animals Hospitals and a Clinic, which give over 60,000 free treatments annually, and perform over 6,000 lifesaving operations.

Every year, loving new homes are found for over 8,000 cats and dogs, through the eleven Blue Cross Adoption Centres which take in unwanted and abandoned animals. We believe no healthy animal should ever be put to sleep simply because it has no home.

This promise can only be kept if we have your support to provide care for the many animals at risk.

Tangibles and Other Investments

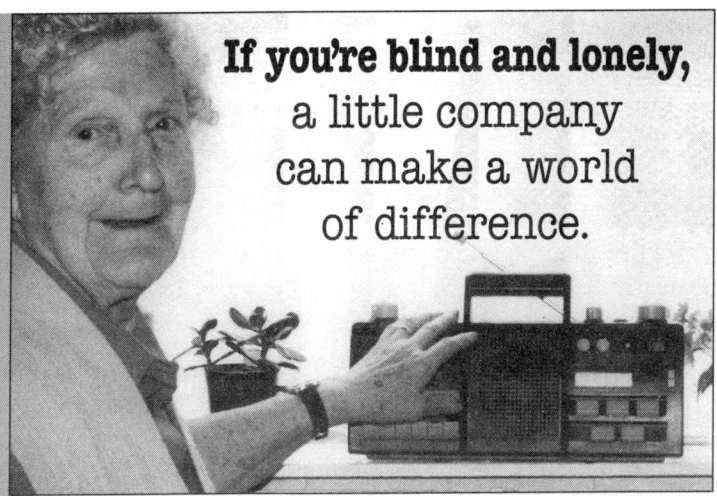

If you're blind and lonely, a little company can make a world of difference.

" To someone who is blind, lonely and in need, a radio means so much.

It brings complete entertainment; the comfort of a friendly voice, and constant companionship, around the clock, at the touch of a button.

Nearly half of all UK registered blind people live alone. Many are elderly, many exist on very limited incomes. The simple pleasure of a special radio or radio cassette provided by the British Wireless for the Blind Fund, free for life, can make all the difference in the world.

If you would like to help - with a donation, a covenant or legacy - please write to the address below. "

Richard Baker

For full details about the Fund and its work, please contact:
BRITISH WIRELESS FOR THE BLIND FUND
Gabriel House, 34 New Road, Chatham, Kent ME4 4QR Tel: (01634) 832501.
Fax: (01634) 817485. Reg. Charity No: 211849

KEEPING BLIND PEOPLE IN TOUCH WITH THE WORLD

Lump-Sum Investment

For further information about the Charities Aid Foundation's Charity Account Scheme telephone 01732 771333; or to find out more about the trust service contact 01892 512244.

Tangibles and Other Investments

PLEASE HELP US TO HELP THEM

Holly belonged to the owner of a public house and when the pub was sold, the new landlord had no idea of her existence. Holly was 35 years old and going blind. Eventually her plight was brought to our attention but in the two months since the sale, she had lost weight dramatically and was covered in lice.

Holly is now safe with us and has learnt the touch of kind hands and the sound of gentle voices. 6,700 donkeys have been taken into our care. To continue this work, we really need your help - either by a direct donation or a legacy.

Please send donations to:
The Donkey Sanctuary,
(Dept CG 96), Sidmouth,
Devon, EX10 0NU
Tel: (01395) 578222
Fax: (01395) 579266   Reg. Charity No. 264818

Over 6,700 donkeys have been taken into care, many from lives tormented by cruelty and neglect. A donkey is never turned away from our Sanctuary and never put down unless there is no longer any quality of life.

We need your help to continue rescuing donkeys as we must purchase an additional farm to ensure their future where they can spend their remaining days grazing peacefully and receiving loving care.

Any donation, no matter the amount, is gratefully appreciated and our donators' list is jealously guarded – we never release details to other organisations. Administration costs are kept to a minimum – just under 6p in the £1.

If you would like to receive further information, including a copy of our "Will Making Guide", please do not hesitate to contact us. A legacy is of great value to us to ensure the future of our large donkey family – many of the donkeys live to 40/50+ years. In return we remember with deep gratitude those who have made a bequest, not only inscribing their names on the Memorial Wall but also holding a Memorial Service every year on St Francis of Assisi Day.

The Donkey Sanctuary, Sidmouth, Devon, EX10 0NU. Tel. (01395) 578222. Fax. (01395) 579266. Administrator and Founder – Dr Elisabeth Svendsen, MBE

Advertisement feature

Lump-Sum Investment

PAYROLL GIVING AND VOUCHER ACCOUNTS

With a cache of money to dispense or save as you please you may wish to consider opportunities to give regularly to charity either as and when you like or through your salary. Payroll giving is a tax-free way to give from your pay. The voucher account system offers a versatile and flexible way to give to charity. Both schemes are administered by the Charities Trust.

Charities Trust is incorporated and registered as a charitable company to operate as a payroll giving agency in accordance with Sections 505 and 506 of the Income and Corporation Taxes Act 1988. Charities Trust aims to provide a high quality payroll giving service, which is non-profit making. The trust acts as a clearing house, sending donations to the chosen charities. Money is taken directly from the donor's pay with the benefit of tax relief. Any one of a quarter of a million causes can benefit. All contributions have to be distributed within 80 days of receipt and the interest obtained on deposit during that time helps to offset costs.

The administration fee is designed to cover the cost of the processing of the donor's requirements and the distribution to the selected charities. The fee is currently 5 per cent or 30p per donor per month, whichever is the greater. The breakdown of a single donation of £10 would be as follows: agency charge of 50p, cost to tax payer of £7.50, charity receives £9.50.

How the payroll giving system works

A maximum of four charities per person is permitted. The minimum donation per charity is 25p per week or £1 per month. Donors can vary their choice of charity or stop giving at any time. A statement of donations can be provided to employers on request at the end of each tax year.

Employers provide to employees a facility for a pre-tax deduction for charitable donations. Employers send those donations to Charities Trust monthly together with a list of donors. It is recommended that the donor code used is the employer's

Tangibles and Other Investments

Alzheimer's Research

The **Bristol Alzheimer's Research Centre** is internationally recognised for its development and evaluation of new treatments whilst providing support to sufferers and their families.

Funds are urgently needed for research into this devastating disease

To make a donation or for further information, please contact the

BRACE Appeal Office, Blackberry Hill Hospital, Fishponds, BRISTOL, BS16 2EW
Telephone: 0117 975 4831. Major credit cards accepted.

Bristol Research into Alzheimer's and Care of the Elderly, Registered Charity Number: 297965

ALZHEIMER'S RESEARCH – BRACE
(Bristol Research into Alzheimer's and Care of the Elderly)

BRACE supports an internationally recognised Alzheimer's Disease research centre (established in 1984) where a multidisciplinary team, including doctors, scientists, nurses, psychologists, psychiatrists and counsellors, works under the direction of Professor Gordon Wilcock who heads the Department of Care of the Elderly in the University of Bristol.

Statistics show that dementia affects approximately 750,000 people in Great Britain of middle age and beyond, and in particular 1 in 5 of those aged 80 years and over. Alzheimer's disease is the commonest cause of dementia, cruelly afflicting as many as 500,000 people in the UK. The Bristol research team is playing a key role in understanding the biochemical changes which take place in the brain, and over the past eleven years has been evaluating new treatments and methods of improving care for sufferers and their families. Scientists in the Department have been developing another avenue of treatment which will shortly be used in clinical trials.

The challenge and urgency of the work is considerable.

The charity BRACE is campaigning vigorously to create an Endowment Fund for the Department to ensure the ongoing research into this intractable and tragic disease which is causing such overwhelming distress and problems of care amongst our increasingly elderly population.

BRACE urgently needs your support.
Gifts, legacies or covenants are all deeply appreciated.
For further information please contact the BRACE Appeal Office (DT), Blackberry Hill Hospital, Manor Road, Fishponds, Bristol BS16 2EW. Tel. 0117 975 4831

Lump-Sum Investment

payroll number or National Insurance number. Donations are sent before the 19th of the following month in line with PAYE.

Employers should note that to achieve maximum tax benefits, they need to enter into a contract with an agency charity and register with the Inland Revenue. Charities Trust can undertake this on their behalf. Donors leaving a company's employment are entitled to request from the employer a statement of their contributions made during the tax year.

Employers may elect to match employee donations and/or pay their administration fees. To ease administration, personnel departments are advised to produce easy-to-follow forms to input for submission to Charities Trust and use constant donor/employee reference numbers. Inland Revenue regulations prohibit the return of any money withheld from employees.

Voucher accounts

Alternatively, you can open a voucher account. The minimum monthly donation is £120 per annum – £10 per month. The maximum individual donation is £900 per annum. With the tax advantage, a £10 donation would cost only £7.50. The scheme gives you the flexibility to give to whoever you want, whenever you want.

The money is paid into a 'pot' and whenever you wish to make a donation, whether it be to the local hospice or a TV extravaganza, the money is paid out. A book of vouchers or a charity cheque book is issued to you to enable this to happen.

A group voucher scheme runs alongside the individual voucher scheme. A 'group' is considered a minimum of five individuals. These contribute to a 'pot'. The minimum and maximum donations by the group are the same as for the individual's scheme: £120 and £900 per annum respectively. One employee is nominated to complete and return a group voucher account registration form to the Charities Trust. An account number will then be issued.

In addition, each employee donating to the group completes a Charity Choice Form but nominates the group account number rather than a specific charity. Once the group or individual account is established a book of vouchers will be supplied.

The vouchers are completed at the individual's discretion like a cheque book and forwarded to the charity. The charity will complete its section and return the voucher to the Charities Trust for processing. Please remember that the charity must be or become registered with Charities Trust. A statement of account is provided on a quarterly basis to the account holder(s). Statements show donations made (less an administration charge of 5% maximum), vouchers issued and balance available to use.

Charities Trust can also offer personal advice to companies on how employers can save time and money, how voucher accounts can be set up, enabling irregular donations to be made to an assortment of charities. The trust is the second largest payroll giving agency in the United Kingdom. It currently handles over 800 employers and more than 100,000 donors. Funds are distributed to over 2,000 charities.

For further information contact: Charities Trust, PO Box 15, Liverpool L23 0UU. Telephone: 0151 949 0044.

WILLS, LEGACIES AND CHARITABLE GIVING

Making wills is an age old occupation. It is quite impossible to say when the first will was made, by whom and under what circumstances. There are of course copies of ancient wills still in existence or records of what they contain. The purpose of wills has, however, never changed as it represents the inalienable right of people to leave their lifetime possessions to whomsoever they wish. For some it also provides an opportunity to speak from beyond the grave and throughout history all manner of people have used their wills to express unflattering observations about their kith and kin. Equally some of the sentiments expressed in wills about friends, relatives and reasons for leaving money to charity are loving and heart warming and depict the best features of human nature.

The style and nature of wills has of course changed down the centuries.

Here is an example of a will by Joshua West of the Six Clerks' Office in Chancery Lane, made in the 18th century. He wrote:

> Perhaps I died not worth a groat;
> but should I die worth something more,
> then I give that, and my best coat,
> and all my manuscripts in store, to those
> who shall the goodness have
> to cause my poor remains to rest
> within a decent shell and grave.
> This is the Will of Joshua West.

With the passage of time the collection and storage of wills became more regularised and a system evolved whereby probate matters in England and Wales were dealt with by a mixture of almost 400 ecclesiastical and secular courts. Some of these, including the Prerogative Court of the Archbishop of Canterbury were situated at the famous Doctors Commons near St Paul's Cathedral and it was there that the Principal Probate Registry was first located.

In 1857 Parliament passed The Court of Probate Act which established the Principal Probate Registry and 40 District

Probate Registries in England and Wales with effect from 12 January 1858. In October 1874 the great collection of wills stored in old Doctors Commons were transported through the streets of London in vans and wagons to Somerset House in the Strand into offices vacated by the Admiralty in the previous year. One hundred and twenty two years on, Somerset House remains the central repository for wills proved in England and Wales.

The case for challenging a will

In most respects the law in England and Wales provides the greatest freedom of choice for will makers in comparison with other countries. In other words, anyone from the age of 18 onwards can make a will disposing of their worldly goods in any way they choose. This of course can and does lead to injustices and where this occurs claimants have a right to challenge the will under the Inheritance (Provision for Families and Dependants) Act 1975. The basis of any claim is failure by the deceased to make reasonable financial provision for any person or persons who had some degree of financial dependence upon them prior to death. In other words, the plaintiff can claim compensation for the loss of benefit out of the estate.

The legal position is that claims should be made within six months from the date of grant of representation (probate) but the court can extend this time limit in very special circumstances. In order for the Act to be applied the deceased must have died domiciled in England and Wales. Currently the classes of persons who may challenge a will under the 1975 Act are:

- wife or husband of deceased;
- former wives or husbands of deceased who have not remarried;
- a child of the deceased;
- any person (not being a child of the deceased) who, in the case of any marriage to which the deceased was at any time a party, was treated by the deceased as a child of the family in relation to the marriage;
- any person (other than those above) who immediately before the death of the deceased was being maintained, either wholly or partly, by the deceased;

Lump-Sum Investment

- for deaths on or after 1 January 1996, a new category: persons living with the deceased in the same household and as the husband or wife of the deceased, during the two years immediately prior to the date of death (Law Reform (Succession) Act 1995).

The first Act of this kind was introduced in the 1930s since prior to that date a will in England and Wales could only be challenged on the basis that the legator was not of testamentary capacity – in other words they were not considered to be of sound mind, memory and understanding. This was a very unsatisfactory state of affairs since in order to gain redress for any injustice created by the will the plaintiff could only in effect allege that the deceased was of unsound mind. This could be deeply distressing when the testator or testatrix was a loved relative. It still remains a fact that wills are occasionally contested on the basis that the deceased did not have testamentary capacity, but in most cases wills are now challenged under the 1975 Act.

In Scotland the position is markedly different. Under Scottish law a will can be challenged on a number of grounds – for example if the person were insane when it was made, if children were born after the will was made, if the person had been improperly influenced by another person when making the will. The 1975 Act referred to earlier does not apply to Scotland in that there are inbuilt rights to protect the immediate family. Basically, whatever the will says, a surviving husband, wife or children can if they wish, after 'prior rights' have been satisfied, claim further 'legal rights' to a proportion of any property excluding house and land.

The amounts designated under 'prior rights' are changed from time to time but the current provision is as follows.

Prior rights
These are the surviving husband's or wife's rights to (a) the house (up to the value of £110,000); (b) furniture in the house (up to £20,000); (c) a payment of £30,000 if there are children, £50,000 if there are not.

Legal rights
After prior rights have been dealt with, a surviving husband or

National Benevolent Fund For The Aged

Giving direct practical help to older people on low incomes. Lord Tonypandy asks you to remember us when giving to charity or making your will.

The NBFA provides:
EMERGENCY ALARMS:
for peace of mind.
TENS MACHINES:
for pain relief.
HOLIDAYS and OUTINGS:
for pleasure and friendship.

For more information please contact:

1 Leslie Grove, Croydon CR0 6TJ
Tel: 0181-688 6655. Fax: 0181-688 1616
Registered Charity Number 243387

THE NATIONAL BENEVOLENT FUND FOR THE AGED

The National Benevolent Fund for the Aged (NBFA) is a small national charity founded nearly 40 years ago to provide direct help to older people. We help those on low income to improve their quality of life in a very practical way.

EMERGENCY ALARMS
The NBFA's provision of Emergency Alarms for older people living alone is a reassurance for them and their families that help is on call at the touch of a button in the event of an emergency.

TENS (Transcutaneous Electrical Nerve Stimulation)
TENS machines provide effective long term pain relief in conditions such as arthritis and rheumatism without the use of powerful drugs. The NBFA has provided many TENS machines for older people to use at home on long-term loan.

HOLIDAYS
For more than 25 years the NBFA has been providing holidays for older people – over 35,000 so far – giving enjoyment, a change of scene and good companionship. NBFA Holiday Clubs continue these benefits when the group returns home.

wife and children have certain 'legal rights' to a proportion of the 'moveable estate' – that is, all things such as money, shares, cars, furniture and jewellery.

Where there is an intestacy (no will) and any prior or legal rights have been dealt with the remainder of the estate is given to surviving relatives according to a strictly laid-down sequence – for example, any children have first claim; if there are no children half goes to the parents or parent and half to the brothers and sisters; if there are no children or parents all goes to the brothers and sisters and so on. In the event of there being no qualifying relatives in the case of an intestacy the estate will pass to the Crown.

Because of the complexities in the law relating to claims and contested wills it is imperative that plaintiffs, defendants and lay (non professional) executors seek legal advice from qualified solicitors.

Having set out the ways and means by which disputes over wills can be resolved it is important to remember that the overwhelming majority of wills create no problems at all and the intended beneficiaries receive their bequests as the will maker intended.

Why make a will?
Let us now consider the reasons why people make wills. As already stated, anyone over the age of 18 in England and Wales is eligible to make a will, whereas in Scotland girls from the age of 12 and boys from the age of 14 are able to make wills. Some people make a will at quite an early age, perhaps because they are involved in a dangerous job, pursuit or hobby or serving in Her Majesty's forces. Long distance travel or going abroad as a family often motivates people to make a will. Another strong reason for making a will is marriage or partnership or buying a house. It is also very important for people to make a will when their children are born, both to provide financial security and, deal with guardianship issues. Divorce does not totally invalidate a will except where it effects the provisions made for the former husband or wife. As life moves on the marriage or partnership of children may motivate parents to make wills, as may the birth of grandchildren. The problems associated with the ageing process are often the main reasons for making wills such as illness, the

If the beauty of bird song gives you pleasure

then ensure that future generations share your enjoyment by leaving a legacy to the BTO.

For over 60 years, the BTO's network of thousands of volunteers has collected vital information on the birds around us.

Leave the legacy of bird song for future generations.

Please remember the BTO in your will.

For information on how to secure the future of birds in the UK, and to receive a copy of our free booklet *A Will to Act*, please contact:

The Director of Development, Room 103B, BTO, The National Centre for Ornithology, The Nunnery, Thetford, Norfolk IP24 2PU.

The BTO is a registered charity no 216652

The British Trust for Ornithology
The National Centre for Ornithology – Room 103B
The Nunnery, Thetford, Norfolk IP24 2PU
Tel: 01842 750050. Fax: 01842 750030. RCN 216652

The BTO cares for the well-being of all our wild birds by encouraging a wider understanding through studies carried out by birdwatchers.

The information collected by thousands of BTO volunteers provides the basis upon which conservation policies and practices are based. The BTO has recently started a large-scale garden bird survey, called *Garden BirdWatch,* to study our best-loved birds. The BTO has also highlighted the declines of many of our farmland birds and has launched the *Save Our Skylarks* campaign to help bring them back.

Please support our work with a donation or a legacy to safeguard the future of our birds.

death of loved ones and the general desire to put one's affairs in order. Experience of dealing with an intestacy is another strong motivator for making a will. Moral – don't make life harder for the loved ones you leave behind.

Above and beyond all else it is important for people to realise that the only way to ensure their worldly possessions pass to the beneficiaries of their choice is to make a will. It is often presupposed that there is no need to make a will because the immediate family will benefit anyway, which is to some extent true where the estate is of modest size. In the case of high value estates it has been known for husbands or wives in particular to find that the provisions under the Intestacy Rules do not sufficiently cater for their needs and it may then be necessary in England and Wales to seek further and better provision under the 1975 Inheritance Act.

Tax considerations

For some people tax planning is important and anyone wishing to make special arrangements to reduce or avoid tax should seek expert advice. Bequests to a surviving husband or wife are totally exempt from inheritance tax as are gifts through wills to charities. Other beneficiaries, such as children, are liable to pay tax on any inheritances they receive in excess of the inheritance tax threshold. With effect from 6 April 1996 the inheritance tax threshold was raised to £200,000 from the previous level of £154,000. This will clearly release quite a few more estates from tax completely. For estates over £200,000 a flat rate tax of 40 per cent is levied on the excess unless it passes to exempt beneficiaries as mentioned earlier.

There are other ways of reducing the burden of tax on estates but because of the unique nature of each person's affairs it is always advisable to obtain professional advice on the legitimate ways in which this can be done. Whilst many solicitors have knowledge in this field, it is sometimes better to consult accountants who probably have the greatest skills in this area of tax planning.

At the moment, for instance, we have what is generally known as the seven-year rule. This relates to any personal gifts made during a person's lifetime in excess of the annual or other specific exemptions, such as gifts on marriage, known as 'potentially exempt transfers'. These transfers are subject to inheritance tax only if the person who makes the gift dies within a seven-year period from the time of making the gift. Tax is reduced on a sliding scale depending on how many years have elapsed before the donor's death as shown below:

Years before death	Percentage of full tax charge
0–3	100
3–4	80
4–5	60
5–6	40
6–7	20

The wealth factor

It is impossible to say how many people place a high priority on tax planning when making their wills but, looking at the wealth statistics produced by Smee & Ford, the vast majority of people who die each year do not leave large estates. For instance, in 1994 there were approximately 544,000 adult deaths in England and Wales. Of these fewer than half (247,491) left estates worth over £5000. The probate value of these estates was £17.66 billion. 53,409 or 21.6 per cent died intestate, the cumulative value of their estates being £2.02 billion. The 194,082 will makers together left £15.64 billion. Furthermore, detailed analysis indicated that 85 per cent of the will makers had estates worth between £5000 and £125,000, suggesting that the great majority could be described as cash poor but asset rich. In other words, for most of them their house would have been their most valuable possession. Just under 15 per cent of will makers had estates valued between £125,000 and £1 million. People leaving estates in excess of £1 million totalled 690 or 0.4 per cent of all will makers. Fourteen millionaires died intestate and of course their estates would be distributed in accordance with the Intestacy Rules.

Professional involvement

Although available evidence indicates that relatively few will makers take financial advice from accountants when making their wills, it is very important that they consult a solicitor who will be able to give sound legal advice, particularly when complicated provisions are required. The research carried out by Smee & Ford reveals that the majority of will makers still appoint lay executors only but in most cases these executors engage solicitors to obtain the Grant of Probate and carry out the subsequent estate administration on their behalf. Many will makers appoint non-professional executors because they believe it will reduce the cost of administering their estates but for the reasons stated above legal charges are incurred by the employment of solicitors who will require a written undertaking from the lay executors that their proper professional fees will be deductible from the estate. When solicitors are themselves appointed executors their charging clause will automatically be written into the will. All the main banks provide a will making and probate service but have only a very tiny percentage of the executorship market, possibly due to the fact that their charges are for the most part higher than the fees charged by solicitors.

It is of course quite feasible for people to make home-made wills or use the standard forms which can be obtained from stationer's shops. Providing people observe the basic legal requirements such wills are perfectly valid and raise no problems in implementation. Even so, the best advice is to consult a solicitor who will be prepared to give prospective clients a quote for making their will. The cost of a solicitor made will is not nearly as high as some people believe. In some cases it can be less than £50 with special deals for joint wills made by husbands, wives or partners.

Legal requirements
The basic principles for making a valid will are that it must be in writing and must appoint executors. The attestation clause must follow the legal requirement that the testator and two witnesses be together and sign the will in the presence of each other. In the case of Scotland only one witness is now required, but there the testator is required to sign each page of the will, whereas in England and Wales the testator need only sign the attestation clause on the final page along with the two witnesses. Although it is possible to have up to four executors, one is sufficient, but on

Tangibles and Other Investments

THERE'S NO BETTER EXERCISE FOR THE HEART THAN BENDING DOWN TO PICK UP A CHILD.

Children in Crisis believes every boy and girl has the right to a healthy and happy childhood. Our aim is to provide relief wherever we find hardship, distress, sickness and poverty.

We help children in any part of the world, irrespective of race, religion or politics. Our work seeks to restore dignity and hope. We are active in Former-Yugoslavia; we also provide aid in Poland, Albania and Britain.

And while children depend on us, we depend on you. Your generosity makes the difference between a pitiful existence and a life worth living. So please lift up your wallet and shed a few pounds.

Please send your donation to:
Children in Crisis, 4 Calico House, Plantation Wharf, York Road, London SW11 3UB.
Or telephone Juliette Smith on 0171-978 5001 for details on tax effective ways to give.

children in crisis

Charity Registration No. 1020488

balance it is preferable to choose two people such as a solicitor and a younger adult relative or close friend. Remember, a will may be declared invalid if it has not been signed and dated by the testator in the presence of the witness or witnesses who must also sign the will. Witnesses do not need to know the contents of the will they are witnessing nor should they be beneficiaries, since being a witness or a spouse of a witness could invalidate any gift bequeathed to them if the will is made in England and Wales. In Scotland it is preferable not to have the will witnessed by a beneficiary but this will not invalidate the attestation or (as in England and Wales) the gift. On the other hand, an executor may be named as a beneficiary in any will.

As indicated earlier the sole purpose of making a will is to dispose of one's lifetime possessions and to decide on the list of beneficiaries who are to inherit your estate. There are three main types of legacies. The first is a specific gift such as a car, house, item of jewellery or other household effect. If at the time of death the gift described in the will cannot be found or identified it will fail. The second type of legacy is a pecuniary (cash) gift of any size (for example £1000). The third type of legacy is what is called a residuary bequest, which is all or part of the balance of the estate after all debts, taxes, expenses and other legacies have been paid. With the passage of time pecuniary legacies will lose value because of inflation and legators may therefore wish either to index-link their cash gifts to family, friends and charity or divide the whole estate into shares or percentages so that all classes of beneficiaries will gain if the value of the estate increases between the will being made and the time of death.

Charitable giving through wills
Despite the growing incidence of divorce and the increasing numbers of people who live alone, the strong allegiance to family and other loved ones is still reflected in the provisions of wills, but there have always been a minority of legators who make charitable bequests. Although this amounts only to about one will maker in seven, Smee & Ford estimate that in England and Wales alone charitable will makers collectively leave £1 billion to their favourite causes each year. It is the second most productive form of voluntary income for charitable organisations and any

diminution in this source of funding will have very serious implications for most of the United Kingdom's leading charities. To illustrate this point further, the following charities amongst many others receive over 50 per cent of their total voluntary income from legacies: RNLI, Imperial Cancer Research Fund, Cancer Research Campaign, Guide Dogs for the Blind Association, Barnardo's, RNIB, Salvation Army, RSPCA and British Heart Foundation. A number of smaller charities are also heavily dependent upon legacy income including the Dogs' Home, Battersea which every year receives more than 90 per cent of its income in the form of legacies.

It may well be that far more people could be influenced into leaving charitable gifts, bearing in mind the tax benefits to both the giver and the receiver. Charities have been influential over the years in promoting the concept of will making since there is no provision for charities under the Intestacy Rules. No will equals no charitable bequest.

It is to be hoped that with the passage of time and continuing growth of individual wealth more people will see the wisdom of making a will and not allow the law to have the final say in their affairs. I began this article by quoting an ancient will and I will end with a few lines from a very recent will:

> O, grant me, heaven, a middle state,
> Neither too humble, nor too great,
> More than enough, for nature's ends,
> With something left to treat my friends.

Bernard Sharpe is Director of Consultancy with Smee & Ford Ltd, having previously worked in the charity sector for over 20 years, promoting and administering legacies for the RNLI and SCOPE.

13

Where to Go for Professional Advice

One question often asked by investors is where to go to get reliable financial advice. In practice, there is no shortage of people or organisations willing to offer advice, from stockbrokers to solicitors and accountants, banks and various kinds of intermediary. The services offered also cover a wide range, from advice on specific types of investment, such as life assurance plans or stocks and shares, to overall financial management, including tax planning and long-term strategies as well as day-to-day affairs.

As well as scope, services differ in terms of independence, cost and the type of client they are aimed at. Traditionally, for example, stockbrokers, merchant banks and accountants focused on the top end of the market, so-called 'high net worth individuals', while smaller investors dealt mainly with insurance brokers and agents, or the local bank manager.

These two extremes have now come much closer together. The top end has spread downwards, as stockbrokers have made efforts to enlarge their appeal and appear more user-friendly. Some are even advertising on commercial radio in order to spread the message to a wider audience. At the same time, smaller firms of advisers have been expanding the range of services they offer, moving up the scale from simple life assurance into the realms of investment and, in some cases, tax planning.

There are perhaps three main reasons for these changes. In the first place, the substantial growth in home ownership before and after the Second World War has meant that far more people are now inheriting property. In many cases, they already own their own homes, so the inheritance translates into a sizeable capital sum – even despite the recent fall in property prices. This creates a need not only for investment advice, but also tax planning; the nil rate band for inheritance tax of £200,000 can easily be surpassed where the estate includes a house.

Redundancy, sadly, is another source of increased demand for advice. Again, there are two sides to this. First, the redundancy payment may be a sizeable sum that needs careful investment, particularly if the redundancy happens fairly late in life and the person is not expecting to find another job, or not at the previous level. Second, the tighter job market has encouraged younger people to set up their own businesses, with a consequent need for advice on matters such as tax and pension arrangements.

Third, the spate of privatisation issues over the last few years has enticed many first-timers into the stock market, some of whom have then caught the bug and gone on to other share dealing. A good number, of course, have not stayed in the market, particularly as some issues gave exaggerated opportunities to take a quick profit. But this in itself encouraged the growth of cheap share-dealing services; while the issues could be bought very easily through application forms in newspapers, selling was more of a problem and 'no-frills' services sprang up as a convenient solution.

The Financial Services Act

In addition to these social changes, a major influence on the development of financial services, and the cause of much upheaval, has been the Financial Services Act, which became law in 1988. This is founded on the principle – which has been much questioned ever since – of self-regulation by the industry rather than statutory control by the government.

Nevertheless, it has still spawned a substantial amount of bureaucracy and one suspects that vast acreages of forest must have been expended on producing rule-books, which are continuously needing to be updated for amendments, and which are so complicated that further reams of paper are devoted to clarification of what it all might mean. If there has been one growth area during the recent recession, it has been the compliance departments of financial services companies, which are responsible for ensuring that all these rules are followed.

At the top of the regulatory tree is the Securities and Investments Board (SIB), which is responsible for supervising the whole show. At the next level down are the Self Regulatory Organisations (SROs), which take their authority from the SIB and carry out the day-to-day tasks of regulation. Prior to 1994, there were four of these bodies: the Financial Intermediaries, Managers and Brokers Regulatory Association (Fimbra); the Life Assurance and Unit Trust Regulatory Organisation (Lautro); the Investment Management Regulatory Organisation (Imro); and the Securities and Futures Authority (SFA).

In July 1994, a new SRO came into operation: the Personal Investment Authority (PIA). This is responsible for retail investment services and is in effect an amalgamation of Fimbra and Lautro, plus Imro members who deal primarily with private clients.

The PIA was originally conceived as an answer to funding problems experienced by Fimbra, particularly in relation to the Investors' Compensation Scheme. It was felt that a single regulator would be more cost-effective and financially sound; it would also offer a measure of control to life assurance companies, which had been repeatedly asked to subsidise Fimbra while having no say in how it was run. The SIB also saw the creation of the PIA as an opportunity for raising regulatory standards.

In addition to the SROs, there are also Recognised Professional Bodies (RPBs). These cover professionals who offer investment advice and management services as part of their business, such as solicitors, accountants and insurance brokers. The Law Society, the Insurance Brokers Registration Council and various accountancy bodies act as RPBs.

Anyone who gives financial advice must be authorised through one of these various organisations. The PIA covers independent financial advisers, life assurance companies and their agents, and unit trust groups, while investment managers dealing mainly with institutional clients continue to come under Imro and stockbrokers are governed by the SFA.

Anyone who offers financial advice without being authorised is

Where to Go for Professional Advice

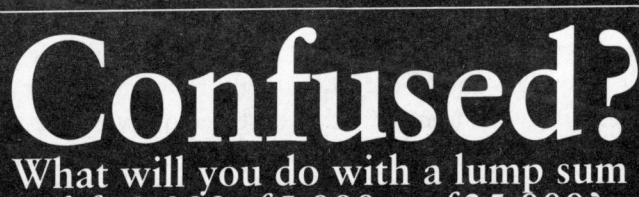

breaking the law, unless it is on a casual, one-off basis and unpaid. This was once explained to me by a regulator as follows: if you are in the pub one evening and a friend asks you for some advice, you may obviously offer your opinion. But if you hold court at the bar every night, offering advice to all and sundry and perhaps accepting a few drinks in return, that would, strictly speaking, be against the law.

Polarisation

Authorised firms must display on all their literature, stationery, business cards and so on which of the regulatory bodies they belong to. In addition, they must make it clear whether they are offering advice in a wholly independent capacity, or as the representative of one particular company.

This distinction, which is known as polarisation, was one of the main planks of the Financial Services Act when it was first drawn up. Before then, it was quite common for some advisers to recommend products supplied by more than one company, but without professing to cover the entire market. For example, they might limit their suggestions to just a handful of companies because they lacked the resources to research all of them. Alternatively, they might act in the main for a single company, but occasionally recommend others if the required product was not offered by that one company.

The powers that be decided that this could prove much too confusing for the customer, who would not be sure whether the advice he was getting was genuinely free range or in fact limited to a small sector of the market. So they came up with the principle of polarisation, under which an adviser must be either completely independent and able to offer the products of any company in the market, or tied exclusively to one company and barred from offering the products of any other. Since then, there have been occasional proposals to modify the principle; for example, to allow 'multi-ties', under which an adviser could represent several specified companies, but so far it has not been changed.

To be independent, the cardinal rules laid down were 'know your customer' and 'give best advice'. The former still holds: advisers must complete a fact-find on their clients, covering circumstances such as age and tax position, the range of their financial needs and other relevant factors such as attitude to risk.

The 'best advice' principle has since been toned down to 'good advice'. The adviser is not expected to have a crystal ball to show which product will produce the best results at the end of the day – which could be 20 years hence – but he must select the most appropriate for his client from all those available, in terms of both the type of product and the track record of the company on charges, past performance and so on.

In practice, this means that the adviser may focus on particular companies if they are seen to be the market leaders. For example, if he identifies one company as being good for endowment policies, there is nothing to stop him recommending it to several different clients, but he must be prepared to justify his choice to inspectors from his regulatory body, who will make periodic visits to check that the rules are being satisfied.

While this is basically a sound concept – and what any good adviser should be following anyway – there are certain drawbacks in practice. First, advisers may be tempted to stick to big name companies, the choice of which would not be queried, rather than face having to justify a recommendation which might be based on gut feeling as much as hard facts.

Second, the considerable costs and pressures of being independent have meant that a large number of advisers have simply given up and become tied, so the availability of independent advice has shrunk considerably. It is arguable that the quasi-independent advice that existed before, for all its faults, at least gave investors a degree of choice.

Those tied to one company may work as part of a direct salesforce or be self-employed but acting as an appointed representative. Either way, they can offer only the products from that one company's range but, within that, they are still expected to recommend the most appropriate product. The obvious drawback is that the company may simply not provide the type of product that would best suit the client, in which case he may be persuaded into a poorer substitute.

In practice, the competition between companies to attract and retain good quality representatives does influence the product range, although it is still true that any single company is unlikely to be a market leader across the board. Naturally, both independent advisers and representatives will argue fiercely for their own merits: the former point out that they are free to select the best product on the market for any given need, while the latter claim that the closer relationship they have with the company can work to the client's advantage. The truth is that there are good and bad in both sectors; what really counts is honesty and competence.

For banks and building societies, polarisation presented a difficult problem. On the one hand, they did not want to give up offering independent advice, as that might mean losing their more discriminating (and more valuable) customers, but on the other, the branch network represented an excellent outlet for business from an associated operation.

Midland, Barclays and Lloyds already had associated life and assurance and unit trust companies and a number of others have set up subsidiaries since: among them, NatWest Life, Abbey National Life, Woolwich Life, Halifax Life and N&P Life. In fact, 'bancassurance', as it is known, is becoming a growing force in the market and represents considerable potential competition to traditional operators because of the huge opportunities afforded by high street outlets.

Of the major banks, National Westminster was the only one to retain independent status at the outset, which it has now given up, while among the top ten building societies, only Bradford & Bingley offers independent advice. To some extent, though, banks and building societies have cut across polarisation by offering tied advice through their branches and independent advice through a separate arm. But where they have associated operations of their own, these would not normally be recommended through the independent side; the rule for that situation is that the recommendation would have to be 'better than best advice', which in practice would be almost impossible to prove.

With so many developments in the market, it is difficult to be categorical about what sort of advice is available from where. What follows is therefore just a basic guide to current sources and the services they offer.

Merchant banks

Merchant banks still tend to operate very much at the top end of the scale, offering investment services mainly or wholly for six and seven figure portfolios. These would be based on UK equities and gilts and also on overseas investments, either directly into equities or, particularly for smaller markets, through the medium of unit trusts and other pooled funds.

Commonly they provide services on a discretionary basis, which means that they will take the decisions without previously referring to the client. You do, of course, have the chance to specify your aims and requirements; for example, whether you are primarily seeking income or capital growth and the degree of risk you are prepared to take.

**Phone ShareLink for the best
0121 200**

Where to Go for Professional Advice

REDMAYNE BENTLEY
STOCKBROKERS

MEMBERS OF THE SECURITIES AND FUTURES AUTHORITY
MEMBERS OF THE LONDON STOCK EXCHANGE

MERTON HOUSE 84 ALBION STREET LEEDS LS1 6AG
TEL: LEEDS (0113) 243 6941 FAX: LEEDS (0113) 244 5516

YOUR FRIEND ON THE STOCK EXCHANGE

**"WE WON'T DO IT FOR YOU,
WE WILL DO IT WITH YOU!"**

BRANCHES ALSO AT: BEVERLEY BURY ST EDMUNDS GLASGOW HARROGATE HENLEY-ON-THAMES
INVERNESS LEIGH-ON-SEA LOCKSBOTTOM LONDON MANCHESTER PERTH STROUD

The firm will take care of all the paperwork, but you will be kept informed of all the transactions and in addition will receive regular reports and valuation statements. The management fee will generally be based on a percentage of the portfolio value on an annual basis.

Stockbrokers

At one time, stockbrokers were generally regarded as inhabiting a rarefied world of high finance which had little to do with the man in the street. In recent years, though, the mystique has been

---

introduction to stocks and shares.
2242.

Lump-Sum Investment

Choosing and using Investment Advisers

Given the bewildering array of investments available, it makes sense to take specialist advice when investing a lump sum. The right choice could make you lots of money. Conversely the wrong choice could mean you lose out. This decision therefore needs very careful advance thought.

Financial advisers will either be a company representative (sometimes called a tied agent) or an independent financial adviser (IFA). A company representative can only advise you on the products of one company which limits the range of advice that can be given. An IFA can select any product from a wide range of companies to recommend to you. The flexibility this offers cannot be under-estimated. For example,

(i) You might want a specific type of investment, perhaps with some form of guarantee.
(ii) You may wish to include an extra benefit – perhaps a lump sum investment with some protection benefits or wrapped inside a trust for extra tax savings.
(iii) Are you concerned about charges within a product? An IFA can use products with the competitive charging structures.
(iv) An IFA can recommend companies that have proven track records – very important when investing a lump sum.
(v) IFAs regularly deal with several companies and can compare their relative administration merits.
(vi) Most IFAs will monitor the financial strength of the companies they recommend.
(vi) Company representatives will generally be remunerated by commission. The IFA will also normally be entitled to commission but may alternatively be prepared to accept the payment of a fee.

Therefore, it will normally be in your interest to choose an IFA. But how do you choose between different IFAs?

Check how long the adviser has been in business and with which firms. It would be reassuring to deal with somebody who is likely to be around in the future and hopefully with the same firm.

You should be absolutely certain as to the adviser's ability to provide quality investment advice. For example,

• Can he analyse the suitability of different products to meet your financial needs?
• Can he appraise the financial strength of all investment companies?
• Has he the ability to investigate and appraise, across the market, good quality investment performance and good track records?
• Can he compare the differing initial and ongoing charges of companies?
• Does he know the quality of differing companies' administration services?

Continuing investment advice is just as important as the initial advice. Markets and outlooks change and if action is not taken this can damage the value of your investment. Your adviser can regularly review your investment objectives and requirements.

The IFA should also make use of modern technology and research in order to give you the best possible advice. This can be a major cost and for this reason a number of IFAs have joined together under the umbrella of a Network. The Network then provides information based on in-depth sophisticated research and development to all Network members at a shared cost, thus giving the best possible information on which to base investment recommendations. The Burns-Anderson Independent Network is committed to this process and provides up-to-date electronic information comparing products, investment track records and companies' financial strengths, to all their Network members in order that they can provide the best possible investment advice.

The Burns-Anderson Independent Network PLC is regulated by the Personal Investment Authority.

Advertisement feature

Where to Go for Professional Advice

FOR MANY PEOPLE CHOOSING THE RIGHT FINANCIAL PRODUCT CAN BE A GAMBLE. WE'VE REDUCED THE ODDS.

With literally thousands of pension schemes, unit trusts and insurance plans to choose from, the odds are the product you choose may not be the most suitable for your personal requirements. Unless of course you seek professional, independent financial advice. This is where we come in.

The Burns-Anderson Independent Network PLC is a nationwide network of independent financial advisers committed to providing you with professional and impartial advice. All our advisers have access to our unique computerised Best Advice System.

Our Best Advice System, combined with our professional advisers ensures you get the best possible advice on the comprehensive range of financial products.

Our research team, working with leading investment specialists, carries out an in depth analysis of each product area to ensure that only the top quality products are included.

So before making your next financial decision talk to us first. We can ensure you receive independent, unbiased and professional advice. And of course the right product for you.

Call Helen Spiller at Burns-Anderson now on **0117 927 6954** or write to her at:

The Burns-Anderson Independent Network PLC, 27 Great George Street, Bristol BS1 5QT.

A QUALITY NETWORK

 Regulated by the Personal Investment Authority

all but dispelled. For one thing, Big Bang brought greater potential for competition between firms, stimulating the wider publicity of their services. For another, potential clients are no longer just the upper classes whose families have placed business with the same broker for generations. With privatisations, all kinds of newcomers have been drawn into share-buying and most stockbrokers are keen to attract this new business.

As a result, where choosing a broker was once largely a matter of personal recommendation, a number now advertise their services and provide information on what they offer. For example, the Association of Private Client Investment Managers and Stockbrokers produces a directory in which members set out brief but alluring guides to the facilities they provide. All this is very welcome, as it makes the choices much clearer.

Most brokers offer a range of services, from the very basic to the fully comprehensive, as follows.

1. *Dealing or execution-only service.* This is for people who simply want the broker to buy and sell shares, generally without any advice being given. Because there are no added frills, this is generally much cheaper than management facilities.
2. *Discretionary or portfolio management service.* This is suitable for those who have an overall idea of what they want, in terms of income or growth and degree of risk, but do not want to take part in the decision process. The broker will take full responsibility for managing the investments, but the client will be kept informed of the transactions carried out and will receive regular valuations and reports. While some brokers only offer this type of service to wealthier clients, many are happy to take on quite small portfolios and there may be no fees above the dealing commission.
3. *Advisory service.* This may cover dealings in individual shares or the whole of your investment portfolio. Unlike the discretionary service, the client takes responsibility for decisions; the broker will offer advice, based on the client's needs and objectives, but no transactions will be carried out without reference and express permission. Although some brokers specify a minimum portfolio size, which might be

anywhere between £20,000 and £75,000, others are happy to consider any amount.
4. *Comprehensive financial planning.* In addition to investment management, this would include advice on any other financial needs; for example, retirement planning, school fees, tax planning, mortgages, life assurance and general cash management. In fact, it could go right down to advice on bank and building society deposit accounts and some brokers also offer banking facilities themselves.

Now that standardised commission scales no longer exist, costs can vary from one firm to another. As a rule, those based in the provinces are likely to be cheaper than those in London, simply because they have lower overheads, and with modern communications technology, location should not have any impact on the quality of service. If you are using an advisory service, it may be more convenient to choose a local firm; for a discretionary service, this is not particularly necessary, although you may need to make the occasional visit to update your objectives.

Accountants and solicitors

Traditionally, accountants have focused on tax affairs, while solicitors have touched on financial matters only indirectly, through business such as conveyancing and wills. Nowadays, however, the distinctions are becoming blurred and accountants in particular may offer overall financial planning services, generally on a fee basis.

Solicitors are becoming more involved in investment business and there is now a trade association for those who specialise in giving financial advice – the Association of Solicitor Investment Managers. A directory of members can be obtained free by telephoning 01892 870065. Work is undertaken on a fee basis, as solicitors are required by the Law Society to disclose and repay any commission earned.

Independent financial advisers

Independent financial advisers will generally come under the auspices of the PIA, but that, and the fact of independent status,

Keep it simple!

by John S. D. Shorter ALIA(Dip), FLIA of Shorter Byrne & Co

Over the past fifteen years, I must have asked literally thousands of people what they are looking for from their ideal investment. Some people say they are seeking the maximum income they can obtain from their nest-egg. Others, being happily awash with surplus income from other sources, are far more interested in maximising capital growth for their future or that of their family. *Everybody* I speak to justifiably requires absolute security (i.e. protection against fraud) and the majority of people, when asked, admit that they would prefer the strategy which is to be adopted for them to be SIMPLE.

In my view, it is to be applauded that the world of financial services has, through the medium of the press over the past couple of decades or so, been going out of its way to make the whole area of lump sum investment seem very much less mysterious than it previously appeared to be. The problem now seems to be that we are all suffering from a new disease; Information overload! The national newspapers and lately the TV are bombarding us (especially at weekends) with a seemingly limitless range of differing ideas on how our precious capital could be invested.

Imagine for a wild moment that you have just learned that you are this week's Lottery Jackpot winner. Where are you going to go for advice on how to invest it? Some people would immediately put it on deposit in the High Street Building Society or Bank without a second thought and will entertain a vague thought that they will probably do something "better" with it when they get round to it. Others will speak to a firm of Stockbrokers to see what they recommend as the current "best buys". Still others, mindful of the dangers of ignoring the destructive effects of inflation upon deposited money over the long term, would respond to those seductive newspaper advertisements which appear to them to offer the solution to their requirement for income or capital growth or both.

Yes, the whole world of investment *does* appear to be incredibly complex and dangerous to many people. Perhaps that's the very reason for the phenomenal success of the Building Society movement in this country over so many years. People feel that the money will, at least, be safe there.

Safe from what, I wonder?

Certainly not from the ravages of inflation. Leaving all your Lottery winnings in the jolly old Building Society into the years ahead could be rather like leaving a block of ice in the sun. Even modest rates of inflation will certainly, if slowly, destroy its buying power bit by bit. Perhaps it's the comforting thought that Building Societies and Banks don't either collapse or run off with people's money, do they? . . . and of course it's a nice simple way of investing.

Giving the matter a little thought, most people would agree that investing a lump sum of money just cannot be as easy as merely asking which Building Society is paying the highest interest rate on a given day. If that were the case, why would the great investing institutions of this country, like pension funds and insurance companies, employ armies of investment managers, analysts and other experts to spread the billions of pounds of savers' money across all the world's Stock-markets, industrial and commercial property markets *and* the money markets? The answer, of course, is that history shows us again and again that, given a reasonably continuous period of time, investing in real assets (as distinct from simply placing money on deposit) has always proved to be a successful antidote to the relatively modern phenomenon of inflation.

Making a decision on where to invest the money is however only part of the problem. Another key issue is that of the TERRIBLE TAX TRIO – Income Tax, Capital Gains Tax and Inheritance Tax. It seems to me that there is little point in helping a client to build up a substantial amount of money for the next generation through highly successful investment strategies, if no heed is taken of the demon Tax Man and the damage he can inflict. As an example, Inheritance Tax, will snatch a pretty fair chunk of your estate away from your nearest and dearest if you fail to do anything about it. Because of the clever and effective mitigation schemes on offer from the ever-inventive Insurance Companies, IHT could be referred to as a voluntary tax. Are these schemes simple enough, though, to understand?

An experienced Independent Financial Adviser (duly regulated by the Personal Investment Authority) is not only in a position to ascertain from you precisely what your desires from the lump sum happen to be, but also to help you to select financial products which are *appropriate* to your needs. To do this successfully, it is necessary to take careful account of information gleaned from you regarding your family circumstances, your short- and long-term requirements from the capital involved, your attitude towards investment volatility, your tax position and many other related matters. Therein lies the skill of the adviser. In brief, his (or of course her) responsibility is to express in as simple and straightforward a way as possible the advantages and disadvantages of the solutions which may be suitable in your particular case. Moreover, most IFAs worth their salt are keen to ensure that you are offered an on-going service into the years ahead in order to ensure that any relevant changes in your circumstances or in the tax rules are taken into account within your chosen strategy and any relevant changes swiftly put in hand.

Remember, a good Independent Financial Adviser will always KEEP IT SIMPLE!

Where to Go for Professional Advice

Associate Member of
The Independent Financial
Practitioner's Group

SHORTER, BYRNE & Co.
INDEPENDENT FINANCIAL ADVISERS
(Est. 1980)

**CONFUSED OVER CHOICE OF INVESTMENT?
WANT SOME RELIABLE HELP?**

**WE SPECIALISE IN MAKING THINGS PLAIN
AND SIMPLE**

'PHONE (01323) 725624 FOR THE NO-NONSENSE APPROACH

Regulated by the Personal Investment Authority

---

are more or less the only things that any one may have in common with any other. In other respects, this group has enormous diversity, ranging from one-man bands to large firms and offering a wide variety of services.

In the first place, there are different categories of authorisation, depending on the type of business carried out. At the lower end, the adviser will not actually handle your money; you simply make out your cheque direct to the company supplying the product. Firms that do handle clients' money have to undergo more rigorous checks designed to ensure that they are not likely to make off with it.

New entrants to the industry must undergo 'Stage 1' training before they are allowed to give any advice. This includes passing an examination, commonly the first paper of the Financial Planning Certificate, which tests knowledge of regulation and products. They may then give advice under supervision as part of Stage 2 training. To become a 'competent' adviser, a person must obtain Stage 2 qualifications such as the second and third papers of the Financial Planning Certificate.

Arbitration or Ligitation?

The Personal Investment Authority was established following upon a recommendation by Sir Kenneth Clucas made in March 1992 that a single self-regulating body be established to regulate investment business carried out for private investors. The Personal Investment Authority commenced operation on 18th July 1994, as did the Personal Investment Authority Ombudsman Bureau Ltd, a company limited by guarantee and the body established to provide an efficient and cost-effective source of redress for persons with legitmate complaints relating to investment business carried out by members of the Personal Investment Authority.

The procedure adopted by the Bureau as set out in the Ombudsman's terms of reference is a mixture of conciliation and adjudication designed to provide a swift and cost-effective forum for dispute resolution and intented to provide an attractive alternative to litigation as a means of resolving disputes within the Bureau's terms of reference. The Bureau has two jurisdictions. The mandatory jurisdiction which covers mainstream investment business as defined by the financial Services Act 1986 binds all Personal Investment Authority members and enables the Bureau to award a maximum of £50,000 by way of compensation.

The voluntary jurisdiction, which came into being on 1 April 1995, is one to which members of the Personal Investment Authority can elect to be subject and covers matters such as the administration of long-term insurance business and other investments and events which occurred before 29 April 1988, being the date upon which the Financial Services Act came into effect. Somewhat surprisingly, the voluntary jurisdiction enables the Bureau to recommend that a maximum figure for completion of £100,000 is paid although, unlike awards made under the mandatory jurisdiction, compliance cannot be enforced by the complainant and will be secured by the peer and moral pressure exercised by the Personal Investment Authority upon its members.

The procedure adopted under both, jurisdictions is a model of clarity and revolves around initially encouraging reconciliation by means of a statement of complaint by the complainant to the Personal Investment Authority member which requires a reasoned response from the member. The Bureau's early experience suggests that better communication between members and their customers could avoid many complaints arising and this is clearly an area requiring application by the industry. If matters cannot be resolved at the complaint stage, the matter formally becomes a "case" and is taken over by a case officer who investigates, attempts conciliation, and if conciliation fails, then provisional agreement is made. It is only if either party rejects the advice contained in the provisional assessment that the matter is referred to the Ombudsman who considers the matter afresh and issues an adjudication which will be binding on the member if accepted by the complainant. Adjudication by the Ombudsman will usually be based upon documents only, although the power to hold a personal hearing does exist if the Ombudsman considers that to be necessary.

The period covered by the first annual report of the Bureau was 18 July 1984 to 31, March 1995, during which period the Bureau received 2,376 enquiries, of which 1,500 became complaints and 330 became cases. Although the second year of the Bureau operation has, at the time of writing, yet to be completed figures for selected periods within the second year show a drastic but expected growth in busineses. During the eight months from 1 April 1995 to 30 November 1995, the, Bureau received 11,100 contacts, of which 5,900 became complaints leading to 1,400 cases. The growth pattern is expected to be maintained as the voluntary jurisdiction of the Bureau is adopted by Personal Investment authority members, and the jurisdiction of the former self-regulating body replaced by the Personal Investment Authority declines.

The declared aim of the Bureau is to provide an efficient, swift, impartial and cost-effective forum for the resolution of dispute involving Personal Investment Authority members. Has this been achieved? It is, of course, early days to pass judgment upon the scheme, particularly as the first Annual Report reviewing the voluntary jurisdiction of the Bureau is, at the date of writing, awaited. However, initial indications woult appear to signify success. Certainly, as an alternate to civil litigation within the Court system the alternative offered by the Bureau is very attractive, not lost on account of the fact that the average time for case resolution is eleven weeks and that the average award, made by the Bureau is under £2,000, which, under the new Court rules, would place such cases within the County Court Arbitration "small claims" scheme in any event. The procedure adopted is informal and positively encourages complainants to pursue their complaints personally and certainly it would be difficult to imagine a more user-friendly environment in which to pursue such a complaint.

Where to Go for Professional Advice

MIDAS LEGAL

INVESTMENT LOSSES

You may be entitled to Compensation.

An investor is entitled to receive a high standard of investment advice. Most do.

However if you are a victim of bad investment advice **-MIDAS LEGAL-** can guide you through the legal minefield and advise you on your rights.

MIDAS LEGAL is a comprehensive legal advice service designed to review the investment advice which you have received at a minimum cost to you the investor.

If you think you have been badly advised ring **FREE PHONE 0800 515959** for a confidential discussion entirely free and without obligation.

What have you got to lose? Not even the price of your call!

-MIDAS LEGAL-
A dedicated legal service by
James Jukes Dodd & Co, SOLICITORS,
1 Starkie Street, Preston, Lancashire PR1 3QL
Tel: (01772) 253993 Fax: (01772) 250753

Lump-Sum Investment

WISE INVESTMENT OF YOUR LUMP SUM
By Alan Steel, Managing Director of Alan Steel Asset Management

For as long as I can remember, lump sum investors have been driven by one of two conflicting forces; fear or greed. This fact has not been ignored by the financial services industry in its marketing material or advertising campaigns.

The end result of buying products based on emotional response has been disappointment in performance, one way or another. It has led investors to remain in deposits at the wrong time, or to invest in equities near the top of a stockmarket rise to experience short term losses, or to rush for guaranteed products when asset investment offers the best value. Link all of that to grossly inefficient tax strategies, and a fuzzy impression of what they are trying to achieve in the first place, and it is little wonder that the majority of investors have become disillusioned.

There is only one successful way to invest. It involves a focussed assessment of short and long term requirements from the investment, and then testing various options available against key areas which include tax, risk, available products, charges, and past performance. Above all, however, you need to find the right independent financial advisers in the first place. Their role is to recommend investments appropriate to your overall financial and family circumstances.

The best way to find one is to ask around for recommendations, or speak to existing customers. Once an adviser has been selected, he or she should help you assess your requirements, establish your attitude to risk, source the market place, find the best short and long term ways forward, and then put the various investments in place.

Of the key areas mentioned, the most important is the correct tax strategy. There is little point receiving good growth that is taxed too highly, receiving income subject to more tax, or amassing wealth without regard to Inheritance Tax ramifications. Many opportunities exist to add value by reducing exposure to tax, and most packaged investment products sold off the page ignore this fact.

Much has been made in the National Press about the high costs attached to commission based advice, as against fee based advice. Both systems can be flawed. Being charged fees is no guarantee of receiving appropriate advice, or value for money. Commission based advisers can reduce charges to a fair level to the client. What consumers really want, is good advice from experienced advisers sympathetic to their short and long term needs.

A good independent financial adviser will have knowledge, experience, and a capability and desire to provide pro-active on-going service to report progress, and to recommend changes as new taxes and developments occur.

We now live in a world of increasing complexity. One way of recognising that you found the right financial advisers is that they make complex matters simple to understand. Find such an adviser, and your investment programme should go smoothly, and your investment returns should be well sheltered against tax.

Where to Go for Professional Advice

One Name Ensures You Don't End Up in a Financial Scrabble

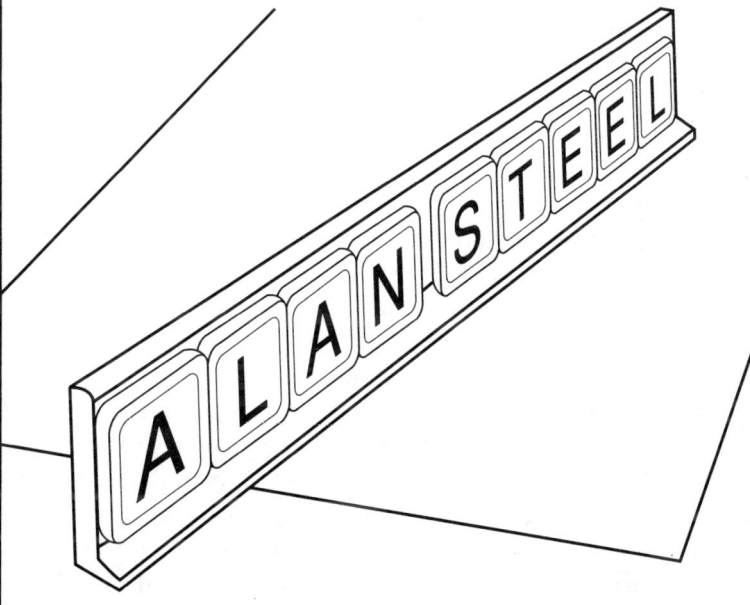

A LAN S TEEL A SSET M ANAGEMENT

-Independent Financial Advice throughout the UK for over 20 years

TEL: 01506 842365

FAX: 01506 845074

ALAN STEEL (ASSET MANAGEMENT) LTD.,
NOBEL HOUSE, LINLITHGOW, SCOTLAND EH49 7HU

Lump-Sum Investment

Existing advisers who have not yet passed Stage 2 examinations may give advice under supervision as long as they have at least one year's appropriate experience. They must undergo training for the exams and pass them before 1 July 1999 at the latest.

Once qualified as competent, advisers must undertake a minimum amount of ongoing training as continuing professional development. There are also additional examinations that are required for certain specialist activities, such as discretionary portfolio management, broker fund management and dealing in options and warrants.

The Financial Services Act has led to greater costs for independent advisers and a considerable burden in time and money to comply with the morass of rules. One response has been the establishment of networks, linking together anywhere between a dozen and 1200 advisers. Through either centralised or decentralised administration, a network can take over much of the burden of compliance with the rules, leaving advisers to concentrate on their main business, and may also offer technical support and training. Generally, network members will deal with their clients in the normal way, but they may also cross-refer for specialist products, which may be an advantage for the investor.

The range of services offered by independent advisers can include any or all of mortgage arrangements and related products, life assurance, pension planning, school fees planning, unit trusts and investment trusts. In the last two categories, some firms provide portfolio management facilities on a discretionary as well as an advisory basis. However, they do not normally offer advice about individual stocks and shares, or get involved in sophisticated tax planning techniques.

The majority operate wholly or mainly on a commission basis, but some are fee-based or may offer the client a choice. The organisation IFA Promotion runs a telephone service which can supply investors with the names of three independent advisers in their local area.

Insurance brokers

Insurance brokers are members of the Insurance Brokers Regis-

Where to Go for Professional Advice

Where's the *best place* to invest a *lump sum?*

Call now - we'll help you find a better deal

0800 591115

Say you've inherited some money. Or had a bonus. Or you'd like to make some of your savings work harder. Where can you invest with confidence? And what if a high return is the most important consideration?

Quality Financial Planning from Bradford & Bingley Building Society will give you free unbiased advice to help make sure your money is invested to your best advantage.

Call us now to arrange an appointment. When you have told one of our advisers your objectives we'll research a wide range of investments and provide you with our recommendations on your best options, whether you're looking for capital growth or a regular income. Our advice comes free of charge without obligation.

So phone us today or complete the coupon and make sure *your* money is working as hard as it should be.

BRADFORD & BINGLEY
BUILDING SOCIETY

Regulated by the Personal Investment Authority for Investment Business

Lines are open 9.00am-5.00pm, Monday to Friday.

Bradford & Bingley Building Society, P.O. Box 88, Crossflatts, Bingley, West Yorkshire BD16 2UA.

I 18

tration Council (IBRC). In addition to general insurance, such as motor and household, they may also deal with life assurance, pensions and a certain amount of investment business. In the case of those who are authorised only by the IBRC, this last is currently limited to a maximum of 49 per cent of total business, but a number of insurance brokers are also members of the PIA, hence are not subject to this restriction.

Choosing an adviser

In addition to the above categories, financial advice is also offered by banks and building societies, although, as mentioned above, the majority of these act on behalf of one particular provider and can only offer its products. Similarly, the appointed representatives and direct salesforces of life assurance companies can offer advice within the range of the company they represent. Unit trust groups may also offer portfolio management services within the scope of their own trusts.

All advisers must clearly notify the investor of their status, whether they represent one company or act as an independent. The Securities and Investments Board maintains a central register of authorised firms, so if you are in any doubt, you can check whether a firm is authorised and the types of service it is allowed to provide. The information can be obtained by telephone or through Prestel.

In principle, independent advisers offer the widest choice, because they can select any product on the market. But if you are happy to deal with one particular product supplier, a tied agent can offer equally valid advice and, by virtue of his relationship with the company, may be better placed to sort out any problems that arise.

Types of service

Discretionary
With a discretionary service, you are effectively handing over all control to the adviser. At the outset, you will, of course, set out your basic requirements, your investment aims and the degree of risk you are prepared to accept in trying to achieve them. But

thereafter you must trust the adviser to carry out your wishes faithfully and effectively.

On the other hand, there is the advantage of speed of action. Since the adviser is not having to refer decisions to you for approval, he can act immediately on opportunities which might otherwise be missed.

Advisory

Advisory services give you complete control, while you still have access to professional advice. Of course, if you are simply going to agree to everything the adviser suggests, you may as well give him discretion and have done with it. But an advisory service can also provide a useful learning process, so that you gradually come to take a more active role.

Since every transaction will require your prior authorisation, it is important that you should be accessible to your adviser. Equally, he should be readily accessible to you whenever you need advice or to deal.

Execution-only

Execution-only services are aimed at those who are confident that they know what they want and do not want to pay extra for added frills. Since no advice is being given, the choice may be largely cost-based, but if you plan to deal actively, then you need to be sure that you can place an order easily and that it will be carried out quickly. Also, some execution-only share-dealing services do offer a few additional facilities, such as company reports or recommendations, and may also deal with the paperwork; for example, looking after share certificates and providing composite tax vouchers at the end of the financial year.

Commission versus fees

The commission versus fees issue has always been a sensitive one and has become more so lately. From the start of 1995, all independent advisers and insurance company salespeople have to disclose what they stand to earn from a product sale before the client signs the application form. This will include not only

Lump-Sum Investment

Exploding the myth

"Stockbrokers only deal for the very rich". Wrong! Around ten million people already own shares and many more know something about the stockmarket through the Government's privatisation programme.

Stockbrokers are far removed from the stereotyped images often portrayed in the popular press and above all are approachable, friendly and accessible. You would probably be surprised to learn that about 95% of the population lives within 10 miles of a stockbroker's office.

Almost all of the firms who look after individual investors in shares are members of the Association of Private Client Investment Managers and Stockbrokers (APCIMS), the trade association which promotes those firms and, by extension, the interests of the private investors who use their services.

What makes APCIMS members different?

Direct Access to the Market – the majority of our firms are members of the London Stock Exchange and are therefore unique in having direct and immediate access to the stock market for buying and selling shares. The computerised systems used mean that brokers do not have to be located in the City of London – they can be in your local high street. Professionalism – the breadth and depth of investment experience and knowledge which APCIMS members make available to their clients contrasts with that of many other financial advisers whose expertise is limited to the selling of a handful of "packaged" products offered by the big insurance companies.

Genuine Independence – APCIMS members are truly independent unlike other financial advisers many of whom are "tied" to a particular company. The advice given by our members is completely impartial and their charges are disclosed to you in advance.

Tight Regulation – most APCIMS members are regulated by the Securities and Futures Authority (SFA) or the Investment Managers' Regulatory Organisation (IMRO). They are subject to demanding tests of their financial resources and are obliged to meet the most rigorous procedural standards and management controls. Only those individuals who are personally registered with the regulators as being "fit and proper" are authorised to give investment advice.

Individually Tailored Services – APCIMS members operate on the basis of providing services which are tailored to suit your individual circumstances and requirements

THE MAIN SERVICES AVAILABLE ARE:-
Advisory Services – almost all APCIMS members offer an advisory service in which the professional advises on the purchase, sale or retention of individual stocks.

Dealing or "Execution-Only" Service – this service is designed for investors who do not require advice but who do need a stockbroker to buy and sell shares for them.

Discretionary Investment Management Service – to put it simply, this service gives the manager the authority to buy and sell investments for you without obtaining your prior approval on each and every occasion.

Comprehensive Financial Planning – this can include advice on the placing of cash deposits, pensions, mortgages, life assurance, Personal Equity Plans (PEPs), Tax Exempt Special Savings Accounts (TESSAs) and so on.

How To Find Out More

A comprehensive brochure and a directory of APCIMS members detailing the range of services they offer are available free of charge by writing to APCIMS at 112 Middlesex Street, London E1 7HY, quoting reference DT96.

Advertisement feature

Where to Go for Professional Advice

For professional and impartial investment advice ...

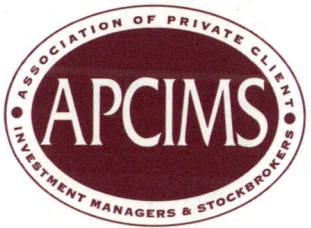

choose a financial advisor who is:

- **Expert in stockmarket investment**
- **Genuinely independent**
- **Regulated to the highest standards**
- **Qualified by examination**

An APCIMS member meets all these requirements

APCIMS members have over 300 offices throughout the British Isles and specialise in looking after private clients.
Our brochure and directory contain full details of the services they offer and where to find them.
Write to us at the address below quoting reference DT96 for a free copy.

APCIMS - the representative body for private client investment managers and stockbrokers.

112 Middlesex Street, London E1 7HY

You've worked hard for your money, now make it work hard for you.

Since beginning life as a firm of accountants over 25 years ago, R J Temple PLC has grown to become one of the UK's leading independent financial advisers. Specialising in investment planning for retirement, the company now advises over 25,000 people throughout the UK with investments totalling more than £300 million. Through a network of Financial Planning Managers under the control of seven Regional Directors, independent advice is available on all individual investment circumstances without cost or obligation.

Many people approach retirement with significant capital assets, including pension funds, which have been steadfastly built up during their career. The immediate concern at retirement is to derive an income from that capital but there the generalisation usually ends. Almost everyone has differing requirements and priorities at retirement and it is therefore vital to obtain independent financial advice at this time if your hopes and aspirations are to be achieved. Some typical questions that arise at this time are:

"Can I increase my investment income?"

"Will my capital/income keep up with inflation?"

"Am I claiming all my tax allowances?"

"Are my retirement plans adequate?"

"How will inheritance tax affect my family?"

"Could I afford long term care?"

These questions and many others can be answered simply and efficiently by taking expert independent financial advice. R J Temple PLC frequently runs local seminars at which effective ways of investing for and during retirement are very clearly explained. They also offer a free guide to investing for income and saving tax which can be obtained by responding to their advertisement or by telephoning 01273 821177.

Where to Go for Professional Advice

Is it still possible to receive 8%, 9% or even 10% p.a. on your money?

Yes it is! R J Temple PLC is one of the UK's leading independent financial advisers and is regulated by FIMBRA. We can provide details of investments that offer these levels of return – free of basic rate tax. For more information and a FREE copy of our special publication "A Guide to Investing for Income ... and Saving Tax", please complete and return the coupon below or telephone us on

01273 821177

RJ TEMPLE PLC
Independent Financial Consultants

Lyndean House, 43-46 Queens Road,
Brighton, East Sussex BN1 3XB
Telephone: (01273) 821177 Fax: (01273) 821296.
Registered in England No. 1468366

To: R J Temple PLC, Lyndean House, 43/46 Queens Road, Brighton BN1 3XB.
Please send me a copy of your "Guide to Investing for Income ... and Saving Tax."

Name_____

Address_____

_____ Postcode_____

Telephone_____

commission but, for company salespeople, any relevant additional benefits provided by the company.

As there is no longer a maximum commissions agreement, companies are free to pay whatever levels they choose, which means there is the potential for advisers to be biased in their recommendations. In practice, rates are still based on the old scales and the differences between providers tends to be small. A more important issue is possible product bias, as products with similar functions may carry quite different rates of commission. In particular, if an adviser has spent considerable time checking a client's circumstances and requirements, he may be reluctant to recommend something like National Savings Certificates which carry no reward.

Commission disclosure, however, will not prove whether a product is good value for money. That depends on a number of factors, including the overall level of charges, the service provided and the total returns one might expect. To judge impartiality, an investor would need to know not only the levels of commission on all the possible alternative products, but also their relative merits in different circumstances; without that knowledge it would be difficult to prove a case of commission bias.

The obvious solution would be to move to a fee basis for all advice. But while this would increase independence, it is no guarantee of good advice. There is also the key question of whether people would be prepared to pay realistic fees. For those who are, there are a growing number of advisers who work on a fee basis or offer clients the choice. But this route is likely to prove more expensive for small investors, for whom percentage commissions can offer very good value.

Making complaints

If you feel that you have been badly treated by a company, or given inappropriate advice, the first step should be to take it up with the company itself, explaining why you are not happy and what action you expect. Always keep copies of any correspondence and also make a note of any telephone calls – when they were made, who you spoke to and what was said.

Where to Go for Professional Advice

If you are not satisfied with the response, the next stage is to take your complaint to the appropriate SRO. Advisers and companies must indicate which SRO they are authorised by.

If you believe you are entitled to compensation, and this is not forthcoming from the adviser, you can take your case to an ombudsman. There are now ombudsmen covering each sector of the financial services market: banks, building societies, insurance, investment and pensions, plus a PIA ombudsman.

In some cases, you may be able to make a claim from the Investors Compensation Scheme. Claims should be made within six months of a default being declared and the maximum for any individual claim is £48,000. The main criteria for eligibility are:

- that you are a private investor;
- that the firm involved is fully authorised;
- that the firm cannot pay out claims;
- that the firm owes money or was holding investments on your behalf;
- that your claim relates to business regulated by the Financial Services Act.

But the Scheme cannot help in the following cases:

- the firm is not fully authorised;
- the firm has gone into liquidation but has not been declared in default;
- the firm is still in business;
- the business was conducted before 18 December 1986.

Bear in mind, too, that you cannot claim compensation simply on the grounds of bad performance if you have been fairly advised and warned of investment risk.

The various ombudsmen publish guides to their services, which are provided free of charge to investors. Product providers – whether life assurance companies, unit trust groups, banks or building societies – can also supply information on their complaints procedures, but if you have any doubts, further guidance is available from the Public Information Office at the SIB.

Useful contacts

Investment Management Regulatory Organisation: 0171 390 5000
Personal Investment Authority: 0171 538 8860
The Securities and Futures Authority: 0171 378 9000
The Securities and Investments Board, Central Register: 0171 929 3652; Public Information Office: 0171 638 1240
The Banking Ombudsman: 0171 404 9944
The Building Societies Ombudsman: 0171 931 0044
The Insurance Ombudsman: 0171 928 7600
The Investment Ombudsman: 0171 796 3065
The Pensions Ombudsman: 0171 834 9144
The Investors Compensation Scheme: 0171 283 2474
IFA Promotion: 01483 461461
The PIA Ombudsman: 0171 928 4488

Sharedealing made simple, 7 days a week.
Phone ShareLink on 0121 200 2242.

Further Reading from Kogan Page

Finding and Funding Residential Care for the Elderly, Terry Fruin, 1995
Good Retirement Guide 1996, Rosemary Brown
How to Write a Will and Gain Probate, 6th edition, Marlene Garsia, 1996
How to Understand the Financial Press, 2nd edition, John Andrew, 1993
Letting Residential Property, Frances M Way, 1993
Living Abroad: The Daily Telegraph Guide, 9th edition, Michael Furnell, 1996
Splitting Up: A Legal and Financial Guide to Separation and Divorce, 3rd edition, David Green, 1995
Tax Facts 1996/97: A Quick and Easy Guide to Your Business and Personal Tax Matters, Kidsons Impey, 1996

Index

Accountants, 345
Accumulator funds, 74-5, 147, 176
Additional voluntary contributions (AVCs), 266
   contribution limits, 266
   free-standing, 266
Advice
   finding an adviser, 334-62
   types of service, 354-5
Age allowance, 28-9
   limits, 24
Alternative Investment Market (AIM), 96-7
Annuities, 234-40
   capital protected, 238
   compulsory purchase, 235
   guaranteed, 235
   hybrid plans 239-40
   increasing, 239
   joint life, second death, 238
   purchased life, 235
   rates, 238
   taxation, 235
   temporary, 239
   unit-linked, 239
   with profits, 239
Appointed representatives, 339
Arts and crafts, 270

Association of Investment Trust Companies (AITC), 184, 187, 195
Association of Private Client Investment Managers and Stockbrokers (Apcims), 105, 119, 344
Association of Solicitor Investment Managers, 345
Association of Unit Trusts and Investment Funds (Autif), 126, 150

Back to back plans, 239
Bancassurance, 339
Banks, 39-42, 340
   collapse, 20
   current accounts, 39-40
   higher interest accounts, 40
   money market accounts, 41
   Ombudsman, 362
   term deposits, 42
Bear funds, 138
Bed and breakfasting, 23
Big Bang, 32, 105
Bonds, *see* Broker bonds, Guaranteed bonds, Guaranteed equity bonds, Local authority bonds,

Personalised bonds,
Premium bonds, Single
premium bonds
Broker bonds, 234
Broker unit trusts, 172-4
Building societies, 42-5, 339
  account rates, 43, 45
  Association, 64
  banking accounts, 42-3
  closed accounts, 44
  fixed term accounts, 44
  instant access accounts, 43-4
  notice accounts, 44
  Ombudsman, 362
Bull funds, 138
Business angels, 282

Capital gains tax, 25
  allowances, 24
  bonds, 222
  gilts, 84
  investment trusts, 177
  National Savings, 39
  offshore funds, 74, 147
  pensions, 256
  personal equity plans, 198
  unit trusts, 140
Cash unit trusts, 70, 134-6
Charitable giving 285-6,
  307-21, 332-3
Classic cars, 272
Collectables, 272
Collective investments, 123
Commercial property, 297, 304
Commission
  on equities, 94, 112-13, 345
  versus fees, 355, 360
Complaints procedures, 361-2
Compound Annual Rate (CAR), 44
Coupon, meaning, 79-80

Crest, 34, 95
Critical illness insurance, 249

Dealing services, 101, 105-6,
  110-13, 344
  advisory, 110, 112, 344-5
  costs, 112-13, 345
  discretionary, 112, 344
  execution-only, 110, 344
  financial planning, 112, 345
  nominee service, 95, 112, 119
Derivatives, 116-18
Diamonds, 274, 279
Distribution bonds, 231
Distributor funds, 76, 147, 176
Dividends
  cover, 103
  on shares, 103
  scrip dividends, 104
  taxation, 20, 103

Enterprise Investment Scheme
  (EIS), 282-3
Enterprise zone trusts, 283-4
Equities, 93-122
  blue chip, 119
  buying and selling, 105-6,
    110-13
  commission, 94, 112-13
  convertible shares, 118
  dealing services, 101, 105-6,
    110-13
  debentures, 118-19
  dividends, 103-4
  indices, 97, 100
  ordinary shares, 101-3
  personal equity plans, 114,
    199, 202-3, 206
  preference shares, 118
  price/earnings ratio, 104-5
  for private investors, 100-1
  privatisations, 100-1

Index

rights issue, 119
rolling settlement, 94-6
scrip dividends, 104
share prices, 102
stamp duty, 113
yields, 103
Ethical investment, 286-95
 ethical banking, 294-5

Fees versus commission, 355, 360
Financial Intermediaries, Managers and Brokers Regulatory Association (Fimbra), 34, 336
Financial planning services, 112, 345
Financial Services Act, 34, 335-7
Fixed capital investments, 36-64
Forestry, 280-1
Friendly societies, 217-20, 242
 Friendly Societies Act, 242
 tax exempt plans, 242
Futures contracts, 116-17
 in unit trusts, 134-9

Geared futures and options trusts, 138
Gilts, 18, 78-92
 buying and selling, 89-90
 coupon, 79
 flat yield, 80, 83-4
 index-linked, 18, 80, 87-8
 and interest rates, 82
 long-dated, 80
 medium-dated, 80
 prices, 81-2
 redemption yield, 83-4
 short-dated, 80
 taxation, 84-6
 terminology, 78-80
 undated, 80

Gold
 coins, 272
 offshore funds, 274
 options, 274
 shares, 274
 unit trusts, 274
Guaranteed bonds, 66-70
 growth bonds, 68
 income bonds, 66-8
 interest rates, 68
 taxation, 68-70
Guaranteed equity bonds, 226-30

High income bonds, 230-1
Hybrid plans, 239-40

IFA Promotion, 352, 362
Income tax
 allowances, 24
 annuities, 235
 dividends, 103
 gilts, 84-6
 guaranteed bonds, 68-9
 investment trusts, 177-80
 local authority bonds, 66
 National Savings, 38
 offshore funds, 74-6, 147
 pensions, 256
 single premium bonds, 222-4
 unit trusts, 139-40
Independent financial advisers (IFAs), 34, 338, 345-52
 networks, 352
Independent taxation, 28
Index
 betting on indices, 118
 FT-SE-Actuaries All Share, 19, 97
 FT-SE 100 (Footsie), 97
Index-linked gilts, 18
Inflation, 18-19

break-even rate, 88
and index- linking, 18, 51
Inheritance tax, 29
  reliefs on transfers, 29
Insider dealing, 103
Insurance brokers, 352-4
Insurance Brokers Registration Council (IBRC), 336, 352-4
Insurance Ombudsman, 269, 362
Interest
  fixed versus variable, 36-8
  and gilts, 82
  receiving gross, 38
  and tax, 20, 38
Investment
  definition, 15
Investment Management Regulatory Organisation (Imro), 34, 336, 362
Investment Ombudsman, 362
Investment trusts, 123, 177-96
  annuity income shares, 188
  buying and selling, 186
  capital shares, 188
  categories, 184-5
  charges, 182
  discount, 180-1
  gearing, 181-2
  highly geared ordinary shares, 188
  housing investment trusts, 193-4
  income shares, 188
  lifestyle products, 194-5
  limited life, 187
  Lloyd's trusts, 191-2
  net asset value, 180
  performance comparisons, 185, 187
  premium, 180
  price listings, 187
  savings schemes, 186
  share exchange, 186-7
  split capital, 187-90
  spreading risk, 177
  stepped preference shares, 190
  take-overs, 181
  taxation, 177-80
  venture capital trusts, 192-3
  warrants, 190-1
  zero dividend preference shares, 188
Investors Compensation Scheme, 112, 361-2
  eligibility, 361

Jewellery, 272
Jobbers, *see* Stock markets

Law Society, 336
Life assurance, 217-55
  annuities, 234-9
  hybrid plans, 239-40
  and pensions, 257-60
  planning services, 352
  second-hand endowments, 240-1
  single premium bonds, 220-34
Life Assurance and Unit Trust Regulatory Organisation (Lautro), 34, 336
Lloyd's investment trusts, 191-2
Lloyd's of London, 284-5
Local authority bonds, 65-6
  and interest rates, 66
  taxation, 66
London International Financial Futures and Options Exchange (Liffe), 116-19
Long-term care (LTC), 249

Index

Managed funds, 220-1
Margin trading, 95-6
Market value adjustment (MVA), 222
Merchant banks, 340-1
Monthly income portfolios, 141-2

National Savings, 38, 48-64
  capital bonds, 54
  First Option Bond, 60
  income bonds, 54
  index-linked certificates, 18, 51-4
  NS Bank investment account, 58
  NS Bank ordinary account, 57
  ordinary certificates, 50-1
  past issues, 51
  Pensioners Bond, 58-60
  premium bonds, 60-1
  product guide, 62-3
  taxation, 38
National Savings Stock Register, 39, 86, 89-90
Nominee Service, 95, 112, 119

Occupational Pensions Advisory Service (OPAS), 269
Offshore investments
  accumulator funds, 74, 147, 176
  commodity funds, 174-5
  compensation, 148
  currency funds, 174
  deposit accounts, 70-1
  distributor funds, 75-6, 147, 176
  money funds, 74
  offshore funds, 143-50, 174-5
  regulated funds, 146-50
  regulation, 143
  roll-up funds, *see* Accumulator funds
  SIB recognised funds, 146
  SICAV and SICAF, 143, 150
  taxation, 74-6, 147
  UCITS, 146, 148
  umbrella funds, 148-9
  unregulated funds, 146
Ombudsman
  Banking, 362
  Building Societies, 362
  Insurance, 269, 362
  Investment, 362
  Pensions, 269, 362
  PIA, 362
Open-ended investment companies (OEICs), 150
Options, 116-18
  call options, 117
  premium, 117
  put options, 117
Ordinary shares, 101-3

Past performance
  comparative figures, 35
Pensioners Bond, 58-60
Pensions, 262-9
  early retirement, 267
  final salary, 256-7
  how much to save, 267-8
  investment trust plans, 194-5
  life assurance, 257
  Ombudsman, 269, 362
  and personal equity plans, 266
  tax relief, 256
  transfer values, 260
  widow's/widower's, 257
  see also Personal pensions, Additional voluntary contributions

368

Index

Pensions Ombudsman, 269, 362
Pensions Register, 269
Permanent interest-bearing shares (PIBS), 90-2
Permanent health insurance (PMI), 248-9
Personal equity plans, 197-216
  advisory, 202
  charges, 213-14
  corporate, 206-8
  corporate bond, 198
  and equities, 113-15
  growth versus income, 212-13
  investment limits, 197-8
  managed, 199-202
  mortgages, 194-5, 215
  and pension planning, 266
  performance, 214-15
  rules, 198-9
  self-select, 202-6
  share exchange, 215
  single company, 208-10
  taxation, 25
Personal Investment Authority (PIA), 33, 336, 362
  ombudsman, 362
Personal pensions, 257-64
  contribution limits, 260
  deposit, 261
  investment trust, 261
  self-invested, 261-2
  unit-linked, 261
  unit trust, 261
  with profits, 261
Personalised bonds, 231-4
Platinum, 273
Polarisation, 34, 337-40
  appointed representatives, 339
  banks and building societies, 339-40
  independent advisers, 34, 338
  multi-ties, 338
  tied agents, 34, 338
Policy auctions, 240
Policyholders Protection Act, 242
Portfolio management services, 172, 344
Pound-cost averaging, 140-1
Precious metals, 273
Premium bonds, 60-1
Price/earnings ratio, 104-5
Private health care, 242-55
Private medical insurance (PMI), 243-8
Privatisation issues, 100-1
Property funds, 221
ProShare, 106
Public limited company, 101-2

Recognised Professional Body (RPB), 336
Retirement planning, 256-69
  early retirement, 267
Risk
  and protection, 16-20
  spreading, 177
Rolling settlement, 94-6

Scrip, 104, 119
Second-hand endowments, 240-1
Securities and Futures Authority (SFA), 34, 112, 122, 336, 362
Securities and Investments Board (SIB), 34, 336, 362
  central register, 354, 362
  public information office, 362
Self-invested personal pensions, 261-2
Self-regulatory organisation (SRO), 34, 336
Shares, *see* Equities

Index

Share exchange schemes
  and investment trusts, 186-7
  and PEPs, 215
  and unit trusts, 140
SICAV and SICAF, 143, 149-50
Single premium bonds, 220-2
  broker bonds, 234
  distribution bonds, 231
  guaranteed equity bonds, 226-30
  high income bonds, 230-1
  personalised bonds, 231-4
  taxation, 222-4
  versus unit trusts, 224-6
Software for investment, 106-10
Solicitors, 345
Stamp duty, 113
State Earnings Related Pension Scheme (Serps)
  contracting out, 262
Stockbrokers, 341-5
Stock Exchange, 93-4, 122
  Crest, 34, 95
  rolling settlement, 94-6
  settlement day, 95
Stock markets
  brokers, 94, 110-12
  capitalisation, 32
  indices, 97-100
  jobbers, 93-4
  market makers, 94
  private investors, 100-1
  share prices, 102
  software for investment, 106-10
  terms, 119
  wider share ownership, 100

Tangibles, 270-81
Taurus, 34, 94

Tax
  age allowance, 28
  allowances, 24
  on dividends, 29
  on interest, 20
  independent taxation, 28
  and investment, 20-9
  tax-free investments, 20, 38
  see also Capital gains tax, Income tax, Inheritance tax
Tax exempt special savings accounts, 38, 45-8
  taxation, 46
  transfers, 46
Theatre productions, 281-2
Timeshares, 296-7

Umbrella funds, 148-9
Undertakings for Collective Investments in Transferable Securities (UCITS), 146, 148
Unit trusts, 123-43, 152-74
  accumulation units, 132
  bid and offer prices, 129-32
  broker trusts, 172-4
  bull and bear trusts, 138
  buying and selling, 143
  cancellation price, 129-32
  cash trusts, 70, 134-6
  categories, 153-8
  charges, 128-9
  commodity and energy, 156
  convertibles, 156
  distribution units, 132
  equalisation, 132
  exempt, 156
  exit fees, 132
  financial and property, 156
  franked and unfranked income, 139
  funds of funds, 134, 156

futures and options trusts, 136-9
geared futures and options trusts, 138
gilt and fixed interest, 154
growth trusts, 165-8
historic pricing, 142
income trusts, 158-64
index trusts, 136
international, 154-5
international income, 154
investment trust units, 156
money market, *see* Cash trusts
performance comparisons, 156-7
portfolio management services, 172
pound-cost averaging, 140-1
property, 304
regular savings schemes, 140-1
regulation, 126
share exchange schemes, 140
smaller companies, 154
taxation, 139-40
UK equity and bond, 154
UK equity and bond income, 153
UK equity income, 153
UK growth, 154
UK growth and income, 153
versus bonds, 224-6
warrant trusts, 139

Venture capital trusts (VCT), 192-3

Warrants, 115-16
  on investment trusts, 190-1
  unit trusts, 139
Wills, 322-34
Wine, 279-80

Index of Advertisers

Abtrust Unit Trust Managers Ltd, *160-1*
AIB Fund Managers, *77*
Alan Steel Asset Management, *350-1*
Alzheimer's Research, *319*
Amnesty International, *311*
Anchor Housing Trust, *209*
APCIMS, *356-7*
Aspire, *75*
Association for International Cancer Research, *69*

Bank of Scotland, *301*
Barclays Bank, *49*, *59*
Beale Dobie & Company Ltd, *232-3*
Binder Hamlyn, *26-7*
Blue Cross, *314*
Boys' Brigade, *171*
Bradford & Bingley Building Society, *353*
Breakthrough Trust, *313*
British Trust for Ornithology, *327*

British Wireless for the Blind Fund, *315*
Burns Aderson Independent Network plc, *342-3*

Chesham Building Society, *298-9*
Children in Crisis, *331*
Children in Distress, *133*
Children's Hospice South West, *313*
Church Army, *312*
Cinnamon Trust, *175*
Co-operative Funeral Bond, *271*
Colonial Direct, *305*
Concern Universal, *37*
CPRE (Council for Protection of Rural England), *183*

Devon Air Ambulance Trust, *57*
Donkey Sanctuary, *317*
Dunfermline Building Society, *52-3*

Ecclesiastical, *263*
Erskine Hospital, *87*

Index of Advertisers

Family Assurance Friendly Society Ltd, *236-7*
Fidelity Brokerage, *111*
First National Building Society, *178-9*
Furlong Research Foundation, *137*

Garrison Investment Analysis Ltd, *204-5*
General Accident Life Assurance Ltd, *120-1*

Hanley Economic Building Society, *306*
Health Care Matters, *244-5*
Hearing Dogs for the Deaf, *312*
Help the Aged, *167*
Henshaws Society for the Blind, *309*
Home Farm Trust, *55*
Homeowners Friendly Society Ltd, *227*

Inland Revenue, *21-3*
Inspire Foundation, *115*
Institute of Chartered Accountants, *11*
Investor Intelligence, *337*
Irish Life International, *225*

James Jukes Dodd & Co, *348*
Just Tax, *31*
Jyske Bank, *72-3*

Kent Air Ambulance Trust, *61*

Leathes Prior Solicitors, *5*
Leeds & Holbeck Building Society, *47*
Lloyds Bank, *124-5*

M & G Group, *200-1*
Market Data Centre Ltd, *107*
Merchant Investors Assurance Company Ltd, *264-5*
MGM Assurance, *219*

National Benevolent Fund for the Aged, *325*
National Deposit Friendly Society Ltd, *228-9*
National Savings, *inside front cover*
Natural Medicines Society, *81*
Neville James Ltd, *302*
Not Forgotten Association, *79*
NPI, *289, 303*

Ohra UK Ltd, *250-2*
Old Mutual Life Assurance Ltd, *253*
Ostrich Centre, *173*

Portman Channel Islands Ltd, *145*
PPP, *223*
Premier Cru International Ltd, *276-8*
Prime Health Ltd, *246-7*

R J Temple plc, *358-9*
Redmayne Bentley Stockbrokers, *341*
Rippon Boswell and Company, *275*
Royal Free Hospital, *2*
Royal Insurance Ltd, *13*
Royal London Society for the Blind, *85*
Royal Navy Submarine Museum, *195*
Royal School for the Blind, *213*
RSPCA, *151*

Index of Advertisers

Sailors' Families' Society, *241*
ShareLink, *16-17, 45, 67, 96-7, 105, 110, 118, 119, 139, 170, 186, 211, 216, 340-1, 360*
Shorter Byrne & Co, *346-7*
Southernhays, *292-3*
Special Olympics UK, *261*
St Anne's Shelter and Housing Action, *135*
St Mary's Hospice, *33*

Start (Skin Treatment & Research Trust), *267*
Stocktrade, *98-9*
Sun Alliance, *258-9*

United Trust Bank Ltd, *6*

Wise Investment, *290-1*

YorkSHARE Ltd, *189*

**One call is all it takes.
Phone ShareLink on 0121 200 2242.**